KU-131-065

COLLECTED T.V. PLAYS

PLAYS

VOLUME TWO

A Suitable Case for Treatment
For Tea on Sunday
And Did Those Feet
Let's Murder Vivaldi
In Two Minds
The Parachute

DAVID MERCER

JOHN CALDER
LONDON

822·025 MER
added entry at
822·914 MER

820-293·9
MER
MER

First published as *Collected T.V. Plays Volume Two* 1981 by
John Calder (Publishers) Ltd.,
18 Brewer Street,
London W1R 4AS

A Suitable Case for Treatment, For Tea on Sunday and *And Did Those Feet* were
originally published as *Three TV Comedies* in 1966 and *The Parachute, Let's
Murder Vivaldi* and *In Two Minds* as *The Parachute* in 1967 by Calder and
Boyars Ltd.

© David Mercer 1966, 1967, 1982

All performing rights in these plays, whether for amateur or professional
performance, are strictly reserved and applications for performances
should be made in writing to Margaret Ramsay, 14a Goodwin's Court,
London WC2.

No performances of these plays may be given unless a licence has been
obtained prior to rehearsal.

All Rights Reserved.

BRITISH LIBRARY CATALOGUING IN PUBLICATION DATA
Mercer, David, *b. 1928*
     Collected TV plays.
     Vol. 2
     I. Title
     822'.91'4   PR6063.E7

ISBN 0 7145 3814 0 casebound
ISBN 0 7145 3817 5 paperbound

b811079b

No part of this publication may be reproduced, stored in a retrieval
system, or transmitted in any form, by any means, electronic,
mechanical, photo-copying, recording or otherwise except brief extracts
for the purpose of review, without the prior permission of the copyright
owner and the publisher

Any paperback edition of this book whether published simultaneously
with, or subsequent to, the casebound edition is sold subject to the
condition that it shall not, by way of trade, be lent, resold, hired out or
otherwise disposed of without the publisher's consent, in any form of
binding or cover other than that in which it is published.

Printed and bound in Great Britain by Redwood Burn Ltd.,
Trowbridge & Esher

1.7.91   244353

CONTENTS

THE POLYTECHNIC OF WALES
TREFOREST

By the same author
The Generations
Ride a Cock Horse
The Long Crawl Through Time
   (*New Writers 3*)
Three TV Comedies
The Parachute

A SUITABLE CASE
FOR TREATMENT

CAST:

MORGAN DELT	Ian Hendry
LEONIE DELT	Moira Redmond
CHARLES NAPIER	Jack May
MRS DELT	Anna Wing
MR HENDERSON	Norman Pitt
MRS HENDERSON	Helen Goss
JEAN SKELTON	Jane Merrow
POLICEMAN	John Bennett
ANALYST	Hugh Evans
TICKET COLLECTOR	David Grahame (Film only)
MR DELT	Harry Brunning

BBC Transmission: October 21st, 1962

SCENE I: GORILLA'S CAGE AT ZOO

Morgan approaches the gorilla's cage and stands looking rather disconsolately at the gorilla. The gorilla looks at Morgan. There appears to be some sort of mutual understanding. Morgan puts on dark glasses and walks away.

SCENE II: DIVORCE COURT

Leonie is giving evidence.
Counsel: Would you tell the Court, Mrs Delt, what your husband did then?
Leonie [*air of haughty wretchedness*]: He shaved the dog in such a way that it had a hammer and sickle on its back.

SCENE III: LANDING OF LEONIE'S FLAT

Morgan is contemplating the nameplate to one side of the door. It says 'Morgan and Leonie Delt'—but the 'Morgan' and the 'and' have a single line struck through in ink. Morgan removes the card from its frame, takes another from his pocket and slips it into the frame. It says 'Morgan and Leonie Delt'. He is carrying an L-shaped parcel and a long cylinder. He takes a key and puts it in the lock and turns.

SCENE IV: DIVORCE COURT

Counsel: And the er . . . the breed of dog?
Leonie: A poodle.

9

Counsel: Your husband in fact hated the poor dumb creature?
Leonie: I wouldn't say that. [*Pause*] It's me he was getting at.

SCENE V: LEONIE'S FLAT. BEDROOM

The bedroom is tastefully and expensively furnished, with a feminine emphasis. On the bed is a woolly dog. Morgan puts his parcel on the bed beside dog, sits on the bed and begins to unwrap the parcel.

SCENE VI: INTERIOR TAXI

Leonie and Mr Henderson are sitting in the back of the taxi.

Father: It wasn't too painful, darling, was it? A foregone conclusion of course. [*Pause*] I never liked Morgan.
Leonie: I know, father.
Father: He's brutal, lazy, dirty, *and* immoral. I've also heard he's a Trot, whatever that may be.
Leonie: It's a kind of communist, father.
Father: Indeed? I wouldn't have said he had the moral fibre for *any* sort of belief.
Leonie: In any case it's not true. Morgan isn't a Trot. [*Pause*] He isn't anything.
Father: Well—when you get the decree absolute, you'll be free of him. [*Pause*] Why don't you buy yourself something nice on the way home? Celebrate.
Leonie: I think I might. You've been terribly good about all this.
Father: Thank God none of us will have to put up with him any longer.

SCENE VII: LEONIE'S FLAT. BEDROOM

Morgan now has the parcel unwrapped. It is a replica in wood of a gallows, with a noose hanging from the arm. Morgan sets it upright on the floor. Takes the woolly dog, puts it in the noose. Pulls it tight, pushes it and watches it swing. Steadies it. Rises and walks out. Morgan goes through the hall to the living-room. Crosses towards chair and drinks table. As he crosses:

Morgan: Hullo Room.
   [*He takes a large roll of paper from chair, crosses to wall above gramophone and pins up a notice . . . 'Napier go home'.*]
Morgan: Pins . . . wall . . . notice . . . [*turns into camera*]
   Have a drink, Morgan? Don't mind if I do.
   [*He goes over to drinks table, pours himself out a tot and sits in the chair. Leonie comes in the front door carrying large dress bag, goes across and into bedroom. Leonie comes towards the bed, throws down parcel and coat on seeing dog hanging. Goes towards it. She picks up the gallows and dog and goes back towards the bed. She throws the gallows and dog on bed and walks away quickly towards the hall.*]
Leonie: Morgan. . . .
   [*She stops as she sees him sitting in the living-room. Crosses to him.*]
Leonie: Morgan! I told you not to come here. I also asked you for your key. Will you give it to me please.
   [*Morgan indicates notice and Leonie turns and sees it. Walks over to it and takes it down.*]
Leonie: I suppose you think that's funny. [*Unpins it and rolls it up.*]
Morgan: Not at all. I mean what it says.
Leonie: I divorced you this afternoon.
Morgan: How did my image come over in court?
Leonie: Will you *please* go?
Morgan [*scratching*]: Did you see what I did to your woolly dog?
Leonie: I did.
   [*Pause.*]
Morgan: Is Charles Napier living here?
Leonie: You know perfectly well he isn't. [*Morgan rises and goes to her.*]

Morgan: I've been to see a psychiatrist. He was fat, and extremely furry. Furry suit . . . furry hands . . . furry—

Leonie: If it's money you want, I can let you have twenty pounds.
   [*Leonie crosses over to desk drawer but changing her mind takes cigarettes.*]

Morgan [*shouts*]*:* This is my flat as well, you know!

Leonie: Not yours, darling. Not now.
   [*Morgan crosses back to drinks table and sits deliberately in chair.*]
   [*Pause.*]

Leonie: This is tiresome, Morgan—

Morgan: Tiresome! A human life destroyed? A soul eviscerated?
   [*There is a piano in one corner. Morgan goes to it. Sits, picks out a tune: the Red Flag.*]

Leonie [*Moves in to drinks table*]*:* I don't think you loved me at all until I asked you to leave.

Morgan [*singing*]*:* Now Hitler's dead and Stalin's gone—

Leonie: Will you please go, Morgan.
   [*Crosses to end of couch and sits. She lights a cigarette.*]
   [*Pause.*]

Morgan: I've nowhere *to* go. I've given up dossing on people's
   · floors. Living in their flats when they're away. [*Lights cigarette*]
   I live in the car now.

Leonie: My solicitor is writing to you about that too. I bought it. And I want it back.

Morgan: I went to see a psychiatrist today.

Leonie: I won't have you back.

Morgan: I have fantasies.

Leonie: Nothing new about that.

Morgan: I believe my mental condition's extremely illegal.

Leonie: I'm tired of loving you and keeping you and admiring you. If it turns out that you're a psychopath, I'm sure it's the best thing for all our sakes.
   [*She rises and goes up to alcove in window. Morgan drinks up, rises and comes to drinks table. Sets down his glass and sits. Leonie walks quickly down to telephone.*]

Morgan: There are two toothbrushes in the bathroom. And one of them is neither mine nor yours. And when did you start using hair-cream?

Leonie: Welton, Booth and Welton? Mr Booth, please. Mr Booth?

Leonie Delt. Yes, yes it was. But when I got home my husband was here. Yes. Yes. You said something last week about a court injunction. Well, he's here now, he's pretending to be mentally ill. I beg your pardon? Yes, he has a key. Yes. That's terribly kind of you. Thank you. Goodbye—[*She puts the phone down and turns*] —Perhaps you'll understand now, Morgan, that I—
[*Morgan has walked out during her conversation.*]

SCENE VIII: UNDERGROUND STATION

We see Morgan, in dark glasses, coming up the escalator. He hums the National Anthem, peers at the posters. He comes off the escalator and walks up to the ticket collector.

Morgan: Have you ever killed a man?
Collector: Just you watch it.
[*Morgan walks quickly through the barrier.*]

SCENE IX: HALLWAY OF CHARLES NAPIER'S OFFICE.

A glass door with the name on. Morgan opens it, walks round desk right up to Napier. Napier is seated at his desk. The room is tiny, filled with books. There is a desk, an office chair and an armchair. Napier is looking at some galley proofs. He looks up. He has an amused air but he is apprehensive.

Napier: Good afternoon, Morgan.
Morgan: Although you used to be my best friend, I can't allow you to sleep with my wife. I don't like it. It makes me feel funny in

the head, and whereas it's a run of the mill job for a shrinker it
will still cost me money.

Napier: Wife in name only, Morgan—

Morgan [*smiling*]*:* I shall stave your ribs in and plant a boot in your
guts.

Napier: Can't we be civilised about all this?

Morgan: One of the things I came to tell you is that in future you
can't count on me to be civilised. I've lost the thread.

   [*He rises, strolls round and sits on edge of desk.*]

I should warn you that I am becoming dangerous. This afternoon
I hanged a woolly dog. Tomorrow I might hang you. [*Pause*]
I'm getting fed up with symbolic gestures.

   [*Pause.*]

Napier: Why the dark glasses, Morgan?

Morgan: My eyes hurt. [*Pause.*]

Napier: Where are you living nowadays?

Morgan: I live in a car. My address is now BCD 801.

Napier [*rising*]*:* Leonie's car, I believe—whisky?

   [*Napier comes round to Morgan. Morgan takes knuckledusters
   from jeans pocket. Napier continues down to filing cabinet R.*]

Morgan: A small one. And then to brass tacks.

   [*Napier gets the whisky and two glasses. He is nonchalant, but
   the bottle rattles against the glasses.*]

Napier: How's your novel coming along?

Morgan: Have you got a sort of acid taste at the back of your throat?

Napier: You have a wonderfully bizarre imagination, Morgan.

Morgan: I'm conducting a war, I've decided to carry my art into
my life. Why should I be driven to psychiatrists by people like
you and Leonie? Think of all the people who really need treatment. People with obsessions, phobias, delusions and so on. I'm
busting the queue.

Napier: You started it. If you hadn't gone to France with that
pug-nosed little socialist girl [*He has rejoined Morgan*] Leonie
would never have turned to me. She's very loyal.

Morgan: You're after her money—admit it.

Napier: I doubt if she makes more than twenty-five hundred a year.

Morgan [*stands*]*:* Twenty-five hundred and seventy. She married me
to achieve insecurity, and when she'd got it she didn't know
what to do with it.

Napier: Violence will get you nowhere, Morgan.

Morgan: Where has gentleness got me? Where has love got me? Violence has a kind of dignity in a baffled man. The rich have the law, the poor a simple choice between docility and brutality. I am full of love. I shall punch you with love. Will you have love between the eyes or in the teeth?

[*He takes Napier by the shirt.*]

Napier: Now be reasonable, Morgan.

Morgan: But I am being reasonable. I could stand here and tell you to keep away from my wife till I was blue in the face—but would you?

[*Morgan releases him. Napier shrugs. Morgan goes R. to drinks and Napier goes back to the desk.*]

Morgan: I counted four haircream stains on the wallpaper in my flat. Did you think me unobservant?

Napier: I don't care what you are, Morgan. I'm very sorry for you and all that, but you don't exactly reach me. Not in the solar plexus. Not where the dark gods are located.

Morgan: Leonie bites in her sleep. She growls at dawn. Without make-up she looks like a wizened parsnip. Her stomach rumbles when she dreams. Her motto—I bath, therefore I am.

Napier [*rising*]: This has been a most interesting little chat, Morgan.

[*He goes to end of desk. Morgan comes in to him.*]

Morgan: They tell me you keep yourself in petty cash by robbing drunken writers in Soho drinking clubs.

Napier: That is apocryphal, I assure you.

Morgan: Then I must be off.

Napier: And I.

Morgan: To Leonie?

Napier: To the theatre.

Morgan: With Leonie?

Napier: With a client.

Morgan: Exactly.

Napier: Little insinuations please little minds.

[*Morgan goes towards door but stops and comes back to Napier.*]

Morgan: I definitely meant to bash you.

Napier: Goodbye then, Morgan.

Morgan: Goodbye—

Napier: One day—

Morgan [*at door*]: One day we shall strangle the last publisher with the entrails of the last literary agent.
Napier: No hard feelings.

SCENE X: GREEK CAFE

A seedy Greek cafe in Charlotte Street where Morgan is being given a free meal by his mother who is a waitress there. Morgan finishing his prunes. 'Olympos' in neon is flashing in the background.

Mrs Delt: Your dad was run down by the mounted police in Bristol in nineteen twenty-six. [*Pause*] That's nothing to be ashamed of. But you! Marry a rich woman, live in luxury on your backside. [*Pause*] And me slaving away in this dump. Look at me. Those aren't lady's hands—
   [*Holds out hands, which Morgan looks at.*]
Morgan: One of these days, Ma, they'll be coming for me with a strait-jacket.
Mrs Delt: I thought you was going to write for the telly and make a fortune. [*Pause*.]
Morgan: You know what a strait-jacket is, don't you?
Mrs Delt: Don't I! I've been living in one for years. Son, your dad saw himself waving the red flag on the rubble of Buckingham Palace. Don't ask me when. [*Pause*] Now look at us. You aren't the militant little lad that tried to set fire to Stepney Police station. Where's he gone?
Morgan: Things are very dicy just now on the ideological front, Ma.
Mrs Delt: Your dad was on to you the day he drowned them kittens. You knew what'd happen to them if he gave them away. But oh, no! Drowning was cruel. He says to me the day after: you've given birth to a bleeding liberal!
Morgan: It's your afternoon off tomorrow. I thought we might take a trip down the river to Greenwich.
Mrs Delt: I was thinking of going to the cemetery with his flowers. Ah son, the mess you've made of your life.
Morgan: You're a funny old woman, do you know that?

Mrs Delt: You wait and see. [*Pause*] It'll all come crashing down.
  [*She reaches down and massages her legs.*]
Morgan: What? [*Pause.*]
Mrs Delt: Everything. [*Pause*] I hope I live to see it all in ruins.
  Then I shall die happy. [*Pause*] I'm just the same as I was about
  religion when I was a girl. I couldn't bear it all to turn out untrue.
  [*Pause*] Well, I've still got me self-respect. Which is more than
  you have I should think.
Morgan: It's very difficult to retain a coherent view of life.
Mrs Delt: Your dad wanted to shoot the Royal Family, abolish
  marriage and put everybody who'd been to a public school in a
  chain gang. [*Pause*] He was an idealist was your dad.
Morgan: It's time you gave up working in this caff. Why don't I
  come home and take a job and let you retire in peace?
  [*Mrs Delt is much affected. Sniffs at her tears.*]
Mrs Delt: Oh I am tired, Morgan—
Morgan: Now, Ma—
Mrs Delt: When I look at you. You've grown into a peculiar sort
  of a feller—
  [*Pause.*]
Morgan: I consulted a trick cyclist yesterday—
Mrs Delt: What's that?
Morgan: A specialist in mental troubles.
Mrs Delt: And what did he say?
Morgan: He said—I'm a suitable case for treatment.
Mrs Delt: What sort of treatment? Electric shock and that?
Morgan: No. You lie on a couch and say whatever comes into your
  head.
Mrs Delt: Well let's hope he makes a man of you. [*Gets up*] I never
  did like your Leonie. [*Pause*] Ah, I shall never have peace in this
  world, Morgan. And I don't believe in the next.
  [*Morgan goes and puts his arm round her.*]
Morgan: I'll call for you at two then?
Mrs Delt: All right, Morgan.
Morgan: We'll go and see the Cutty Sark—
Mrs Delt: All right, Morgan.
Morgan: Cheerio then, Ma—
Mrs Delt: Cheerio son.
  [*She sits on at the table as he leaves her.*]

SCENE XI: MORGAN'S CAR IN STREET

CUT IN: *Sequence of gorilla film. The gorillas parade through sunlit jungle.*
CUT BACK TO: *Car, where Morgan's Mickey Mouse alarm clock is ringing on the dashboard. Morgan wakes up. With hot water from a thermos he begins to shave in the driving mirror.*

Morgan [*singing*]: Don't ask me why I'm dreaming . . . don't ask me why.
> [*A Policeman comes along the street—stops and stares at Morgan. He comes to the offside door and crouches at the window. Morgan dabs a blob of shaving soap on the policeman's nose. The policeman takes out his handkerchief and wipes it off.*]
Policeman: That's an assault, technically speaking—
Morgan: Is there anything which is not, technically speaking, an assault? Birth. School. Work. Sex. Life. Consciousness. Death—
Policeman: This your car?
Morgan: No.
> [*The policeman takes out a notebook.*]
Policeman: Begged, borrowed or stolen?
Morgan: Property of wife.
Policeman: Got any proof of identity?
Morgan: No. Have you?
Policeman: I'm asking the questions.
Morgan: You were until just now. Now, *I'm* asking them as well. That's an indisputable fact.
Policeman: It's funny how many of you think that's an original line. Address?
Morgan: How do I know you're a real policeman?
Policeman: You'll just have to take me on trust.
Morgan: Haven't you got a little card with your photo on it? And an official stamp?
Policeman: No.
Morgan: If I was Prince Philip, do you know what you'd do?
Policeman: What?
Morgan: You'd . . [*Peering*] have you got a forelock? Well, you'd pull your forelock and straighten your helmet and back the hell out of it. Confess.

Policeman: Do you usually shave in this vehicle of a morning?

Morgan: Is it against the law?

Policeman: I shouldn't think so.

Morgan: Then what's all the fuss about?

Policeman: You're the one that's making the fuss—

Morgan [singing]: Come into the garden Maud . . . for the black bat night hath flown.

Policeman: I'm asking you to show legitimate right of usage of this vehicle.

Morgan: You could always ring my wife.

[*The policeman wanders round the car and copies down the number.*]

Policeman: [*States car number.*]

Policeman: You want to watch it—

Morgan: I know. But where *is* it?

[*The policeman eyes Morgan for a moment then goes off down the street. Morgan wipes his face with a towel and switches on the radio. We hear the fat stock prices.*

Morgan opens a packet of sandwiches, and from a second thermos pours a cup of coffee and settles back in seat to eat them. Jean comes along the street. She stops by car and she and Morgan stare at each other. She goes and leans on window.]

Jean: I *wish* you'd go away.

Morgan: You shouldn't have changed the lock. I would go away. But I can't drive.

[*Jean is fiddling with door handle. She gets into the car.*]

Jean: That copper seemed very interested in you.

Morgan: Just passing the time of day.

Jean: Do you love me, Morgan?

Morgan: Yes.

Jean: This won't be much fun when it's winter, you know—

Morgan: They'll have come for me before winter.

Jean: They don't put neurotics in mental hospitals. Only psychotics and psychopaths.

Morgan: But I'm not a bit neurotic. I'm happy . . . integrated . . . friendly . . . tractable . . . and I'm extremely loving.

Jean: Your sunflower's very high now. Nearly as tall as me.

Morgan: It must be nice to have a bit of garden. Fill it with sunflowers . . . babies . . . empty whisky bottles . . . copies of *The*

Observer—

Jean: I wish you'd get a divorce.

Morgan: Will you have some breakfast?

Jean: I love you such a lot. That's why I have to keep you out of the flat.

Morgan: That's what they call a *non sequitur.*

Jean: I know.

Morgan [singing]: Girls . . . were made to love and kiss . . . and who am I to interfere with this. . . .

Jean: I'd better go in. I'm tired. I'm going to give up this telephone job.

Morgan: I wonder how much I could get for this car.

Jean: You could try working—

Morgan: Yes. Got to pay for this mental medication. Got to get the mind working. Supple.

Jean: How's your mother?

Morgan: She refuses to de-Stalinise.

[*Jean yawns and stretches her arms.*]

Jean: Oh, I love her. [*Cuddles to his shoulder.*]

Morgan: I'm a bad son. Is it the chromosomes, or is it England?

Jean: It's your wife.

Morgan: It all started in the pram with me.

Jean: What?

Morgan: I used to lie there gurgling in the sun. Innocent. Laughing at the rabbits and bears on my blue blanket. My mother'd leave me outside the shops chewing a piece of coal or something else for the teeth. Somebody would park a pram with a girl in it next to mine. Then boarding stations. It's been boarding stations for me ever since.

Jean: Leonie's been good to you.

Morgan: Yes. I attract people who are good to me. It's my burden. I wish I was eighteen months again, cooing at the butterflies.

Jean: You can't have me *and* Leonie, that's all. That's what I've decided. I'm monogamous. What are you going to do about it?

Morgan: What I'd really like is to go to Africa and build hospitals for picaninnies.

Jean: About Leonie and *me.*

Morgan: Oh, yes—

Jean: Yes what?

Morgan: I mean, I think I can guarantee the Minister's full and careful attention to the problem.

Jean: You infuriate me. I shall find somebody else—you see. I'm not going to hang about waiting for you to make your mind up.

Morgan: Is it degrading?

Jean: Is *what* degrading?

Morgan: Hanging about waiting for me to—

[*Jean gets out of the car and bangs the door.*]

Jean: You owe me six pounds ten, by the way.

Morgan: Impossible.

Jean: Oh no it isn't. My landlady saw the rug. The one you shaved the hammer and sickle on. I've had to pay for it *and* she thinks I'm a communist now, as well as a tart.

Morgan: You could have told her it was the Turkish national flag.

Jean: Oh, Morgan, please leave Leonie. I'll have you back if we can be together properly. We can live on my money till you've finished your book.

Morgan: I'm surprised at you—wanting to be the agent of another woman's unhappiness.

[*Jean bursts into tears. She rushes across the pavement and into the house. Morgan stands up.*]

Morgan: You can't kill the idea—

SCENE XII: LEONIE'S FLAT

Morgan comes out of the living-room where he has been fixing some wires on the radiogram. He opens the closet door and goes in.

Morgan [*singing*]*:* Morgan is sad today, sadder than yesterday. . . .

[*He picks up a small attache case (a tape recorder) opens it and picks up microphone. He begins to recite into the microphone.*]

Morgan: They fought all that night neath the pale Tartar moon,

The din it was heard from afar.

And the bravest of all

Was that wily kelmuk—

Morgan, Skavinsky-Skavar.

[*Morgan's voice stops.*]

[*A variety of loud jungle noises—screams, squawks and roars are emitted. These stop and are replaced by several bars of Purcell's Trumpet Voluntary. Morgan scuttles into the living-room. Looks at gram and smiles.*]

Morgan: All shall be well and all manner of *thing* shall be well. Thing. Thing. Thing thing thing. [*Sings*] Morgan is sad today. [*Speaks*] Very sad. Sad man.

[*Goes to a large flat brown paper bag leaning in the chair. Takes from bag a huge blow-up of a gorilla's face, and goes up into dining alcove, to Picasso, which he removes. Hangs the picture, setting it straight and stepping back to dig the effect. Collects carrier bag etc. Puts the Picasso into the bag. And goes quietly away.*]

SCENE XIII: LEONIE'S FLAT

The room has been returned to its normal state. The radiogram is playing softly the M.J.Q. Napier and Leonie are at the table. They clink their champagne glasses.

Napier: Cheers, darling.
Leonie: Cheers.

[*Morgan and stepladder appear outside the window. Napier and Leonie lean back in their chairs. Dinner has been very satisfactory. Morgan has his dark glasses on as usual. Napier and Leonie are absorbed in each other and unaware of Morgan.*]

Leonie: Fruit, darling.

[*Napier takes grapes—begins to peel one.*
Morgan pushes back his dark glasses.]

CUT IN: *Film of gorilla eating grapes.*

[*Morgan's glasses drop over his eyes and he climbs down ladder.*]

Napier: Do you know darling, I wouldn't have met you if it hadn't been for Morgan.
Leonie: Poor Morgan.

Napier: Don't waste your pity on him.

Leonie: I don't pity him.

Napier: One of society's throwouts I'm afraid.

Leonie: Can he write, Charles?

Napier: Oh yes. He can write. He's very talented. Never get him published though.

Leonie: But why? Why does everybody say the same thing?

Napier [lighting his cigar]: The man's aberrated. Bonkers. No sense of structure. I can't understand why you ever married him—

Leonie: I adored Morgan. In the beginning.

Napier: He's a parasite.

Leonie: I learned a lot from Morgan. It's no use ignoring his—his positive side.

Napier: I don't really want to talk about Morgan.

Leonie: We've got to be good, Charles.

Napier: What do you mean?

Leonie: The proctors.

Napier: Proctors?

Leonie: My solicitor definitely said something about discretion, and proctors.

Napier: Really, we do live in an archaic society, don't we? In some respects. [*Puffs at cigar.*] You know, I feel rather guilty about old Morgan sometimes.

Leonie: Why? You never even touched me, before he ran off with that nasty little thing with the stringy hair.

Napier: I was waiting to pounce though. I knew Morgan would go too far one day. So I simply waited.

Leonie: It made it easier to send him packing. Morgan has no sense of values at all. [*Touches his hand.*] I feel secure for the first time in years now.

  [*They look at each other.*]

  [*Morgan in the hall is sitting listening at the keyhole. He sits up in a Buddha position and lights a joss stick.*]

Leonie: I wouldn't say Morgan is exactly immoral. No. He never meant to hurt me. There are some men who help women to mature, whilst remaining adolescents themselves. Morgan's one of those, poor darling.

Napier: Let's dance. [*He rises and goes to her. Escorts her down into the main room by the radiogram.*]

Leonie: I'm sure the only dancing Morgan would have approved of is negro fertility rites—

Napier: I notice you still haven't had the lock changed

Leonie: No. I suppose it's terribly Freudian. You know, by leaving that picture of a gorilla on the wall I think Morgan was trying to tell me something.

Napier: A postcard would be more efficient.

Leonie: He had an awful childhood you know. That blowsy old mother. And his father working in the sewers.

Napier: Is that what Morgan told you?

Leonie: Yes . . . well didn't he?

Napier: He once told me his father worked in a gasworks.

Leonie: He's an awful liar of course. [*Breaking away from him*] Do you think I'm bourgeois, Charles?

Napier: Darling, of course not. [*They kiss.*]

[*In the hall Morgan is dancing with Leonie's coat.*]

Morgan: Do you think I'm bourgeois, coat?

[*In the living-room Napier and Leonie have sat down on the sofa.*]

Leonie: I think you'd better not go on being his agent.

Napier: It hardly matters. He'll never finish anything.

Leonie: Oh it has been nerve-wracking these past few years. One gives and gives. I feel desiccated.

Napier: Poor Leonie . . .

Leonie: You do love me, Charles—? [*She turns to him.*]

[*We see Morgan at the keyhole. He gets up and goes to the closet. Napier is about to kiss Leonie. Morgan opens the tape recorder and turns the switch. As Napier's lips touch Leonie's the record keeps turning but there is silence. Napier and Leonie are frozen with surprise. We now hear an American rocket count-down.*]

Voice: Six, five, four, three, two, one, *zero*.

[*This is followed by a loud recording of a rocket launching. Napier and Leonie spring apart.*]

Leonie: Morgan!

Napier: Where?

[*They cross to gram and turn the record off then go out into hall. Leonie goes into dark bedroom and switches on light. Goes out to hall. And goes to closet door.*]

Leonie: He's in there . . .I know he is . . .

[*She opens door. Morgan stands there holding his tape machine.*

He turns switch. He turns to the light.]

Morgan: Ten years' searching for the substance of art—misled by abstraction, fooled by the lure of style. In fact, I ignored the concrete. Working it out, assuming twelve pounds ten per week for my keep, I have cost you three thousand and seventy-five pounds. A bad investment.

Napier [*moving in*]: I think we've had about enough of this.

[*Leonie cries. Morgan turns switch. Star-Spangled Banner booms out. Leonie rushes into bedroom and Napier follows. Morgan switches off.*]

Morgan: I may be sad—but I'm loving. I constitute a case for life, growth . . . fond of flowers, animals and little children. I even help old policemen across the road. What more do you want?

SCENE XIV: MORGAN'S DREAM

Clip from old Tarzan film—Jane is captured by the apes and Tarzan rescues her. Music.
(1) *Bassoon theme from Britten/Purcell*
(2) *USSR Anthem*
(3) *Bring in Vivaldi's 'Autumn'*
(4) *Fade Vivaldi*
Mix from Vivaldi to USSR Anthem loud.

We now see a table and two chairs. Behind them is a big blowup of Stalin. Mrs Delt sits at the table sipping Russian tea and looking at a dossier on the table. She takes out and looks at a photograph of Morgan prison-style with number BCD 801 along the bottom. Mrs Delt takes a pen and starts to write in dossier. Jean and Morgan approach. Jean has a carbine over her shoulder and Morgan's hands are tied. They come up to table and Morgan goes to stand in front of it.

Mrs Delt: Hullo son.
Morgan: Hullo Ma.

Mrs Delt [*Brandishing dossier*]: Not what you'd call thirty-five glorious years!

Morgan: No Ma.

[*She opens dossier.*]

Morgan: Can I sit down?

[*She motions him to do so.*]

Mrs Delt: How do you feel about it then?

Morgan: Very sad.

Mrs Delt: Is that all?

Morgan: It's a brutal old world, Ma.

Mrs Delt: You started off with every advantage! Born into a decent, working-class family. Good secondary modern education. Nice steady job in a canning factory. [*Pause*] Then you went off the tracks. [*Pause*] Suddenly. For no reason.

[*She scrabbles among the dossier pages.*]

Morgan: I'm looking for a niche, Ma. [*Pause*] I've got symptoms to feed.

Mrs Delt: What symptoms?

Morgan: Anxiety, vertigo, agoraphobia, dandruff, hallucinations, pains in the spinal column, violent impulses, despair, depression, passion—

[*Pause.*]

Mrs Delt: You'll never get yourself put away at this rate.

Morgan: It isn't that I *want* to get myself put away, Ma—

Mrs Delt: What *do* you want then?

Morgan: Or who—

Mrs Delt: It comes to the same thing.

Morgan [*to his Mother*]: It's my distinct impression that you gave me a rough time in nineteen twenty-seven. Aren't you ashamed? [*Pause*] A little, totty, helpless infant. [*Pause*] Still, I suppose you were ignorant. You lacked a theory of the human personality. [*Pause*] There I was. [*Pause*] A small, roaring bundle of sensations in a world of flickering light and shadows. [*Pause*] What it is to inhabit a universe where there are no toes—only tootsy-wootsies. [*Pause*] And faces hanging over the cot like imbecilic moons. [*Pause*] It's an outrage.

Mrs Delt: It's no use blaming me, Morgan.

Morgan: I've already conceded your ignorance.

Mrs Delt: That's not a very nice thing to say, either. [*Pause*] You're

ungrateful. Your father used to read Mayakovsky over your cot—
there can't be many babies grew up with that sort of advantage.

Morgan: You know what happened to Mayakovsky don't you?
[*Morgan closes his eyes.*]

Morgan: I have a distaste for the absolute, Ma. If I've let you down
—blame that.

Mrs Delt: You don't know what it is—a mother's anguish.

Jean: You two are getting on my nerves.

Mrs Delt: I wish I was dead. I wish it was all true about heaven and
I would go to join your dad, Morgan. [*Pause*] You was such a
gay little boy. [*Pause*] What have they done to you?

Morgan: I don't know. Whatever it is, it's very insidious. [*Turns
to Jean.*] What have they done to me?

Jean [*coming round to him*]: It's time you took a hold of yourself.

Morgan: I see. You want me to turn into a babbling extrovert—

Jean: I want you to be a man.

Morgan: Meaning?

Jean: Stop messing about.

Morgan: Meaning?

Jean: Well you're just nothing the way you are.

Morgan: This is very unjust. You're as bad as Leonie. Always
inviting me to step into life—but for *me* it's like stepping off a
precipice. [*Pause*] And put a skirt on.

Mrs Delt: Well I can't see us getting any further than this today.
Take him away.

Jean: Do you love me Morgan?

Morgan: Yes.

Jean: Then *do* something!

[*She cuts Morgan's hands apart and escorts him out.*]

SCENE XV: PSYCHOANALYST'S CONSULTING ROOM

Morgan is lying on the Analyst's couch.

Analyst's Voice: Have you been asleep?

Morgan: Have I?

Analyst: You've had your eyes closed for a long time.

Morgan: I had a dream about my Ma, and a girl I know. [*Pause*] I bet you're tickled to bits to hear that!
   [*Pause.*]

Analyst: Why do you say so?

Morgan: Dunno.
   [*Long pause.*]
 You're a very *dull* psychoanalyst.

Analyst: Why am I dull?

Morgan: I expect it's me that's dull.
   [*Pause.*]

Analyst: Then why are *you* dull?
   [*Pause.*]

Morgan: I could sing something?
   [*Pause.*]

Analyst: You're not singing, are you?

Morgan: It's very boring here.

Analyst: What would you like to do?
   [*Pause.*]

Morgan: Don't you want to hear about my dream?

Analyst: Do you want to tell me?
   [*Pause.*]

Morgan: You know, you drive me up the wall.
   [*Pause.*]
 Well?

Analyst: Well what? [*Morgan sits up*].

Morgan: Did you hear about the woman and the analyst?

Analyst: What about them?

Morgan: She said: Doctor, doctor kiss me!

Analyst: Yes?

Morgan [*brightening*]*:* And he said: Kiss you! I shouldn't even be here on the couch with you. Ha Ha. Huh?
   [*Silence. No response from the Analyst. Morgan looks very dejected. Long pause.*]
 You can't get *me*! [*Pause*] I absolutely refuse to do things here instead of [*Pointing a finger at the wall*] out there.

Analyst: Have I asked you to do anything here?
   [*Pause.*]

Morgan: No.

Analyst: Then.

Morgan [*irritably*]: Then I'm skewered? Eh?

Analyst: Skewered?

Morgan: You're a terrible one for the old symbols, aren't you?

Analyst: Do you think so?

Morgan: All right, all right! *I* am then. [*Pause*] It's all right for you sitting there. [*Pause*] I've got to get up and go out amongst those Anglo-Saxons. [*Pause*] Is it time?

Analyst: Nearly.

Morgan: I'm the one that's exposed to these English. Not you. You're healthy. Healthy mind in a healthy body. Eh? A good match for those types out there. I'm too sensitive for this vale of tears. And then there are the purely technical problems of bread and roof. Women. Marauding policemen. National Health Payments. [*Rises*] Well, cheerio then. See you tomorrow. [*Analyst gets up*] Got cramp have you? Try banging your foot on the floor. You shouldn't sit with your legs crossed.

> [*Morgan goes out—door slams.*
> *Analyst turns to look after him lighting a fag.*]

SCENE XVI: LEONIE'S FLAT. NIGHT

It is 2.00 a.m. Leonie and her mother are just coming in from the theatre. We hear voices:

Mother: I enjoyed that thoroughly . . . so well acted.

Leonie: I'm so glad you liked it. etc. etc. [*She opens the living-room door. Leonie turns the light on as they enter. Shuts door.*]

Mother: It's so good of you to have me, darling. I'd have hated to go back to Maidstone without spending the whole evening with you and Charles.

Leonie: Do you like him?

Mother: He's charming. [*Pause*] The sort of man you should have married in the first place.

Leonie: Oh, Mother!

Mother: I know you're still loyal to Morgan in some way I simply
    can't understand, but—
Leonie: I don't want you to compare them, that's all. [*They cross
    towards the sofa and sit.*]
Mother [*sharply*]*:* There *is* no comparison of course. Charles has
    breeding.
    [*Pauses. Smiles.*]
    He tells me he went to Winchester.
Leonie: Yes.
    [*Pause.*]
Mother: It's all been *most* harrowing, Leonie. [*Pause*] Thank good-
    ness there aren't any children. [*Pause*] One shudders at the idea
    of Morgan having progeny.
    [*Pause.*]
Leonie: Morgan *loves* children.
Mother: He may love them. I'm not saying the man's a monster.
    What chills me is the thought that you might have perpetuated
    the Delt family. [*Pause. Speaks rather cruelly*] I wonder why you
    didn't?
    [*Pause.*]
Leonie: We hoped he'd get somewhere with his writing first.
Mother: I always found him *quite* illiterate. He once told me the
    only person he'd read was Wyndham Lewis. [*Pause*] Your Uncle
    Seaton knew Wyndham Lewis before the war and thought him
    a detestable person.
Leonie: None of which has anything to do with whether or not
    Morgan can write.
Mother: You know, I've never been able to tell you this before,
    Leonie but the one and only time you both slept in my house,
    do you know what I found inked onto the bedspread the day you
    left?
Leonie: A hammer and sickle.
Mother [*taken aback*]*:* Oh, so you knew about it!
Leonie: No.
Mother: Then how did you guess that he—
Leonie: He's got a thing about hammers and sickles.
Mother: Well it's a very silly thing to have a thing about! I'm all
    for social mobility, or whatever they call it. But if some of these
    people can't accept one's standards! [*Pause. Goes to Leonie*] My

poor darling, I do admire you for having taken him on, only please don't think about him any more.

Leonie [*rising*]: Would you like something to eat?

    [*She crosses towards the door. Mother follows her.*]

Mother: I'd rather go straight to bed. I'm so sorry darling. I'm both garrulous and insensitive. I don't know what it is about Morgan . . . he does rather set one off, doesn't he?

Leonie [*laughing*]: Yes.

CUT TO:

Bedroom in darkness except for street light through window. Morgan is climbing in the window, a small square box in one hand. He plants his foot on a box which scrunches under him. His feet knock powder, bottles, etc. to the floor. He looks at his watch and sets a pointer on the bomb he is carrying. Then hears voices from the hall. He crawls under the bed.

Mother: I think I'll take the early train down tomorrow, dear. I have people coming for lunch.

Leonie: All right, Mother, etc. etc.

    [*She opens the bedroom door. They enter and Leonie switches on light. Sees wreckage by dressing table.*]

Leonie: Oh, no! [*She crosses to it.*]

Mother: Oh.

Leonie: Morgan !

Mother: I thought you'd had him stopped coming here.

Leonie: I have. In theory.

    [*She looks round the room. And at clock.*]

Leonie: It's well after two. I think he's mad.

    [*She goes out to the hall and opens closet door. Mother is picking up the wreckage. She has an idea and goes over to the bed and peers under it.*]

Mother: Morgan! Come out—

    [*Morgan crawls out and stands up, leaving the bomb undetected. Morgan stands facing mother as Leonie re-enters after her search.*]

Leonie: Oh Morgan—

Mother: Don't you think you are being rather tiresome?

Morgan: Yes. [*To Leonie*] Where's Napier?

Mother: You surely didn't expect to find Charles here?

Morgan: Why not?

[*He moves down L. Mother following.*]

Mother: Why not? Do you imagine that Charles and Leonie?

Morgan: Yes. That's what I imagine.

[*Leonie crosses and sits wearily on stool at dressing table. Mother moves in on Morgan.*]

Mother: It's a mistake to judge others by one's own standards of conduct, Morgan.

[*Morgan puts his face close to hers.*]

Morgan: You've got real insight! [*Turns away*] I wish I were black.

[*He turns and goes to sit on bed.*]

Mother: I beg your pardon.

Morgan: I'm tired of being white.

Mother: Spare us Morgan.

Morgan: I'm all for negritude.

Mother: He's raving.

Morgan: It's the usual ontological problem.

Mother: Will you go, Morgan? Or shall I ring the police?

Morgan: Silly woman.

Leonie: Morgan.

Morgan: I can't help it. I didn't decide to say it. It just came out. I sometimes doubt whether I'm free at all. [*He stretches out on the bed.*] I'll bet your brains are seething. Both of you. Wondering how to get rid of me. I get lonely you know. I have to have a bit of company.

[*Mother has moved round the end of the bed. She is going towards the door.*]

Mother: We were about to go to bed.

Morgan: It's cold on Parliament Hill. And I get frightened. I need lights. Music. Women.

[*Mother looks scandalised.*]

Morgan: Young women.

Leonie: What's happened to Jean then? Has she kicked you out as well?

[*Morgan sits up.*]

Morgan: Shall we have a cup of cocoa? Get the dressing gowns on. Tell stories about giants, and little chaps in liripipe hats?

Leonie: Can't you just leave me alone Morgan? Why do you come? You're making me hate you.

Morgan: It's entirely your fault that you and I aren't tucked up nice and snug in this bed at this very minute. Man and wife.

Mother: I know you, Morgan. You're all bluff. And behind the bluff—a cringing, dependent lout.

Morgan: First prize to the lady with the hammer nose and the sickle-shaped mouth.

    [*Mother stares at him in outraged disbelief. She goes to telephone on bedside table and begins to dial.*

Leonie: No mother!

    [*Mother hesitates—puts down receiver.*]

Mother: No? Then you can deal with him yourself.

    [*She goes out.*]

Leonie: Were you ever happy with me? I don't think so. I think you wanted it to break up. But you hadn't the guts to do it yourself. I can understand men wanting other women besides their wives. What I can't understand is how a man can make a woman suffer then turn round and say that the actions which caused her to suffer aren't important to him.

Morgan: Yes. It's abominable.

    [*Leonie gets up and crosses to him.*]

Leonie: Is ordinary decency so contemptible?

Morgan: Perhaps it's time we tried something else. Maybe we should let people steal from us, betray us, wreak havoc in general. Learn to yield, to lose, to dispense with judgment.

Leonie: You make my head ache. You always did. When I first got to know you I thought you had a kind of dignity. Something I'd never seen before in a man.

    [*Morgan looks remote. He closes his eyes.*]

CUT IN: *Still of gorilla looking dignified.*

    [*Morgan smiles a little.*]

Morgan: Dignity?

Leonie [*quietly*]: How do you manage to live now?

Morgan: Same as before. The heart pumps, the legs jog along, the kidneys distil, the bowels churn.

Leonie: Don't make fun of me. I mean are you all right?

Morgan: Sound in wind and limb. [*Pause*] Free meals off Ma at the Greek caff. Comfortable back seat in BCD 801. On the whole, tickety boo.

[*Pause.*]

Leonie: I wonder what you'll be like when you're sixty.

[*Pause.*]

Morgan: Pretty squalid, I should think. However, there's a quarter of a century to get things straightened out.

Leonie: And there's always Jean.

Morgan: Yes.

Leonie: Do you love her?

Morgan: Yes.

Leonie: Yet you say you love me!

Morgan: Yes. No one can say I lack the capacity, even if I'm equivocal about the focus. [*Pause*] I also love a wide variety of fauna and flora, e.g. voles, gum trees, dolphins, dandelions, human babies, anthropoids, of all kinds. And certain types of building. Aztec temples, kraals, igloos, wigwams, bronze-age earthworks. [*Pause*] But I can't stand the pyramids. [*Pause. Looks at wristwatch*] I think that's just about all I had to say.

Leonie: I'll never have you back. But I'm glad I had you.

Morgan: I'm glad I was had.

[*Pause.*]

Leonie: I have to have stability.

Morgan: I know.

Leonie: Would you like to give me a goodbye kiss?

Morgan: Why? Am I going?

Leonie: I've got to be up for work.

[*Pause.*]

Morgan: There's just the matter of this anti-Napier device under the bed.

Leonie: The what?

Morgan: A sort of wee bomb. [*Door opens*] More of a thunderflash really.

[*Leonie's mother bursts into the room in her dressing gown, unable to contain her anger.*]

Mother: Morgan, will you leave this house?

Morgan [to Leonie]: It has a time fuse. Made it myself.

[*They take no notice of mother.*]

Mother: If you both propose to ignore me, I shall call the police.

[*Morgan gets up, goes to Leonie's mother.*]

Morgan: Mrs Henderson, you are a grotesque bourgeois lady and the police will get you nowhere. I meant to tell you this several years ago, but I forgot. To invoke the forces of law and order is a very negative attitude. What are we to do then? Shut our eyes and bellow: Constable, arrest that man? Think how bitterness and rancour will shrivel his heart in the loneliness of a prison cell! [*Pause*] No, madam! You must love the wretch. Fatten him up on compassion till his pelt ruptures in gratitude. [*Hisses amiably into her face*] Or he'll blow you sky-high.

Mother [to Leonie]: Surely it's possible to have him certified.

Leonie [gently]: Come on Morgan. I'll come to the door with you.

[*Leonie crosses towards door. Morgan wags his forefinger at Leonie's mother like a metronome.*]

Morgan: Tick tock, poor old Mom. You are standing on a bomb.

[*They go out, the door closing behind them. Leonie's mother stares after them for a few seconds, stunned by Morgan.*]

Mother [venomously]: Ridiculous!

[*She sits on the bed to wait for Leonie. Suddenly there is a flash, a bang, and the room is filled with black smoke. Mrs Henderson shrieks—disappears, enveloped in sooty clouds. Leonie comes into the hall and dashes to bedroom door, which opens. Her mother appears, grim, stark, black-faced and dishevelled, smoke billowing out round her. Leonie's face twitches, she is almost laughing. Puts up her hand to hide her expression.*]

Leonie: Mother! Are you all right?

[*Mrs Henderson pauses.*]

Mother [acidly]: Are you amused?

SCENE XVII: MORGAN'S DREAM

CLOSE UP: *A still of Morgan's face with dark glasses. It begins to spin faster and faster. This turns to a glowing screen in a dark* *room where Morgan enters with his hands tied. We hear drums and music—the USSR Anthem fades up and on the screen—a Tarzan film. Morgan watches, smiling. The film changes to the execution scene from Eisenstein's 'Potemkin'. This changes to a still of a bullet-scarred wall in Spain. Morgan is frightened. Drums beat and Morgan turns as a firing squad approaches consisting of Leonie, Jean, Mr and Mrs Henderson, Napier and Mrs Delt. We track along their faces. A Policeman enters. He ties a black handkerchief over Morgan's eyes. The drums fade.*

Policeman: Got anything you want to say then?
Morgan: Yes.
    [*A long pause.*]
Policeman: Either I've gone deaf, or you're not saying it.
Morgan: It's all gone.
Policeman: We'd better get on then.
Morgan: Wait a minute. It's coming back. Yes. I've got it.
Policeman: Come on then.
Morgan [*clearing his throat*]: Constant revolutionising of production, uninterrupted disturbance of all social conditions, everlasting uncertainty and agitation, distinguish the bourgeois epoch from all earlier ones. All that is solid melts into the air. All that is holy is profaned, and man is at last compelled to face with sober senses his real conditions of life . . . and his relations with his kind.
    [*A long pause.*]
Policeman: Is that all?
Morgan: No.
Policeman: It's a rare old mouthful, and quite enough I should have thought.
    [*Pause.*]
Morgan: Has it clouded over yet?
Policeman: No. It's still a bright blue day.
Morgan: I planted some sunflowers in a girl's garden.
Policeman: Did you now!
Morgan: Am I getting on your nerves?
Policeman: I wouldn't say that.
Morgan: I do get on people's nerves.
Policeman: It's only human.
Morgan: When I was twenty-three, I wanted to marry a beautiful

girl and live on a Greek island. [*Pause*] Watch the kids browning in the sun. Lie besides the honey-brown girl at night with moths banging round the lamp. [*Pause*] I was very wistful, at twenty-three.

[*Pause.*]

Policeman: Have you finished? .

Morgan: I don't want to finish.

Policeman: Nobody wants to finish. Always trying to put it off. But the event *will* take place, young man.

Morgan: Do you love life, constable?

Policeman: I think I can say I do.

Morgan: I'd sing . . . but my throat's dry. [*Pause*] I like singing.

Policeman: We could allow a hymn, possibly. A little hymn.

[*Morgan shakes his head.*]

Morgan: It's very quiet. Are they still there?

Policeman: They're waiting.

Morgan: Have you ever heard cicadas?

Policeman: Once. [*In a surprised tone*] That was in a foxhole in southern Italy. A summer night. [*Pause*] Would you like a cigarette, son?

Morgan: Yes please.

[*The policeman puts a cigarette in Morgan's mouth and lights it.*] Have you ever put your cheek against your wife's nose when she's asleep. Felt her breath?

Policeman: Never.

Morgan: As warm and light as the darkness!

Policeman: Maybe—when you're young!

[*Pause.*]

Morgan: Is the sun high?

Policeman: Straight above.

Morgan: I can feel it on the top of my head. [*Pause*] I like the smell of hair that's hot with sun. The scalp moist. Tiny rivulets of sweat behind the ears. [*Pause*] I get quite nostalgic over these concrete physical things. [*Pause*] Men should throw shadows in history—not offstage, so to speak.

[*Pause.*]

Policeman: You do run on, Mr Delt!

Morgan: Am I holding things up?

Policeman: Well, they'll be wanting to get away for their dinners—

Morgan: And I shall be rotting when they are digesting—
Policeman: Now you mustn't get morbid—
Morgan: Oh, no!
    [*Pause.*]
Policeman: Now then?
Morgan: All right.

    [*Policeman takes cigarette. He walks across to firing squad and raises his hand. The firing squad comes to attention. He lifts his hand higher—they take up firing positions.*]

CUT IN: *Odessa steps sequence from 'Potemkin' as the squad fires at Morgan.*

CUT TO: *Morgan's bloodstained face. A series of stills of Morgan's face as a corpse. Mix to a coffin on trestles with three candles burning on it. Music: Vivaldi's 'Autumn'. Mr. Delt—an old working man in flat cap and muffler—enters. Slowly, he snuffs the candles. Superimpose still of Morgan dead, and mix to:*

SCENE XVIII: JEAN'S ROOM

Morgan is in bed asleep, tossing and being restless. It is a bedsit., with screened kitchen in one corner, an armchair, dressing table, etc. A large stuffed gorilla stands in the centre of the room. It has a large notice pinned on it saying:—
        'Jean, happy birthday, with love from Morgan
             Enclosed one Anthropoid.'
Jean comes in door—home from her night shift on the exchange. She tosses coat and bag on chair. Sees gorilla and goes over to him. She hugs him as she reads the note . . . then sees Morgan asleep on the bed. She goes over to him. He turns restlessly. She kneels beside him. Touches his face softly.

Jean: Morgan. Poor Morgan.
    [*Morgan wakes confused.*]
Jean: You were crying, love. Why cry?

Morgan: What time is it?

Jean: Nearly six. I've just got back from work. Tears.

Morgan: Is it sunny?

Jean: I think it's autumn. The air's sharp. Nearly frosty. Would you like some coffee.

Morgan: I dreamt I was executed by a firing squad. Then I was looking into a room where my own coffin stood on trestles. It had candles on, and my old man came with a snuffer and put them out.

> [*Jean looks at him—kisses his cheek. Stands and goes across to the kitchen corner and switches on kettle.*]

Jean: It's been a rotten summer. I hate London. I hate this rotten telephonist job.

> [*Puts coffee in cups.*]

Morgan [*sitting up*]: You don't reckon much to me, either.

Jean: It isn't that. I want to think I'll arrive somewhere . . . at something. If you'd have me I'd be happy. I'd love everything. But you won't. I'm quite realistic, you know.

> [*Jean is busy pouring out the water and making coffee.*]

Jean: There's a man wants to marry me.

Morgan: William?

Jean: No.

Morgan: Peter!

Jean: No.

Morgan: You must have a pretty seething sort of life when I'm not around.

Jean: I don't think so. But in any case you're not around very often are you? [*She goes over to him*] God knows what you do with your time.

> [*She sits on the bed.*]

Morgan: You haven't said thanks for your birthday present.

> [*Jean looks at gorilla and smiles.*]

Jean: Thanks for my birthday present.

Morgan: They're not easily come by you know, stuffed gorillas.

Jean: I don't suppose they are.

Morgan: Well—I thought you'd be hysterical with pleasure.

> [*Pause.*]

Jean: You're a fool, Morgan—

Morgan: I know.

[*Pause.*]

Jean: Other men I know, I can say they're like this or like that—but I can never say what you're like.

Morgan: I wonder if I've got a brain tumour? [*Pause*] I've had head X-rays and nobody saw anything. [*Pause*] Imagine a little black tumour growing there—dislocating the whole set-up!

[*Jean goes to the sink with her mug. Rinses it.*]

Jean: I think I'm going to marry this man, Morgan.

Morgan: I've always been a hypochondriac. [*Pause*] You know those Victorian glass bells that they used to cover wax fruit with? I sometimes feel as if I've had one put down over me.

Jean: Morgan, somebody wants me. Somebody wants to marry me. Hasn't it sunk in? And I think I nearly love him as well. I wouldn't if you'd behaved differently, but I nearly do. I want to know what you have to say about it—

Morgan: It's extremely complicated.

Jean: Come on.

[*She gets up and goes across to the fire which she lights and sits in front of it on the floor. Morgan sits edge of bed. Then crosses to door and puts his trousers on.*]

Morgan: There just doesn't seem to be anything in this life that comes up to my best fantasies. [*Pause*] Man is an inventive creature—ingenious, industrious, shaping the natural world. Then why the chasm? It beats me. [*Pause*] Have you ever dreamt you were dead? [*Sits beside her.*]

Jean: Millions of times.

Morgan: Well I didn't like it! I do care, Jean.

Jean: Convince me.

Morgan: I'm entombed in love. [*Pause*] I'm essentially outward-directed you know—but I think I'm a bit short in the reach.

[*Pause.*]

Jean: *I* think you're essentially a hole in space, when it comes to love!

Morgan: That's because you interpret me incorrectly. People frequently do. [*Finds his sneakers and puts them on.*] Otherwise I'd be swinging—

Jean: Where are you off to?

Morgan [*coming over to the fire*]*:* I've got a crowded day before me. Got a cig?

[*Jean silently hands him a packet of cigarettes and a box of matches which have been lying on the corner of the fender*.]

Jean: If I could think of any way to keep you—I'd keep you.
  [*Pause.*]

Morgan: What would you do with me?
  [*Pause.*]

Jean: I don't know. [*She laughs suddenly*] Hug you—
  [*Morgan rises.*]

Morgan: Autumn's gone. It's still summer. [*Pause*] There are great shafts of sun—all down the street. [*Pause*] When I was ten, I wanted to be a milkman. [*Pause*] Wanted a striped apron and one of those crates. [*Pause*] I used to think of occupations as if they were little cubicles . . . hundreds of them, waiting for me to choose one and step in. Shut the door. Walk out to the other side a butcher, pilot, doctor, actor, but I never imagined one that was a canning factory. [*To window and opens it*] Perhaps I was under the impression that fruit and vegetables grew in cans. On can trees. [*Pause*] Yes. Life is a great struggle to defy categories. [*Pause*] You've got to equip yourself my father used to say. But for what? Yes. Life became baffling as soon as it became comprehensible. [*Pause*] A sort of invisible fog began to emanate from objects when I got to that stage. It stopped my ears, my eyes—it percolated. [*Jean comes over. Pause*] I complained of this to one of my tutors, and he assured me it was the ontological experience. [*Pause*] People thought me very callow and engaging. I sat over my books at night with a corrugated brow—grappling with the enigmas of those things which are for themselves and those which are in themselves.

Jean: I don't know why you can't simply make up your mind—

Morgan: There has to be a period of mourning—

Jean: Mourning *her*!
  [*Morgan goes back to the bed and sits.*]

Morgan: I have my ritualistic side. I deplore the modern tendency to accept things without making a fuss.

Jean [*stalking away*]*:* Oh, save it for your analyst or whatever he is! [*Leans on bed. Pause*] You're incredible. It isn't therapy *you* need—it's lobotomy!

Morgan: You shouldn't be flippant about these things—

Jean: I know. I'm sorry. [*Pause*] I wish you'd stayed in your flipping canning factory.

Morgan: There are times when I have a twitch of nostalgia for it myself.

> [*Morgan goes over to the gorilla, grabs hold of it. Sings.*]
>> Lovely to look at—
>> And lovely to hold—
>> And heaven to kiss.
>> Can there be—
>
> [*Stops suddenly. Peers into the gorilla's face. Makes a gorilla face at it.*]

Morgan: I'll bet you had fun in life. Lolloping through the jungle. Eating bananas. Standing on dead animals' chests and yodelling away there—

Jean: It's time something was decided one way or the other, Morgan. [*Pause.*]

Morgan: How do I know what I'm going to decide until I've done it?

Jean: You didn't tell me Leonie has already divorced you.

Morgan: It doesn't simplify matters at all. [*Pause*] In fact it complicates them.

Jean: How?

Morgan: I regard that marriage as unfinished business. You can't liquidate a human being with a decree nisi. [*Pause*] Perhaps I should insist on a re-trial. Do they have them? [*Pause*] Then there's also the question of Charles Napier—physically loathsome, mentally retarded and I should think genetically unsound. He uses hair cream—what do you make of that?

Jean: Your treatment of Leonie shrieked out for a divorce!

Morgan: What? [*Crosses to bed.*]

Jean: Oh, I know all about it. She rang me and told me I was a digit in an infinite series—

Morgan: I wouldn't have thought Leonie could formulate such a wry metaphor!

Jean: It's an expression I've heard you use any number of times. You're the *guilty party* Morgan.

Morgan: Putatively—the country's boiling with matrimonial deceit. [*Pause*] That's one thing I never did. I never actually *deceived* Leonie. Whereas Napier slid into our lives like a boa constrictor. You've never seen him with her—he undulates. Turned my back one day and he gulped her down like a rabbit.

Jean: I wish I could have fallen in love with somebody who was integrated—

Morgan [*dejectedly*]: Perhaps I'm not fit for life at all—
    [*Jean goes to the door. Opens it.*]

Jean: Twenty-four hours, Morgan. To get things sorted out once and for all.

Morgan [*tapping his head*]: It's very peculiar and lonely in here. I don't think I'm equipped. [*Rises*] I wonder why people are always showing me the door? Is there no place in the world for the Delt Syndrome?
    [*He slinks past Jean, pauses in the doorway, turns round.*]

Jean: Oh, Morgan!

Morgan: If I'd been planted in the womb of an orang-outang, none of this would ever have happened—

Jean: Please—

Morgan: Man lacks continuity with Nature—

Jean: I'm closing the door now.

Morgan: I'd be sitting in some cosy place all hairy, and primordial, and—
    [*Jean firmly closes the door in his face.*]

SCENE XIX: PSYCHOANALYST'S ROOM

The Analyst is sitting in his chair by the head of the divan, alone. He looks at his watch. Morgan comes in. Closes the door. Stands defensively. Points at the divan.

Morgan: I'm fed up with coming in and lying there. [*Pause*] I don't think I shall, today.

Analyst: Why do you feel like that?
    [*Pause. Morgan goes to the window.*]

Morgan: I like the dusk. [*Pause*] There's a [*sniffs*] a smell of wood-smoke—

Analyst: They're burning the leaves in the square—
    [*Pause.*]

Morgan: I'm very tired. [*Pause*] Do you think you and I'll be together for long?

Analyst: How long do you visualise?

    [*Pause. Morgan rubs his hand across his face.*]

Morgan: Oh, I don't know. [*Pause*] I suddenly wondered if I'd see all the seasons through this window. [*Pause*] Sun . . . wind . . . rain, fog . . . snow. [*Pause*] I've decided to go and live with Jean. [*Pause*.]

Analyst: Are you happy about it?

    [*Pause.*]

Morgan: She's alive.

    [*Pause.*]

Analyst: In what sense alive?

Morgan [*gestures impatiently*]: Ah, lay off it for today will you? [*Pause. Walks up to the Analyst*] Don't think you'll get me to conform! Not to anything—

    [*Pause.*]

Analyst: Perhaps you'll become sufficiently free to decide for yourself—whether you'll conform or not.

Morgan: I think I'll go now.

    [*But he stands waiting. The Analyst stands, comes forward. They look at each other.*]

Did you hear what the white rat said to the other white rat?

Analyst: What?

Morgan: I've got that psychologist so well trained that every time I ring this bell he brings me something to eat—

    [*Analyst smiles and Morgan smiles back.*]

Morgan: Well, goodnight then.

Analyst: Goodnight.

SCENE XX: JEAN'S ROOM

Jean in sweater and slacks is washing a jersey at the sink. Knock at the door. She goes over to answer it. Morgan is standing there.

Morgan: Hullo.

Jean: You've come then.

[*Morgan shrugs.*]

Jean: Are you going to be good?

Morgan: I'm a very disassociated person, basically. I think it's that. Yes.

Jean: Will you love me?

Morgan: Yes. You know, when I was four I wanted to be a pirate. I wonder if I have regressive tendencies? Would that diagnosis be compatible with the facts?

Jean: Oh, Morgan.

Morgan [*sings*]*:* Wanting you, all my life I've been wanting you . . .

Jean: Come in then. [*She goes to sink.*]

Morgan: Hullo room.

[*He closes the door.*]

As the door closes we see it from the hall. It is covered with a huge portrait of Lenin. The hall is crowded with Morgan-type possessions:— A duffel bag; typewriter; machine gun; vase of flowers; Mickey Mouse alarm clock, etc. Credits over film of Guy—the gorilla at London Zoo

FOR TEA ON SUNDAY

CAST:

NICHOLAS	Keith Baxter
BIDDY	Ann Lynn
CHRISTINE	Sheila Allen
SUE	Christine Finn
IAN	Philip Locke
ROBIN	Malcolm Webster
BUS CONDUCTOR	Samuel Mansaray
ATTENDANTS:	Peter Whittaker
	and
	Lee Willis

MUSIC: GOLDBERG VARIATIONS BY J. S. BACH.

BBC Transmission: March 17th, 1963

An expensive flat in Kensington shared by Sue, Christine and Biddy. It has a large balcony with a swinging garden seat, plants, deck-chairs —and overlooks a peaceful square.

The interior is modern—furnished with taste, but displaying little of the girls' individual personalities.

Time: A hot Sunday afternoon in July.

SCENE I

Christine is making sandwiches in the kitchen. Sue comes in holding her hands in front of her, drooping at the wrists. She has just painted her fingernails. She stands just inside the kitchen door waving her hands to dry the nail varnish. Christine looks at her resentfully but goes on cutting bread. Says nothing.

Sue: Did you pay the milkman this morning?
Christine: Yes. [*Pause*] You owe me five and nine.
Sue: He's a sweetie.
   [*Stretches her arms above her head sinuously.*]
   Got lovely hairy arms.
Christine: Look, do you intend to help me with this?
Sue [*examining her nails*]*:* Funny to think they're all people as well. Isn't it? [*Pause*] Milkmen, ticket collectors, window cleaners—
Christine: They're probably robots really. Somebody takes them out of their boxes every morning and sends them trundling off to do all the horrid jobs. There, you can butter that lot.
   [*Pushes over slices of bread: Sue sits—fastidiously takes a knife and begins to butter the bread.*]
Sue: I ought to ring my mother. They're off tomorrow and I said I'd go to the airport. [*Pause*] Daddy's intolerable the last few days before they go on holiday. Thinks the bank'll dissolve into chaos whilst he's away.
   [*Biddy comes in holding a wet and dripping library book. Goes to a clothes horse in the corner and hangs the book on the top rail. She is in her dressing gown.*]
Biddy: I dropped your library book in the bath Sue, I'm sorry—
   [*Sue throws the knife down on the table angrily.*]
Sue: Well you can return it then. I'm not going to do the explaining.
Biddy: I'm awfully sorry—

49

Sue: You can take it back.

Biddy: It was so boring that I fell asleep. I'm fed up with these new writers. [*Taps the book*] He's the sort of person who thinks if you read Winnie the Pooh when you were little, you're the class enemy!

Christine [*wryly*]: Did you?

Biddy [*vehemently*]: I loved it. And so did you. So did she.

Sue: I've always been hazy about what it's supposed to mean—class enemy.

Christine: It's jargon for people who've got what you want.

Biddy: Shall I put the cups and saucers out?

Christine: It would help.

> [*Biddy goes to the cupboard and takes out a pile of saucers, balancing three cups on top. As she brings them to the table she stubs her toe on a chair, yells out, and the crockery goes crashing to the floor. She stands looking down at the pieces.*]

Sue: Biddy, if you do one more *thing*! Honestly—

Biddy: It was an accident—[*Fetches dustpan*].

Sue: But you're so careless—

Christine: I should have thought it part of the definition of an accident that you can't anticipate it!

Sue: She's a blundering menace.

> [*Biddy kneels to pick up the pieces.*]

Biddy: Well I'll get some more next week. It isn't a tragedy.

Sue: I can't stand things getting broken. Those *are* mine you know—

Biddy: But I couldn't help it Sue—

Sue: It's funny how you never seem to break any of your own things. Always somebody else's. [*Going out*] I'll be damn glad when Robin and I get married. I can't wait to get four solid walls between me and people like you!

> [*Exit.*]

Biddy: Robin's a nit.

> [*She straightens up with the dustpan.*]

Christine: Isn't he! [*Pause*] I think all the interesting men have been liquidated by a secret organisation.

> [*Biddy brushes the pieces of crockery into the waste bin.*]

Biddy: Don't you like Ian any more?

Christine [*shrugging*]: He's all right. But—[*Pulls a face*] we bore each other. We're quite honest about it. What keeps us together is that everybody else is just as boring as we are, so we might as well hang on.

Biddy: I'm not sure it was a good idea to ask all three of them to tea—

Christine [*with a little malice*]*:* Are you worried your Nicholas won't fit in?

   [*Pause.*]

Biddy: Why shouldn't he fit in?

Christine: No reason at all. It's you I'm talking about. [*Pause*] You get so anxious about people.

Biddy: I've always been anxious. I find life very precarious. At least I did till I met Nicholas. [*Pause*] Now it's different. [*Goes to window*] Isn't it lovely and hot?

Christine [*starts cutting a cucumber*]*:* If you like heat. It makes me frigid, I don't know why.

   [*Biddy turns from the window, laughing.*]

Biddy: Sexually—or socially?

Christine: Either way, it's one of the few things that jerk Ian out of his torpor. [*Pause*] I've had enough of these bed-now-marry-later relationships!

   [*Pause.*]

Biddy: Do you ever wish you'd started a proper career?

Christine: Are you kidding? London's swarming with women graduates wondering what to do with their education. I'm going to turn up at the registry office one day with Ian between my teeth. Like a spaniel with a dead pheasant.

Biddy: You make it sound awful, Christine!

Christine: It is awful. Never mind. *Che sera, sera*—

   [*Biddy is dejected now. Stands fiddling with the belt of her dressing gown.*]

Biddy: Can I borrow a needle and thread? I've lost mine.

Christine: Top left-hand drawer in my dressing table. And tell that lazy so-and-so she can come and make the lemonade.

SCENE II: SUE AND CHRISTINE'S BEDROOM

Biddy enters and fumbles in dressing table drawer. Sue is lying on the bed reading a Sunday paper.

Biddy: Anything happening in the world?

[*Pause.*]

Sue: The usual.

Biddy: Are Christine's needles in here?

Sue: In that cigarette tin.

[*Biddy finds a needle and a reel of thread. Sits on the bed threading the needle.*]

Biddy: Well what's going on then?

[*Pause.*]

Sue: They're knocking hell out of each other somewhere in Africa. [*Pause*] Ghastly picture of some kids in a Hong Kong gutter.

Biddy: Which reminds me, you promised some of your old clothes for that refugee thing I told you about—

Sue: Rotten revue of what's-his-name's new film.

[*Under her dressing gown Biddy is wearing a slip. She looks along the hem until she finds a place where the frill is torn. Begins to sew.*]

Biddy: What time did you tell Robin?

Sue: Half three. [*Pause*] There's a recipe for moussaka in the other paper—

Biddy: Don't like it.

Sue: I'm going to spit in Christine's eye one of these days.

Biddy: Whatever for?

Sue: Oh you are dim, Biddy! She makes me boil. [*Caricaturing Christine*] I should have thought it part of the definition of an accident that you can't anticipate it!

[*Pause.*]

Biddy: You can't expect three people to live together in perfect harmony all the time—

Sue: Not three women anyway. Men seem to be better at it. [*Pause*] Men are better at everything if you ask me. [*Pause*] Emancipation just isn't natural. [*Pause*] I wish it was time for them to arrive now. [*Pause*] I shall flirt with Ian Graver—you watch.

[*Pause.*]

Biddy: Christine wants you to make the lemonade.

Sue: Does she!

[*Folds the paper, looking bored.*]

How's your father's case coming on?

Biddy: The poor little man whose wife keeps locking him out!

Sue: I expect that's the one I meant.

Biddy: Daddy's hating it. Thinks he ought to show more guts. [*Pause*] It's all rather squalid.

[*Pause.*]

Sue: What's the time?

Biddy: Nearly two.

[*Pause.*]

Sue: What does Nicholas think of Robin and Ian?

Biddy: I've never asked him.

Sue [*wearily*]: I wish you wouldn't be so prissy.

Biddy: You're always accusing me of being things. I'm not prissy.

Sue: Don't get huffy. I like to see you on the defensive, that's all.

Biddy: Well it embarrasses me.

[*Biddy snaps off the thread and puts needle and cotton away in the drawer.*]

Sue: I can't wait to get away from this flat.

Biddy: You as well?

Sue: What do you mean: "Me as well"?

Biddy: I think Christine feels the same way. I must be the only one that's happy here—

Sue: See what I mean? Prissy!

Biddy: I think on the whole I tend to reduce the amount of friction in this flat—

Sue: There, there. Roll on tea time. [*Getting up*] Well, I'm off to squeeze the lemons. [*Yawns*] Wish I was off to Corsica with the parents. Robin has two weeks in September. We might go to Ibiza.

[*Biddy goes to window and looks out.*]

Biddy: I loathed Spain last year. Probably because I had diarrhoea most of the time. The sky's nearly white with the heat. You can smell the tar melting in the road. [*Pause*] I wonder what Nicholas sees in me?

[*Sue shrugs and goes out. Biddy has her back to the room and doesn't see this.*]

I suppose we hardly know each other. [*Pause*] I don't know whether he's a tea sort of person. [*Pause*] Aren't lime trees lovely? [*Pause*] There's a drunken man going through the square. People do *spoil* everything.

SCENE III: SITTING-ROOM. DAY

Christine is arranging some flowers in a vase. Sue is on the swing seat on the balcony. Biddy enters down steps.

Christine: I'll bet Ian's the first to arrive. He's very punctual like a lot of people who've nothing to do with themselves half the time. [*Pause*] These are dying already. It's a cheat.
Biddy: It's funny, paying for flowers, somehow.
Christine: I got them from that man on the corner. He looks shifty. [*Pause*] He was quarrelling with that woman who has the other stand near the tube station. Talk about dog eat dog! [*Flops into a chair*] I don't feel very sociable this afternoon, I must say. Can't we ring them all up and tell them to stay away?
  [*She goes and sits on sofa. Sue wanders in off the balcony, inspects the tea table. Perches on a chair arm, dangling one leg. Looks at the other two, yawns.*]
Sue [*to Biddy*]: Do you like my new bra?
Biddy: Haven't seen it.
Sue [*straightening up*]: I mean the shape, idiot—
Biddy: Oh. Yes. Quite erotic, isn't it?
Sue [*giggling*]: I think Robin's got a fixation—
Christine: Pity every male baby can't be wet-nursed on some great fat peasant girl, and let them get it over with!
Sue: If I have any kids they're getting the bottle!
Biddy: I'd like about eight. And I'm going to feed them myself.
Christine: How dreary can you get!
Biddy: Don't you want any then?
Christine: They're even more boring than adults. [*Pause*] What are they *for*, anyway.
  [*Pause. Biddy rises.*]
Biddy: I sometimes wonder what you want out of life—
Christine: Me? Just to get through it with as little inconvenience as possible.
Biddy: There must be such a lot of marvellous things happening in the world—
Christine: Where, for example? [*Pause*] Ninety per cent of the people in it should have been gassed at birth. Think of China. [*Pause*] Seven hundred million—

Sue: And India—

Biddy: It's bad enough in London.

Sue: I can't see the point in most people's existence at all.

Christine: A nightmare. I wish somebody could wave a wand and make most of them disappear—

  [*Sue gets up, and mimes as she speaks.*]

Sue: They've sent me a new typist at work. All bouffant hair and sticky eyelashes. [*Pause*] She speaks with that sort of cockney whine. You know. When I give her something to do at twenty past five—aaaeeeaaooow! [*Pause*] The lives they must lead!

  [*Goes to table, nibbles a sandwich.*]

Christine: Do you mind?

Sue: I'm hungry. [*Pause*] We had a maid cum nanny when I was little and she always made me leave a clean plate because of the coolies. [*Pause*] I used to wonder how it could help the coolies if I ate all my food. [*Pause*] What's one supposed to do?

  [*Pause.*]

Biddy: What *can* one do?

Sue: You can't exactly shed tears for the starving Asians every time you take a mouthful, can you? [*Pause*] Not that I don't care—

  [*Pause.*]

Biddy: I wish I was out in a boat on Regent's Park lake. Nicholas knows all about the different kinds of ducks—

Christine: Bully for Nicholas!

  [*Sue goes over to Biddy.*]

Sue: What do you and Nicholas *do*?

Biddy: What you mean—do!

Sue: Where does he take you? What do you talk about? He's called for you here three times, and he's barely said a word to me.

Biddy [*defensively*]*:* He talks when he's got something to say. [*Pause*] It's better than listening to Robin re-hashing *The Times*, anyway!

Sue: Now don't you start getting at Robin—

Biddy: Well you're getting at Nicholas aren't you?

Sue [*Going up to Christine*]*:* Have you noticed the way he stares at everything? The last time he came and Biddy was still getting dressed, he wandered round this room *staring*. [*Pause*] Gave me the creeps.

Christine: He's probably short-sighted. [*Pause*] Don't be tedious,

you two—
  [*Biddy and Sue stare at each other, hostile. Biddy turns away,
  sits down and goes on reading. Sue goes to the back of Christine's
  chair. Leans over.*]
Sue: When does Ian go back to the oil wells and things?
Christine: October.
Sue: He seems terribly well off. [*Pause*] Will you go back with him?
Christine: I don't know. [*Pause*] I don't want to leave London.
  [*Pause*] He wants to buy a house in England, anyway.
Sue: Where in particular?
Christine: Oh, I don't know. [*Pause*] Anywhere in the adultery belt—
  [*Sue giggles.*]
I assume he'll get around to other women eventually. And that
I shall get around to other men. You've got to stay sane somehow.
  [*Biddy looks up from her book, closes it.*]
Biddy: Why do you pretend to be so cynical?
  [*Christine gets up, goes to the record rack, looks through the
  records.*]
Christine: There's no pretence about it. [*Pause*] Except I'm not
cynical. I'm civilised. [*Pause*] What time is it?
Sue: Twenty-five past three.
  [*Christine puts a record, Mozart clarinet, on the player and
  switches on. Christine lights a cigarette and sits near the player.
  A long pause. The girls stare vacantly in front of them. Biddy stirs.*]
Biddy: Civilised?
  [*Pause.*]
Christine: Well love, no doubt there's a beast within. All I can say
is, it isn't madly clamouring to be let out.
  [*Long pause.*]
Biddy: Do you ever try to imagine what it will all be like.
  [*Pause.*]
Christine: When?
Sue: All what?
Biddy: When they're all civilised—
  [*Pause.*]
Christine: They?
Biddy: You know what I mean.
Sue: Who, for God's sake—
Biddy: It makes me uneasy.

[*Pause.*]

Christine [*laughing*]: Japanese in bowler hats?

Sue [*giggling*]: Negroes with briefcases.

Christine: Eskimoes getting their whales on easy terms!

Sue [*giggling*]: Head-hunters in girdles.

Christine: Aborigines flying to Switzerland for termination of pregnancy?

> [*Their laughter subsides. Biddy is offended. She gets up and goes onto the balcony.*]

Christine: Now she's hurt—

Sue: Oh, she's too moony!

> [*Pause.*]

Christine: It's probably that man.

> [*Pause.*]

Sue: Nicholas?

Christine: Biddy's the sort that nearly goes into convulsions trying to make herself interesting. [*Pause*] A lot of women are like that. [*Pause*] It's a waste of time.

Sue: Immature, that's all.

> [*Pause.*]

Christine [*yawning*]: To hell with the rest of creation anyway. We've made it. [*Pause*] And look at it.

> [*Pause.*]

Sue: I wish these men would hurry up and get here—

SCENE IV: MIX TO TELECINE

WE SEE: *Robin coming out of his Chelsea home and getting into his car. A pleasant sophisticated young man, well dressed, tolerant, rather entrenched in conventional attitudes, a sort of Bow Group Civil Servant with energy and ambition. He starts the engine, drives away carefully.*

AND CUT TO: *Ian coming out of his exclusive West End Club. A taxi is waiting for him. He is tall, aloof, self-contained, with the confidence of a man of some position, used to giving orders. He gets into the taxi and it pulls away.*

CUT TO: *Int. Large country house, now a mental hospital.*

Vast, bare hall. Staircase preferably ornate baroque. Atmosphere institutional. On a wooden seat at the foot of the staircase three women are sitting. One is old [knitting], one middle-aged [gazing steadily in front of her] one young, [clutching a teddy bear and crying]. There is an air of indefinable shabbiness about them, a touch of wildness.

Nicholas comes down the staircase. He is calmer, has a gentle dignity.

As he passes the seat, he hears the young girl crying and stops . . . looks at her. Slowly, she stands up. Her eyes meet his.

She comes towards him slowly, still sobbing.

Nicholas seems to wait for her. He is calm, but almost clinically attentive.

As the girl reaches him she suddenly throws herself at him, puts arms round him. Gently, he disengages himself. She stands back, hugging the teddy bear.

Nicholas puts his hands to her cheeks, strokes her hair. She quietens. He smiles at her. She does not smile back, but seems calmer. He walks away from her. She walks away up the stairs trailing the teddy bear by one leg.

SCENE V: INT. SITTING-ROOM/BALCONY. THE GIRLS' FLAT

Robin has arrived. He and Christine and Sue are sitting on the balcony sipping lemonade. Biddy is not to be seen.

Christine: She's sulking, rather—
Robin: A funny girl. [*Pause*] Is er . . . what's-his-name?
Sue: Nicholas.
Robin: Yes Nicholas. Is he coming?
Sue: Supposed to be.
Robin: Curious manner, he has—

Sue: I was saying to Christine—this afternoon—

Robin: Never gives anything away. Speaks when spoken to. [*Pause. Grins*] Do you think he finds us catastrophic?

Christine [*coldly*]: Us?

   [*Pause.*]

Robin: Well. I mean—

Sue: Come off it, Christine!

Christine: I don't like that word.

   [*Pause.*]

Robin [*amused*]: What word do you like then?

   [*Pause.*]

Christine: Me.

Sue: I'll bet it's a different story when you're with Ian!

Robin [*being clever*]: Christine's quite right. Antagonism is a natural state. There was an interesting leader in *The Times* last week about—

Sue: It's too hot Robin, honestly!

   [*Robin is affronted.*]

Robin: Not that you ever open a newspaper, of course!

   [*Pause.*]

Sue: I wonder *why* it's warm in the summer and cold in the winter—

Robin: You're quite unbelievably ignorant, Sue. [*Pause*] It's to do with the earth's axis.

Sue: Who gives a damn about those things anyway?

   [*Pause.*]

Robin: It was you who asked the question in the first place.

Christine: The earth can fall *into* the sun for all I care!

   [*Pause.*]

CUT TO: *Interior bus*
CLOSE UP *Nicholas: he is reading a Sunday paper.*

SCENE VI: INT. SITTING-ROOM/BALCONY

Robin: Well. The news isn't good today. I suppose everyone's affected, even if it's in the jolly old subconscious—

Sue: What news?
  [*Pause.*]
Robin: The incipient crisis—
Christine: If nine out of ten situations are critical—they can't be.
Robin: I beg your pardon?
Christine: Nothing.
  [*Pause.*]
Sue: I wish everybody'd get their stupid revolutions and things over with. And settle down.
Robin: It isn't a revolution.
Sue: Well whatever it is then. What does it matter what it is?
  [*Pause.*]
Robin: I was referring, as a matter of fact, to the state of the country's economy.
Sue: You would be, wouldn't you!
  [*Pause.*]
Robin: I wonder what Nicholas does for a living?
Sue: Probably something ghastly.
Robin: Have you noticed that slight inflexion in the way he speaks? Not an accent precisely. [*Pause*] Something provincial, I'd say.
Sue: Even more ghastly.
Robin: I do like to know who people are. Where they come from. What they do. I feel embarrassed if I'm in the dark, though of course it may just be that he's shy. [*Pause*] This is awfully nice lemonade.
Sue: I made it.
Robin: Nice and cool.
Sue: I like making lemonade. [*Giggles*] I like squeezing lemons. I suppose that's full of hidden significance.
Robin [*lazily*]: Silly Sue—
  [*Biddy drifts out onto the balcony looking rather disconsolate.*]
  Hello Biddy.
Biddy: Hello.
Robin: How's Nicholas, Biddy?
Biddy: Fine, thanks. How's your rotten old office?
Robin: Oh, limping along. We keep going. [*Pause*] How's *your* rotten old office?
Biddy: We've got a neurotic computer—I gave it a calculation the other day and I had to pull the plug out. It just sat there chattering

on—
Christine: Robin was just saying how shy Nicholas is—
    [*Pause.*]
Biddy: Is he?
Robin: It was more of a . . . well, a speculation—
    [*Biddy goes to the balcony rail. Looks down into the square.*]
Biddy: Do you think everywhere's going to be like it is here, Robin?
    Eventually—
Robin: I wouldn't be surprised.
    [*Pause.*]
Biddy: That's what I think.
Robin: Given the status quo—
    [*Pause.*]
Biddy: What a relief—
Robin: There's nothing fortuitous about it. Everyone wants the same
    things, and technology's the answer. Bound to be teething
    troubles, of course—
    [*The doorbell rings. Christine goes to answer it.*]
Biddy: Nicholas gets worked up about the animals—
    [*Robin can't quite believe his ears.*]
Robin: Oh? Really? [*Pause*] That's very touching—
Sue: Screwy!
Biddy: Why?
Sue: Well, for goodness' sake—they've got reservations and things
    to live in.

    CUT TO: *Int. shot of bus.*
  A West Indian conductor hands Nicholas his ticket. Smiles at him,
sings a few bars of a song. Laughs and goes downstairs.

SCENE VII: SITTING-ROOM/BALCONY

Ian enters, followed by Christine.

Ian: Who's got reservations to live in?
Sue [*giggling*]*:* The animals.

Ian: Thought you were talking about Red Indians.

Christine: Biddy's being all peculiar and sensitive this weekend. It's her way of being romantic. [*To Biddy*] Isn't it, love?

> [*Long pause. Silence. Biddy goes to Christine.*]

Biddy: You don't like Nicholas, do you?

Christine: Who said anything about Nicholas?

Biddy: You implied—

Christine: What you mean is, you interpreted—

Biddy: Of course, you're all so polite! You say everything by innuendo—

Ian: Not me, Biddy. Hardly me. I've only just arrived, for God's sake—

Sue: The mysterious Nicholas. [*Laughing*] Old Nick!

> [*Pause.*]

Ian: I wish somebody'd put me in the picture—

Christine: Biddy feels persecuted.

Biddy: I do not!

Christine: After all, it's your first serious thing. Isn't it?

Sue [*only half teasing*]: He's afraid of us.

Biddy: You and Christine? That's a good one!

> [*Ian sits down with his legs crossed, one leg jogging up and down.*]

Ian: Now now girls—

> [*Biddy goes back to the balustrade, leans over it, stops listening to the others. They are embarrassed. A long silence.*]

Robin: Wouldn't it be nice to have a private swimming pool?

Sue: Wouldn't it be lovely? In the square. [*Laughing*] We could dive off the balcony—

Robin: That's my ambition. Private everything. [*Pause*] A house at Henley. Bloody great wall round it. Gadgets to do all the work. And then—

> [*He subsides into a daydream.*]

Ian: And then?

Christine [*laughing*]: Nirvana!

Sue [*giggling*]: Bliss—

Ian: What we really need is the perfect robot servant. [*Pause*] Then the masses would be dispensable and we could dispense with them! Half the bore these days is having to go along with the pretence that they're human. You must meet my grandfather. Splendid old man. Patriarchal type. He sees it as a matter of evolution—people are becoming superfluous, let's face it. And what do we do? Fall over backwards to keep them alive. Let them breed . . . finance their housing . . . produce objects for them to consume. Could anything be more fatuous, when you take a good look at what they're like?

[*Pause.*]

Christine: That's my darling!

Ian: Well, it's always interesting to strike an attitude. If I don't talk, I shall go to sleep. If I go to sleep, you'll [*to Christine*] be annoyed. And when you're annoyed you don't talk—

Sue: Maybe we should all just give in, and have a siesta.

Biddy [*turning*]: Personally, I think the whole conversation is rather adolescent.

Christine [*being cockney*]: 'ark at 'er!

Robin: I must say, I often wonder why one makes the effort to be sociable at all. Yacketty-yacketty. It's pleasant when you know people well enough to allow yourself the luxury of silence. Don't you think?

[*Pause.*]

Christine: And *do* you know us well enough, Robin?

Sue [*pouting*]: He knows me—

Ian: We used to play charades, when I was a child. One could always rely on charades.

Sue [*jumping up*]: Who's this?

[*She takes a cigarette, holds it in front of her eyes, staring and blinking her eyelashes. She takes a lighter in the other hand and repeats the performance with that. Putting the cigarette in her mouth, she lights it, holds it out staring at the burning end, vacant-faced. Christine is sniggering.*]

Sue: Go on then—who is it?

Christine: Nicholas—

Sue: Aren't I clever?

[*Pause.*]

Biddy: Nicholas doesn't smoke—

Sue: That was just to make it harder.

[*Pause.*]

Biddy: It's easy to be cruel—

Sue [*suddenly angry*]: You're so bloody solemn! You take yourself so *seriously*!

[*Biddy begins to cry. Sue is immediately and genuinely remorseful. She goes to comfort Biddy. Robin and Ian look rather uncomfortable. Christine watches ironically.*]

I'm sorry. I didn't mean it.

[*Biddy makes an effort to stop crying.*]

Biddy: He isn't coming. I'm sure he isn't.

Sue: Of course he is. Why shouldn't he. [*Pause*] I didn't mean it, Biddy—

[*Pause.*]

Biddy: Why did you say it then?

Sue: You know I'm not cruel—Don't you?

[*Pause.*]

Biddy: I don't know.

Sue: But I'm not though—

[*Pause.*]

Sue [*turning to Christine*]: Shall I go and make the tea?

Christine: I wish you would. I'm dying—

[*Sue goes out. Biddy takes the chair vacated by Sue. She looks round at the others, as if promising to hide any future show of emotion.*]

Ian: Come and sit by me, Biddy. Cheer up. If he wasn't coming he'd phone. [*Pause*] Rather an interesting chap, Nicholas—

Biddy: Stop being nice to me, Ian.

Ian: I'm not, I assure you. I took to him straight away. [*Pause*] When was it? That night I was taking Christine to Covent Garden and Nicholas was taking you . . . where was he taking you?

Biddy: To the Pushkin Society.

Ian: That's right. Pushkin Society. Not my line of country at all, I'm afraid.

Biddy: It isn't Nicholas's either. It's just there's an old man goes there who Nicholas likes to . . .

[*Voice trailing off.*]

. . . likes to watch—

[*Pause.*]

Christine: What gay times you two must have together—

Biddy [*pointedly*]: I'm going to help Sue—

[*She goes through the living room and into the kitchen. Ian stretches.*]

Ian: Some women do have a tedious emotional life—

Christine: Biddy's sweet, but she's gullible.

Ian: How?

Robin: I gather you have dark suspicions about the boy friend then?

Christine: I hardly know him.

Robin: But you have your doubts—

Ian: I don't see you *in loco parentis*, darling!

    [*Pause.*]

Christine: I just took an instinctive dislike to him. That's all.

Robin: So did Sue. [*Pause*] I wouldn't go that far myself. He reminds me of a boy I knew at boarding school. Something coarse. He hardly ever talked, and one always wondered what he was thinking. [*Pause*] When people are as reticent as that, it's almost arrogance. They need taking down a peg. [*Pause*] We certainly had some fun with the silent Cyril. I like people to be open. Gregarious.

Christine: I don't really give a damn what Nicholas is like. Only if she's going to start having him round here very often.

    [*The phone rings in the living-room. Biddy rushes in to answer it. It is Nicholas, and as she speaks she becomes happy again.*]

Biddy: Nicholas? Yes it's Biddy. What? Well I was wondering . . . yes . . . I began to think you weren't coming. [*Long pause*] Oh you silly! [*Pause*] We'll start tea without you then. [*Pause*] How long? Soon? All right. Yes. Yes I do. I am glad. Honestly. Come soon. 'Bye . . . 'bye—

    [*She comes to the balcony laughing.*]

That was Nicholas. He was reading his paper on the bus and he . . [*laughing*] he went half way to the terminus before he realised. He's crazy! Well. You stay here, and we'll bring the tea out—

    [*She runs laughing through the living-room and back into the kitchen.*]

Ian [*scornfully*]: She's got it badly!

Christine: I hope to God I was never like that—

Ian: You weren't with me, at any rate.

Christine: Were you disappointed? Did you want me to be?

Ian: Not at all. [*Pause*] I like hard women.

Christine: Thank you!

Ian: Don't pretend to be offended. You're utterly without feelings of any kind, which is why you and I get on. If either of us dropped dead tomorrow, the other would simply look for someone else.

[*Pause*] We prefer it that way, don't we? [*Pause*] It's a kind of fastidiousness—
　　[*Christine gets up, goes to the balustrade, looks out into the square.*]
Robin: Oh now really!
Ian [*smiling*]: Are you shocked?
Robin: I wouldn't say shocked—
Ian: Then what would you say? You'll have to be quick, or I shall put you down as shocked—
　　[*Pause.*]
Robin: Everyone experiences feeling—
Ian: Then I'm a liar?
Robin: No—
Ian: Then? [*Pause*] You, of course, have feelings about Sue!
Robin: Of course I do—
　　[*Pause.*]
Ian: What's it like?
Christine [*over her shoulder*]: Take no notice of him Robin. He plays this game . . . it's his clever-clever thing.
　　[*Robin is rather annoyed. Rises. Ian smiles to himself.*]
Ian: A house in Henley. [*Pause*] By the river? [*Pause*] Swans at the bottom of the garden?
Robin [*facing him, irritated*]: Anything wrong with the idea?
Ian: Not at all. It even sounds quite elegant. [*Pause*] The nubile Sue bustling about. Summer days on the lawn. And summer nights . . . a little jazz . . . a few couples swaying on the terrace. [*Pause*] I like women's backs, you know. I like those black Italian dresses with narrow shoulder straps . . . and no back. [*Pause*] Yes. I can see you leading quite an Antonioni sort of life, down there in Henley—
　　[*Pause.*]
Robin: Him? He bores me to death.
Ian: Has Sue got a nice back? [*Pause*] She has a very nice front—
Robin: I think we won't discuss Sue, if you don't mind.
Ian: Poor Robin.
Robin: Yes? And what about poor Ian?
Ian: I'm storing up memories to take back to the Middle East with me. [*Pause*] Little bits of London, to keep me amused in the desert. [*Pause*] I find oil tedious. And oil people tend to be—oily. [*Pause*]

I am a very stark person, at heart.

Christine: You can say that again!

Ian: I think some essential gland is missing. Some duct that secretes life.

[*He laughs—to himself.*]

Robin: Well I feel very much alive, I can assure you.

Ian: That's because you're still acquisitive. Beyond a certain level of income, even that little nerve can stop twitching.

Robin: You are beyond that level, I take it?

Ian: It's entirely due to my father. [*Pause*] One could give it away— but the needy have a habit of squandering. No sense of proportion.

[*Christine stares at Ian for a moment, then bursts out laughing.*]

Robin: What's so funny?

Christine: He is. Don't you think?

[*Pause.*]

Robin: Not particularly—

[*Christine goes over to Ian, takes out her handkerchief—dabs his brow.*]

Christine: He's sweating!

Robin: Is that funny?

Christine: It isn't the heat. He's nervous. [*Pause*] We're both nervous. [*Pause*] He talks when we're with other people. I tend to listen. [*Pause*] He always hopes I might hear him say something intelligent. And I always hope he might catch me listening as if I was interested. [*Pause*] How's that for nerves?

[*Robin laughs, but his laughter trails away as he notices how coldly Ian and Christine are looking at one another.*]

Robin: Too deep for me!

Christine: On the other hand, when we're alone there's no problem.

[*Pause. Laughs. Goes close to Robin.*]

We were at a party the other night, and one of those funny little bearded poets that you get at parties trapped me in a corner. He looked over my shoulder, across the room to Ian—and he said, with his little black wet eyes shining: do you have sex?

[*Goes to Ian, kisses him with deliberate savagery.*]

Isn't that marvellous?

Ian: Christine has a secret lust for little bearded poets. She despises them to the point of orgasm. [*Pause*] There's nothing and no one we don't despise, between us.

Robin: I'm flattered!

Ian: You don't want to let us upset you. We never mean what we say—

Christine: You should look upon us as a kind of double act.

> [*Biddy comes in on this last speech. Stands looking from one to the other. Ian blows her a kiss.*]

Biddy: There. It's all ready. Shall I pour?

> [*She begins to pour the tea. Sue comes lounging out.*]

Sue: Have you been having lots of lovely talkies?

Robin: Well—I don't know about—

Ian [*cutting in*]: Lots.

Sue: Biddy lit the gas under the kettle without seeing if there was any water in. It got red hot—

> [*During the following talk, Christine and Sue help their respective men to tea.*]

Biddy: I love red hot metal. I'd like to be a welder.

Sue: If you'd just lay off the kettle, that's all—

Biddy: I know I'm a mess. [*Pause*] I keep offering to go and cook for Nicholas, but we don't seem to get round to it.

Robin: Where does he live?

> [*Biddy goes on eating as if she hadn't heard.*]

Christine: Robin says where does Nicholas live, Biddy?

> [*Biddy is very embarrassed.*]

Biddy: I don't know.

> [*Pause.*]

Christine: You've never been there?

Biddy: No. [*Pause*] Somehow. [*Pause*] Does it matter?

Sue: It strikes me you don't know anything about Nicholas. I mean he might be anything!

Biddy: So what?

Sue: Well it affects us, you know.

Biddy: How?

Sue: Well it's our flat as well—

Biddy: I'm free to know who I like, aren't I?

Robin: The point Sue's trying to make, Biddy, is that you have certain obligations to her and Christine. Then there's your parents. Sue told me how your mother worries about you—

Sue: I've got to say it Biddy, there's something . . . intrusive about Nicholas.

Ian [*deadpan*]: He could be a criminal. A murderer. A sex maniac—
and it may very well turn out that you were the weak point in
the defences!

Biddy: What defences? You mustn't say such things about Nicholas.
[*Defiantly*] He loves me. I love him. I won't have you talking like
this!

> [*The flat bell rings. Slowly, Biddy stands up. They are all watching
> her.*]

I'll never ask him here again. And you'd better start looking for
somebody else to share the flat—straight away!

SCENE VIII: INTERIOR HALLWAY

*She goes to the outer door of the flat. Nicholas stands in the doorway
when she opens the door. He is carrying a large axe, which Biddy
doesn't see at first. Then, as he brings it from behind him:*

Biddy: Nicholas why? What's that for? Nicholas?

> [*He puts his hand out and touches her cheek. Makes for the
> balcony. They pass through the kitchen and down the steps.*]

SCENE IX: SITTING-ROOM/BALCONY

Biddy [*her voice rising*]: Nicholas? Darling what are you . . . what's
that . . . please Nicholas.

> [*Nicholas stands smiling over the tableau on the balcony. At
> first they think the axe is some kind of joke.*]

Nicholas: Good afternoon.

[*Biddy comes up behind him, stands with her hand to her mouth. Christine laughs. They all laugh.*]

Nicholas [*looks at axe blade*]: I don't think it's really funny.

Ian: Put it down and don't be a bore, Nicholas. Rather undergraduate sort of humour, if you don't mind my saying so!

Nicholas: But I'm not an undergraduate—

Christine: What's all this about, Biddy?

[*Everyone looks at Biddy.*]

Biddy: I don't know.

Sue [*giggling*]: The axe-man cometh!

[*Nicholas suddenly raises the axe, and they all spring away from the table. To shrieks from the girls and protests from the men, he smartly chops the table in two, sending the tea things flying. Ian and Robin go for him but he threatens them with the axe.*]

Robin: Just what the hell do you think you're doing?

Christine: A madman—

Nicholas: Do you mean you can't tell what I'm doing?

Robin: Now look here—

Ian: Now put it down, there's a good chap—

Nicholas: What a very soothing tone of voice you have. I've never heard you use that tone before.

Ian: You'll hear a very different tone if you don't stop fooling about!

Nicholas: Ah! You mean the one you use when you're more yourself—

Biddy [*still sobbing*]: Please, Nicholas. Please.

Nicholas [*turning to her*]: Don't cry. There's no need to cry—

Christine: He's insane!

Nicholas: It depends on your point of view.

[*Nicholas rests the axe head on the floor and leans on the haft. He is almost amiable. Stirs the debris with his foot.*]

If I chop your property to bits—is it like chopping *you* to bits? [*Pause*] Think how detached and compassionate you might feel though, if you saw me run amok in the streets. Think of the crowd, frightened—but excited. Think of all those hearts drumming. Until I was caught . . . and dragged away . . . overpowered.

[*Pause. Turns to the living-room, nods at it.*]

I don't like your living-room at all. [*Pause*] I used to daydream of having a room. [*Pause*] High and long, with whitewashed walls and golden, waxed floorboards. [*Pause*] I wanted it to have a tall narrow window with a tree outside. [*Pause*] Each day I would go to work—something manual and exhausting—come home. Bath. Put on a clean white shirt and a pair of dark narrow trousers. I'd make lemon tea and sit in my room until the light faded, the tree was swallowed in darkness. I'd switch on my lamp —it would have an orange shade. [*Pause*] Sit there quietly. Breathing . . . quietly. [*Pause*] Such a gentle vision, I had, of myself in the room. I was hungry for peace. Hungry. [*Pause*] And after dusk, when I knew the city would be a blaze of light—my idea was to pad the streets like a leopard. A good leopard. A leopard out of paradise, one that would not eat babies, or maul their parents . . . or spring at the weak out of the shadows.

[*They react.*]
[*Pause.*]
[*He smiles.*]
I hope I move you. I hope you are touched—

Ian: Listen, Nicholas. Robin and I are going to come for you. We're not going to hurt you.

[*Sharply to Robin.*]
Round to the other side—quickly!

[*As Robin moves, Nicholas inverts the axe so that he is now holding it head uppermost.*]

Nicholas: I don't think you quite understand. [*Pause*] There's always the possibility you see, that I might use this on you. [*Pause*] Mightn't I?

[*Christine steps forward to within a few paces of him.*]

Christine: Go on then. Go on, Nicholas. Why don't you get on with it? Split me from skull to collarbone—

Nicholas [*laughing*]*:* So you're not afraid of me!

Christine: Should I be?

Nicholas: Not afraid of death?

[*Christine shrugs.*]
I expected *you* to be calm.

Christine: Did you? Why?

Nicholas: Because nothing outside you seems real. [*Smiles*] We are ghosts! Brick and mortar are insubstantial. Voices are echoes. Everything comes to you muffled, as if all creation was a shadow

... all the pain and struggle a distant murmur—

Christine: Is it my pity you want? [*Pause*] I take it you are an in-
patient somewhere. And they let you out. So they must be quite
confident.

[*Pause.*]

Nicholas: They may be confident! I'm sure they are. [*Pause*] But
can they be certain? [*Pause*] Can *you* be certain that you don't
want *my* pity?

[*He turns away from them, goes into living-room. Looks round.
He decides on bookcase. He crosses to it, and smashes it. Robin
comes up cautiously behind him. Nicholas turns to face him.*]

Nicholas: Were you going to jump on me, Robin?

Robin: Why don't you pack it in old chap?

Nicholas: What's your normal reaction when things get out of hand?

[*Pause.*]

Robin: I never allow things to get out of hand—

Nicholas: I can't blame you for wanting to appear virile in front of
Sue. In fact there must be whole areas of your personality pining
for expression.

[*Close up Ian at telephone, dialling. Nicholas pounces across the
room and chops through the flex. Begins to chop the sideboard.*]

Ian: Maybe he's sane. And then what would his motives be?

Nicholas [*smiling*]*:* Not motives. Impulses. [*Pause*] The problem
would be—what would my impulses be? [*Laughing*] I'm at a
grave disadvantage. I'm indifferent to—consequences. [*Pause*]
But aren't you? [*To Ian.*]

[*Goes to Sue.*]

Aren't you?

[*To Robin.*]

Aren't you?

[*To Christine.*]

Aren't you?

[*To Biddy, closer.*]

Aren't you, Biddy? [*Pause.*] Do you feel responsible for this
situation?

[*Biddy stares at the floor.*]

Biddy: You told me nothing—

Nicholas: And you suspected nothing?

Biddy: No. [*Shouts*] No!

[*Pause.*]

Nicholas: But you feel responsible!

Biddy [*shouting*]: Yes!

Sue: She brought you here in the first place—

Nicholas: Biddy found me. I didn't find Biddy—[*To Biddy*] Why don't you tell them how? They'll appreciate that. It will be something of a . . . of a delay in the proceedings.

[*Biddy sits down with her face in her hands.*]

Biddy: Leave me alone! [*Pleadingly*] Please, Nicholas . . . please . . . and stop this. And go away—

[*The others, except Nicholas, move in round Biddy. Christine stands over her. Dark and mocking.*]

Christine: Why not? Tell us, Biddy—

[*Pause. Biddy is moving from distress to hilarity. Peers up at Christine between her fingers. Suddenly puts her hands on her lap and sits laughing.*]

Biddy: On a beach. Looking for pebbles, and little crabs. Then I found a hollow in the dunes. And there was Nicholas fast asleep—

[*Pause.*]

Christine: The weekend you refused to come with us to Glyndebourne? [*Pause*] How romantic—

Sue: She's mad herself—

Biddy: Lonely!

Robin: I can remember insisting that you came with us—

Ian: We *all* insisted!

[*Pause.*]

Biddy: I covered him with sand. I made him into a lovely castle. [*Pause*] It was so funny that . . . that I was able to do it. [*Pause*] I was going to run away when I'd finished. [*Pause. Laughs*] I made a flag with a piece of seaweed and a twig. Just when I stuck it in— he woke up.

Nicholas: Excuse me—

[*He goes on chopping. He does it without great exertion or violence—as if it were merely a tiresome job that has to be done. Sue begins to scream, but Ian grabs her and puts his hand over her mouth. She stops screaming and he removes his hand and takes her away.*]

Robin: Nicholas!

[*Christine picks up a magazine and starts reading.*]

Robin: Nicholas, for God's sake. Haven't you any respect for other people's—

Nicholas: Ah—respect!

Robin: I'm tired of all this silly nonsense. I think you're a poseur—

Nicholas: What's the difference between a sane man who acts insanely and an insane man?

Robin: Suppose you tell me!

Nicholas: I can't. I don't know what the difference is.

Robin: You'll be made to pay, I hope you realise. Mental patient or not. And if we can't get it out of you, we'll get it out of who-ever's responsible for you—

[*Pause.*]

Nicholas: Not another cross word. I accept responsibility.

[*Robin goes to Biddy. Nicholas goes on chopping.*]

Robin: Surely you can stop him? I mean, isn't *anyone* going to do anything? Are we all going to hang about whilst he wrecks the place? It's ridiculous!

[*Stands over Biddy. Shouts.*]

Biddy!

[*Biddy stands up.*]

Biddy: Nicholas—

[*Nicholas takes a final swing, then turns to face her. He takes a handkerchief from his pocket and dabs his forehead.*]

Nicholas: Yes?

Biddy: Let me take you back.

Nicholas: That's quite unnecessary. I shall be going back. I always do. [*Pause*] I'm completely reliable.

Biddy: Let me take you back now—

Nicholas: You don't want to let them use you—

Biddy: If I come and . . . and take that thing off you . . . will you hurt me?

[*Pause.*]

Nicholas: I'm afraid I've got to do the whole place.

[*Pause.*]

Biddy: Don't you love me?

Nicholas: Why don't you follow the example of the admirable Christine, and just turn your back on the whole thing. [*Pause.*] Relax. [*Pause*] Try not to . . . not to wince.

Biddy: You've deceived me—

Nicholas: You deceive yourself. [*Pause*] You all do. [*Pause*] Look at them: what do they see? They see their absolute difference from me. [*Pause*] Absolute. [*Pause*] They don't see a good leopard, smiling and whiskered . . . a silky, harmless leopard sniffing the world at night. [*Pause*] The creature is in my head. [*Pause*] And I live with men whose heads are full of creatures. [*Pause*] I *would* be absurd, if I claimed the *mystique* of madness . . . if I subscribed to the divinity of idiots, the holiness of the tortured and the insane.

[*Smiling gently and speaking lightly.*]
But I do not! [*Pause*] We should all be locked up, and many of us are! [*Pause*] To protect you. [*Pause*] To guard your own peculiar dreams.

Biddy: You let me love you. You watched me grow to love you!
Nicholas: I did!
Biddy: You knew what it would come to—
Nicholas: Yes!
Biddy: You let me bring you amongst my friends—
Nicholas: Oh, your friends!
Biddy: Planning some sort of cheap humiliation—
Nicholas: No, not that. No plans. No ideas for the future. [*Pause*] I simply became fascinated by you all. A fresh strand in the lunacy. Lying awake in the ward at night, I thought about you. There I was, as busy as a shuttle . . . weaving in and out of my deductions. I was weaned from paraldehyde. I thought: Such *groomed* people. Educated. Informed. Sophisticated within their limits. I thought: will the visions part like a curtain, and let me be like them?

[*Sue comes forward—she moves and speaks with a kind of sensual hostility. She is the most basic of the three girls, the least sensitive, the least intelligent. There is something rapacious, something sexually brutal in her.*]
Sue: Old Nick!

[*Turning to the others.*]
Didn't I say so. [*Pause*] The cheek. [*At Biddy*] And her! I knew she wasn't like us. [*Pause*] Remember how we got her to share this place? [*Pause*] We *advertised* for her! Why don't you get yourself certified and go with him? Play leopards.

[*She makes clawing motions at Biddy and purrs, rubs her cheek*

against the back of her hand. Purrs. Giggles. Suddenly composes her face, and now it is stiff with dislike.]
He's obscene. Filthy. Loathsome.

Ian: Why do we keep them alive?

[*Nicholas goes and hacks the sofa to pieces. Sue goes towards the door. Nicholas goes to a china mandarin on room divider. He smashes it. Sue slips out. Christine puts down her magazine and rises.*]

Christine: Do you enjoy destroying things? Do you feel you are getting your message across?

Nicholas: Now why should you think there's a message?

Christine: I assume you are trying to tell us something. [*Sneering*] To express something! On the other hand you are quite articulate. Almost lucid.

[*Nicholas gets on with the hacking.*]

Nicholas: I wonder . . . what . . . I could . . . be saying . . . to you . . . that my . . . lucidity . . . can't cope . . . with—

[*He stops. Looks at her.*]

Christine [*with detachment*]: Do you have hallucinations?

Nicholas: Not really—

[*Pause.*]

Christine: What else did you want besides a room?

Nicholas: Nothing—

Christine: Not a girl.

[*Pause.*]

Nicholas: Maybe a girl—

[*Pause.*]

Christine: What sort of a girl?

[*Pause.*]

Nicholas [*looking round*]: So . . . Sue has managed to get out. [*Pause*] It won't be long, then. [*Pause*] Do you think she'll ring for the police, or an ambulance? [*Pause*] Or both.

[*Pause.*]

Christine: You must hate us—

Nicholas: It isn't that.

Christine: Then what?

[*Pause.*]

Nicholas: You're suddenly very unsure of yourself—

[*Christine turns to Biddy.*]

Christine: Biddy . . . Biddy—

[*Pause. Biddy sits staring at Nicholas and Christine for a moment.*]

What happened . . . after, after the beach?

[*Biddy cries.*]

Christine: She's young!

Nicholas: Aren't you?

Christine: Not like her.

Nicholas: Don't cry Biddy. Don't.

Christine: I feel so . . . used . . . and bitter.

[*Turning to Ian.*]

Look at that swine! Look at him!

Ian [coming across]: Naughty, naughty! You're lucky to have me—

Christine [turning to Robin]: And the smooth Robin. The balanced Robin. If I imagine hell—it's full of men like you two!

[*Ian turns away, laughing softly. Goes to the balcony. Stands looking out into the square.*]

Ian [on balcony]: And what are we doing? [*Pause*] In hell! [*Pause*] Burning with women like you?

Robin [puffily outraged]: You can insult each other as much as you like—but you can leave me out of it.

Ian: No.

[*Pauses. Smiles to himself.*]

You won't even get to hell—

Robin: What's the matter with you all? What's the matter?

Ian: But it's been a fascinating afternoon. Hasn't it?

Robin: I'm ashamed of us. Ashamed. We could have stopped him.

[*Robin sits down with his back to them. Christine goes to Biddy.*]

Christine: After the beach . . . Biddy?

[*Pause.*]

Biddy: Every time we met . . . peace. [*Pause*] So I'm frightened now. Obviously. After what he's done. Seeing what he is. [*Pause*] Frightened. [*Pause*] I can't imagine gentleness and violence flowing together. I want them to take him away. Lock him up. I want to scour him out of my mind. [*Pause*] He is—preposterous. He is. He is. [*Pause*] He let me be . . . what I daren't be. And think . . . what I daren't think. [*Pause*] He allowed me to become . . . unreal. [*Pause*] For which I can never forgive. Never.

[*Nicholas looks at Biddy for a long time. Goes to another piece*

of furniture and starts hacking. Biddy shouts.
Stop it! Stop it—
[*She runs at Nicholas and gets him by the shoulders. Tries to shake him. He gets her by the shoulders and holds her until she calms down. Biddy sinks to her knees. Nicholas lifts the axe. Stands over her. She has her hands in her eyes.*]
Nicholas: It's only a question of minutes now. [*Pause*] And it will be over. [*Pause*] When I dream of this, I dream of men with great nets. The sky is full of nets—and the spinning sun glances through them like an eye. [*Pause*] I am shouting to you. [*Pause*] Shouting.
[*Close in on Nicholas's face until it fills the screen.*]
I wonder why . . . I withdrew . . . from your world to mine. [*Pause*] It has been pleasant—coming to see you. Coming here. [*Pause*] The other day I wandered through the woods behind our block . . . to the railings. And pressed my face between two of the bars looking out. [*Pause*] How are they all getting on, I wondered. [*Pause*] How are they making out—in their houses and shops and factories, and all the places where they are. [*Pause*] What are the headlines? [*Pause*] How many are giving birth, and how many closing their eyes for the last time? [*Pause*] I thought of the children doing their lessons, the soldiers dying, the men and women lying in prisons. [*Pause*] I began to cry. [*Pause*] Two old women were waiting at a bus stop a few yards away. One of them saw me. [*Pause*] Poor man, she said to the other. Poor man. [*Pause*] Poor world, I yelled back. Poor world! And they turned away embarrassed.
[*He turns to Christine, his manner changing, he is now laconic.*]
But again I must remind you, it is not my thesis that the truth is inverted—that we are sane and you are mad. Far from it. No. [*Pause*] Yet it makes a curious tableau—a girl on her knees, in the middle of the twentieth century so to speak!
[*He smashes the bookcase, and begins on the table. Biddy gets up. Christine goes to her and puts her arms round her.*]
Christine: You should try again. Try again. [*Pause*] But gently.
[*She moves back. Biddy goes and stands patiently behind Nicholas until he has finished. When he turns, she speaks quietly.*]
Biddy: Do you—do you want to kiss me? [*Pause.*]
Nicholas: Do you think we should kiss?

[*Pause.*]

Biddy: You've got to realise that I don't understand.

[*She goes close to him. He puts the axe down. Stands looking at her. Kisses her. They stop kissing and stand with their cheeks together. Their eyes are closed. Ian moves quickly and silently across the room. Takes the axe.*]

Ian: Now!

[*Nicholas and Biddy spring apart.*]

Kneel down then. By the chair—

[*Nicholas looks at him for a moment, then kneels by the chair. Ian stands over him triumphant.*]

Put your head on the chair. Go on. Go on. [*Pause.*]

[*Nicholas puts his head on the chair.*]

After all, to quote your own words,—there's always the possibility I might use this on you. Isn't there?

[*Ian lifts the axe and gently rests the blade on the back of Nicholas's neck.*]

Christine: Stop this and leave him alone!

Ian [*laughing*]: It's a perfect setting for an execution.

[*Pause. Lifts the axe from Nicholas's neck.*]

The difference being—that I am not mentally afflicted.

[*Ian throws down the axe contemptuously. Nicholas raises his head, remains kneeling. Christine goes on to balcony, followed by Ian. Robin crosses to Nicholas.*]

Robin: I've had enough of this! Enough.

[*He takes Nicholas by the shoulders and hurls him over sprawling on the floor. He walks out. Biddy goes to Nicholas and embraces him.*]

Christine [*at the balustrade*]: I never want to see you again.

[*Pause.*]

Ian: What have *I* done?

Christine: Nothing.

[*Pause.*]

Ian: You can't humiliate a lunatic—

[*Pause.*]

Christine: Perhaps not.

[*Ian takes a cigarette box from among the debris, finds a cigarette left in it and lights up. Stands with his back to her.*]

Ian: The old oil wells are going to be comparatively tame after this!

Christine: I want you to be quiet.

Ian: Why? I would have thought there was still plenty to be said.
   [*Pause.*]

Christine: I'm not concerned with you. Or me. [*Pause*] I'm thinking
   of those two.
      [*Biddy and Nicholas are still kneeling—she has her hands on his
      cheeks.*]

Biddy: You are the only one who knows why—

Nicholas: To smash the objects . . . to tear down the walls . . . to
   have you all as naked as we are. [*Pause*] What else? [*Pause*]
   A most uncivilised urge.
   [*Pause.*]

Biddy: They'll be here in a minute.

Nicholas: Yes.

Biddy: And I shall never see you again.
   [*Pause.*]

Nicholas: You could *come* to see me.

Biddy: And what would we do? [*Pause*] It's too sad.

Nicholas: We are people.
   [*Pause.*]

Biddy: Fragments—

Nicholas: No. Whole. [*Pause*] What we haven't got—we create.
   [*Pause*] There's a fat, amiable nurse who says to me sometimes:
   how's your leopard? Have you seen him lately? [*Smiling*] He
   smiles to himself. [*Pause*] One feels no resentment. There is a
   kind of understanding.
   [*Pause.*]

Biddy: I do love you Nicholas—
   [*Pause.*]

Nicholas: I wonder what you'll think tomorrow morning. [*Pause*]
   In the tube. The tunnel wall clacketing past the window—

Biddy: I don't know—

Nicholas: And in the office . . . good morning, good morning.
   Another lovely day. [*Pause*] Who will say: Did you have a nice
   weekend?

Biddy: Mr Randal. He always does.

Nicholas: And when you open the newspaper—
      [*Biddy suddenly flings her arms round him. They kneel swaying,
      cheek to cheek. The door opens and two hospital attendants*

*come in, followed by Sue and Robin. They stand looking at
Biddy and Nicholas. Christine and Ian come in from the balcony.
Slowly, they all form a circle round the couple on the floor.*]

Nicholas: You see, I found my room. [*Pause*] I remember that
I renounced all ideas of living as you live. I used to be very
confident. I was strong. Muscular. I worked in the open, building
places for people to live and work in. [*Pause*] I was hopeful.
[*Pause*] I had the whitewashed walls, the lemon tea, an orange
rug from a strange country on my bed. I had my routines. I was
always clean and well shaved, and every night a freshly laundered
shirt. [*Pause*] I lived as I told you I wanted to. [*Pause*] I felt life
move in me like a current.

[*The two attendants gently move in on him.*]

I bought a telescope and learned the constellations. I walked on
the moon, I saw the stars floating cold and clear. I bought books
and tried to understand what men were doing. [*Pause*] But
gradually, I came to notice . . . came to notice—

[*The attendants take him expertly and sympathetically by the
arms. Biddy comes close to him.*]

Biddy: Came to notice what, Nicholas? [*Pause*] What?

[*Pause.*]

Nicholas: To notice—

[*His head falls forward onto his chest. He is crying. Biddy
touches the tears on his cheeks. Slowly rubs them on her own
cheeks.*]

Biddy: What love? Tell me—

Nicholas [*whispering*]*:* Noticed . . . noticed. Noticed—

[*The men lead him out. Everyone in the room is immobile,
statuesque. Fade out on empty garden seat swinging gently.*]

AND *DID* THOSE FEET?

CAST:

TIMOTHY	David Markham
BERNARD	Willoughby Goddard
LORD FOUNTAIN	Patrick Troughton
POPPY	Sylvia Kay
LAURA	Jo Rowbottom
MAGGIE	Diana Coupland
TOWSER GRIDDLE	Victor Lucas
NANNIE	Anna Wing
ISHAKI	Kristopher Kum
LADY FOUNTAIN (BLONDE)	Jean Garvey
LADY JANINE FOUNTAIN	Valerie Bell
ZOO DIRECTOR	William Kendall
LORD FOUNTAIN'S DOCTOR	David Langton
BERNARD'S DOCTOR	Donald Morley
HITLER	Carl Jaffe
LUCY	Anna Bentinck
PATRICIA	Angela Harvey
VIVIEN	Jane Knowles
VOICE OF GOD	Jack May
POLICE CONSTABLE	William Holmes
TELEGRAPH BOY	David Palmer
WHELDON	Graham Tonbridge
FLUNKEYS AND REMOVAL MEN	{ James Haswell { Steve Pokel

NARRATION RECORDED BY KENNETH HAIGH

ON FILM ONLY:

LADY HARRIET FOUNTAIN	Araby Lockhart
REMNITZ	Ves Delahunt
GONDOLIER	Mark Penfold
MAID	Delia Abraham
BAILIFF'S DAUGHTER	Verna Harvey
FOUNTAIN'S DOUBLE	Peter Diamond

BBC Transmission : June 2nd, 1965

TELECINE: WOODS AND FIELDS

An ageing man on a horse, dashing wildly through woods and across fields.

Narrator: The man on the horse is Lord Fountain. The year, nineteen-twenty. Lord Fountain is a bad horseman and is about to be thrown. He is also the father of twins, Timothy and Bernard, whose mother is about to leave them. She is leaving them partly because she is bored, and partly because she is not Lord Fountain's wife. [*Pause*] There is an unconscious motive too. Lord Fountain's babies are ugly and their mother wants them to die. Since this is an unconscious motive we are in a dilemma as to whether to hold her responsible for the act of desertion or not. [*Pause*] This is where Lord Fountain gets thrown.

[*The horse shies and Fountain sails through the air into a ditch.*]

SCENE I: INTERIOR OF NURSERY

Nursery, where Nannie stands weeping over the babies' cradles.

Narrator: Meanwhile, in the house, Nannie is in tears. She is frightened of Lord Fountain, and despises the heartless mother who is now on a train to London. Nannie will never forget the things Timothy and Bernard's mother said when they were born.

SCENE II: INTERIOR OF BEDROOM

Maggie, the mother. Head and shoulders only. She is in labour pains. In a rather petulant northern voice she yells her resentment:

Maggie: The little—ooo! You devils. You murdering little—aaah! [*She calms down, panting.*]

85

Nannie's voice: Try a little push now, miss—

Maggie: It's no good telling me to push. What I need is a block and tackle. Oh hell. Hell. Where's *he*?

Nannie: Lord Fountain, madam?

Maggie: Where is he, the sadist—

   [*Pause.*]

Nannie: He's just been recovered from the lower lake, madam. He's all wet and swearing.

Maggie: Not again!

Nannie: His horse threw him in, madam.

Maggie [*groaning*]: I'll kill these things when they get out. [*Pause*] I'd leave him, if it wasn't for the money.

   [*She begins to yell.*]

SCENE III: INTERIOR OF NURSERY

Crying Nannie. Lord Fountain is brought into the nursery on a stretcher.

Narrator: Lord Fountain has heard of his mistress's departure and is rather pleased. He was getting tired of her. He prefers Nannie who adores him in her servile fashion and makes excellent cocoa.

Fountain: Well, Nannie. Good riddance to bad rubbish. How are the little blighters?

Nannie: How are *you*, sir?

Fountain: Nothing serious. The swine chucked me into a ditch the other side of Bassett's paddock. Broken leg. [*Pause*] I hated that woman, anyway.

Nannie: She's left a letter, sir.

   [*Nannie hands over the letter and Fountain begins to read it. The Narrator takes over and the events in the studio take place during the reading of the letter.*]

Narrator: Dear Jeremypops, I am leaving you and going back to Towser Griddle.

SCENE IV: INTERIOR TOWSER GRIDDLE'S STUDIO

In Griddle's studio. Towser is huge, daemonic and bearded. Maggie comes in with her suitcase. Towser has a canvas set up in front of a cage filled with sweets on a dais. When Maggie puts her case down, Towser chases her round the room. Capturing her he drags her into the cage and locks the door on her. Laughing, he goes back to paint Maggie in the cage.

Narrator: He now has a studio in Chelsea and wants me to model for him again. Compared with you, Towser is a sweetie. I have never really liked you, I think I must have been swept away. It was lovely pretending to be a lady, but I must have marriage and security and all these Towser promises without fail. You are a selfish man, Jeremy. Also I could never find my way round in that awful house, nor suck up to your awful friends. Try not to think too badly of your—Maggie Pooh.

SCENE V: INTERIOR NURSERY

Fountain folds the letter and orders the men who carried him in to take him over to the cradles.

Fountain: She's gone back to Towser Griddle, Nannie. Do you remember Towser?
Nannie: Indeed I do, sir.
Fountain: What do you think of a feller taking up art like that?
Nannie: I think it's scandalous, sir.
Fountain: Inbreeding. Half the Griddles are raving. Picturesque but—[*Pause*] The little bitch. Never mind. Let's have a look at the youngsters.
  [*C.U. cradles. One contains a very fat bundle, and the other a very thin bundle. C.U. Fountain's face.*]
Do you prefer the fat one, or the thin one, Nannie?
Nannie: I love both the little darlings, sir—
Fountain: Is it genetic?

Nannie: It started when Miss Maggie lost her milk, if you ask me—
[*Fountain leans over the cradle.*]

TELECINE

A still shot of two children in silhouette. One fat and one thin. Very small. The year nineteen twenty-three superimposed.

Narrator: The seasons came and went. The early formative years passed. The twins grew. [*Pause*] And unaccountably, Lord Fountain began to dislike his natural sons.

TELECINE

Repeat silhouettes for nineteen twenty-five, nineteen twenty-seven, nineteen twenty-nine. As each silhouette comes up we hear Fountain's voice lamenting.

Fountain's Voice: Bastards—little bastards.

TELECINE

Shot of maid going upstairs—the twins peering up her skirts from below. Narrator's voice over.

Narrator: They were innocently precocious, and quite puzzled about certain things to do with grown humans. At the age of eleven they fell in love with the bailiff's daughter.

TELECINE

Still shot of a little girl posed like a Victorian explorer with folded arms and one foot on the back of a fat little kneeling boy. Repeat with thin boy.

Narrator: Lord Fountain was angry when he found out. And one day on a duck shoot—

TELECINE

Shot of Fountain dressed for duck shooting, squatting in a flat bottomed boat.
    CUT TO: *Little girl in white dress skipping through a field.*
    CUT TO: *Fountain with raised gun. He fires.*
    CUT TO: *Sprawled body of the little girl in the field.*

Narrator: Coroner's verdict, death by misadventure. Timothy and Bernard cried for three days, then gradually forgot, and Lord Fountain built his bailiff a new house.

TELECINE
Repeat silhouettes for nineteen thirty-four, nineteen thirty-six, nineteen thirty-eight over shots of clouds.

Narrator: What are known as the clouds of war were gathering. Lord Fountain was marrying into and divorcing out of, several distinguished families. His lust for legal progeny was manic and unproductive, and he tended to work off his frustration against birds. [*Pause*] At Oxford, the twins were renowned for their eccentricity and their pathological fear of Adolf Hitler.

SCENE VI: INTERIOR COLLEGE ROOM

Timothy and Bernard sitting in a college room.

Narrator: Late one night in Hilary Term, Timothy and Bernard were sitting in Timothy's room wondering what they were for.
[*Pause.*]
Timothy: What are we *for*?
[*Pause.*]
Bernard [*irritably*]: *I* don't know what we're for!
[*Pause.*]
Timothy: It makes me sad, Bernard.
[*Pause.*]
Bernard: It makes *me* sad.
[*Pause.*]
Narrator: And they were harmlessly sitting there being melancholy —when Hitler walked in.
[*Hitler comes in, stands facing them with his arm in the Nazi salute. Timothy and Bernard promptly go to a gun case on one wall. Each takes a shotgun and fires.*]

TELECINE: FIELD

Lord Fountain and a Teutonic-looking man stomping through a field, carrying shotguns.

Narrator: Meanwhile, Lord Fountain is hospitably conducting General Remnitz on a wildfowl shoot in Scotland. Remnitz has a bad temper and is a bad shot. On the advice of his doctor, he has abandoned the military cares of the Third Reich for a long weekend. Fountain wishes to placate Remnitz but is infuriated by his bad luck with the fowl. Desperate situations inspire desperate remedies.

TELECINE

Remnitz swings his gun and shoots. His dog goes scurrying off. In a nearby copse there is a gillie with a large crate of dead fowl. As the dog runs into the copse, the gillie thrusts a fowl into its mouth. The dog rushes off and triumphantly lays the bird at Remnitz's feet. Remnitz beams, picks up the bird and waves it spitefully at Fountain.

SCENE VII: INTERIOR COLLEGE ROOM

Hitler, who collapses. Timothy and Bernard stand with smoking shotguns.

Narrator: It turned out that they had both had the same nightmare. None the less, they felt that the occasion should be celebrated.

TELECINE: RIVER

Down the river comes a punt, with a draped coffin. Timothy and Bernard, each in morning clothes and top hat, stand one at each end of the punt, which is poled along by a young man dressed as a gondolier. Sounds of cheering, whistling and shouting. As the punt goes down-river the narrator speaks.

Narrator: Certain young ladies admired this innocuous fun so much that they contrived to meet Timothy and Bernard for breakfast a week later.

SCENE VIII: INTERIOR COLLEGE ROOM

The girls—Lucy, Patricia and Vivien are smoking at the table. Timothy and Bernard stand by the fireplace, basking in the girls' admiration.

Lucy: Honestly, it was just like something by Buñuel—
Patricia: Or Dali!
Vivien: Marvellous!
Lucy: What are you going to do next?
Timothy: I think Bernard and I were meant to be a single person.
Bernard: But something went wrong.
Timothy: Our father is biologically unsound. He keeps getting married and divorced. No one could accuse him of not trying, but he can't legitimately reproduce himself.
Bernard: Our mother lives in a cage.
Timothy: In Chelsea.
Bernard: She makes the best of it, and she's looked after by a charming fellow called Towser Griddle. [*Pause*] Father, on the other hand, is obsessed by primogeniture.
   [*The girls are horrified. They collect their gloves and bags, and begin to withdraw backwards whilst Timothy and Bernard continue their dialogue. As the girls retreat step by step, Timothy and Bernard advance step by step.*]
Timothy: You see, we were born on the wrong side of the coronet. Father supports us out of pique, which is a paradox, but then he's a man of paradoxes.
Bernard: Maturity is going to be a problem.
Timothy: Though we may not survive the war.
Girls [*in chorus*]: What war?
Bernard: Are you out of touch with the European situation?
Timothy: Fascism is the continuation of capitalism by other means—
Bernard: Are we boring you?
Timothy: We do lack a sense of proportion. It's largely because we're bewildered.
   [*The girls open the door and rush out, slamming it behind them. Timothy and Bernard turn to face each other.*]
Bernard: What pretty girls!
Timothy: Very jolly.
Bernard: Do you think we'll ever settle down?

Timothy: We might, if we live.

Timothy and Bernard [*together, singing*]*:* She's only a Mum, in a gilded cage, A bee-hootiful sight to see.

Bernard: Will Griddle keep his mysterious hold on the ageing beauty in the cage?

Timothy: Will Lord Fountain, the dastardly seducer, continue to entertain high-ranking Nazi officers?

Bernard: Will the twins, the bastardly ingrates, plant the Union Jack on the rubble of Berlin?

[*They burst into tears.*]

Narrator: And thirteen months later in Chelsea:

SCENE IX: INTERIOR TOWSER GRIDDLE'S STUDIO

Maggie is in the cage knitting. Timothy and Bernard, in uniform, stand close to the cage. Towser is sulking by his easel.

Maggie: I see your father's just got married again. [*Pause*] He's a bit thick with them Germans, isn't he?

Towser: I won't hear a wrong word against Fountain.

Maggie: Never mind. You two's good proletarian stock on my side. Fountain used to drive me silly with his two thousand years of this and two thousand years of that. [*Pause*] You'd think he'd been *alive* two thousand years. [*Pause*] Have you said bye-bye to your girl friends?

[*Pause.*]

Timothy: I haven't got a girl friend.

Maggie [*shocked*]*:* Bernard?

Bernard: I haven't either.

[*Pause.*]

Maggie: Don't you *like* girls?

Timothy: Yes.

Bernard: Oh, yes.

[*Pause.*]

Maggie: What do you make of that, Towser?

Towser [*airily*]: Oh, they're probably still fixated on you I should think. They can't contaminate your image with sordidness.

Maggie: Towser's very up on people's sexual difficulties.

Timothy: I've often meant to ask you, mother. Why do you stay in that cage?

Maggie: Don't you like it, dear?

Bernard: It isn't exactly normal, is it?

Towser: I won't hear a word against your mother.

Maggie: It's his pictures. He can only paint pictures of women in cages.

Bernard: I don't think you and father have done your best for us by any means. [*Pause*] Why am I so fat? Why is he so thin? What does it *mean*, mother?

Maggie: That's how you come into this world. That's how you'll go out of it. It's the will of God. [*Pause*.] Now don't go and get yourselves killed.

Timothy: Father hates us.

Towser: I won't have that, I won't have it. The man's as sterile as a eunuch, that's *his* trouble,—and when he hits the jackpot, what are the circumstances? Illegitimacy. Mind you, there's something very odd there. Something psychologically unsound. Still, how would you feel if you couldn't procure legitimate heirs?

Bernard: Procure?

Towser: Get. Obtain. Cause. Incite. Produce. Look at you. I've never seen a pair of more lugubrious nitwits.

Maggie: Fountain does give you money, lovies.

Timothy: The point is, we are extremely sad.

Maggie: Why?

Bernard: We don't know.

Timothy: I think it's the world.

Maggie: Have you really *tried*?

Bernard: Tried what?

Maggie: Oh, there's lots of lovely things.

Timothy: Where?

Maggie: Everywhere.

Timothy: Well, if they're everywhere, why can't we see them?

Maggie: It's ever so tedious when people are gloomy. That probably accounts for the girls—

Towser: They aren't men. Fountain's fault, not that I want to blacken the man's name. Look at them. He almost made it—but not quite. He got the form, but not what you might call the content. [*Pause*] You two haven't any *content*.

Maggie: They're half mine you know, Towser!

Towser: Quite. Form from you. Absence of content from Fountain. The poor feller's a kind of creative vacuum. Thank God my lot were yeomen. Like trees. Big thick barky sort of trees—all urge, and sap.

[*Timothy and Bernard begin to cry.*]

Maggie: Now you've *hurt* them—

[*Maggie comes out of her cage to comfort them.*]

Towser: Well, I'm very sorry! They'll probably do something idiotic and get bumped off anyway—

Maggie: Towser!

[*Begins to cry, a keening wail goes up from the boys.*]

Towser: I don't know why you people can't be superficial and jolly. I'm trying to paint, damn you.

[*Silence. Maggie returns to cage.*]

Timothy: I don't want to fight. I want to look after animals. Furry ones.

Bernard: Same here, only with me it's fish. Lovely shining choreographic fish.

Towser [*with steely exasperation*]: Can't the animals and fish look after their bloody selves?

[*Pause.*]

Timothy [*primly*]: The green-crested gibbon is practically extinct in Sumatra.

Bernard [*grimly*]: And what about the whales? Spiked, harpooned, dynamited! I mean; you Griddles would soon complain if people came after *you*.

Towser: Twelve Griddles lost their lives in the last war, I am proud to inform you. I hope you have the same luck.

Maggie: Towser!

Towser: I can see it. Two gun-carriages, one with a fat coffin and one with a thin coffin. Union Jacks. Salvo. The last of the crypto-Fountains. [*Pause*] For King and country boys! If it weren't for my aluminium leg I'd be there with you.

Timothy: There wasn't even a fieldmouse left in Flanders.

Towser: Who wants mice?

[*Pause.*]

Bernard: There were lice.

Towser: There you are then! Where there's lice there's hope.
[*He laughs uproariously at the joke.*]

Timothy: He makes me feel dejected, mother.

Maggie: He doesn't mean it, darling.

Bernard: Things that upset Timothy upset me. [*Pause*] I was upset *anyway.*

Towser: Can't you be positive? What's the matter with you? If old Tunny Crook has any sense he'll post you two in opposite directions. That'd be a lesson. Then you'd have to be independent.
[*Pause.*]

Bernard: But we like each other.

Towser: You're a disgrace to a fine regiment. Maggie, come out of there and boil my egg.
[*He gets up and stalks out.*]

Maggie: He's a lovely man really. When you get to know him. [*Vaguely*] He has to have his egg, round about now.

Timothy: He doesn't keep you locked in then?

Maggie: He did at first. I'm glad to say he doesn't need to now. I know my place.

Bernard: Yes. Well. We'd better be off then. Bye-bye, mother.
[*Kisses her through the bars.*]

Timothy: Bye, mother. [*Also kisses her.*]

Maggie: Cheery bye lovies—
[*They cross the studio waving to her.*]
You'll hang out the washing on the Siegfried Line, won't you?

TELECINE

Film of jungle warfare.

Narrator: But Lord Fountain was against the idea of any sons of his shooting at the people who managed his factories in the Ruhr. He knew some people at the War Office, and they managed to find a nice battle for Timothy and Bernard in the Far East. It was very green and wet and exciting, but during a retreat, Timothy and Bernard got lost. Whilst they were trying to find out where they were, Lord Fountain contracted his sixth marriage.

TELECINE

Lord Fountain and his new wife Harriet on horseback. Lord Fountain is now a parched myth of a man, hideously old.

Fountain: What I want to know, Harriet, is—are you fecund woman or are you not?
Harriet: I don't know, Jeremy.
Fountain: Have you got any opinions on the matter Harriet?
Harriet [*with horsy coyness*]*:* Well it may be superstitious of me Jeremy—but I can make things grow. I really can.
Fountain: I'm talking about babies, gel, not vegetables!
Harriet [*deflated*]*:* I know, Jeremy.
Fountain: I told your father. I don't want just any old rubbish, I said. I want a *woman*. A buxom, breeding, lively sort of gel.

TELECINE

Cackling away to himself, Fountain cracks her horse with his whip. It bolts, and Fountain goes galloping after it.

Narrator: This is where Lord Fountain gets thrown again.

TELECINE

Fountain's horse sends him sailing into the air.
    CUT TO: *Jungle clearing. Timothy and Bernard are sitting with piles of fruit, eating.*

Narrator: Back in the jungle, Timothy and Bernard went on being lost. They forgot about the war and became vegetarians, since they were getting very friendly with the animals.

TELECINE

A chimp appears in the clearing. Timothy holds out a banana. The chimp takes it and eats.

SCENE X: EXTERIOR THE BURMESE JUNGLE

Narrator: One day they met a little Japanese.
    [*A Japanese soldier springs yelling from the bush into the clearing, with fixed bayonet. There is no reaction from Timothy and Bernard, which leaves the Japanese rather crestfallen.*]

When Timothy and Bernard didn't try to kill him, the Japanese
was very frightened. Fright often causes tantrums, and he had a
tantrum. He threw his rifle on the ground.

[*The Japanese chucks his rifle on the ground and bursts into tears.
Timothy pulls out a handkerchief and gives it to him. The Japanese
stands wiping his cheeks. Starts grinning.*]

No one should be misled by this smiling foreigner. The rest of
his platoon was burning a village and raping its women. On the
other hand, the survivors from Timothy and Bernard's platoon
were disembowelling some Japanese at a place called Tan-Yang,
three hundred miles away.

[*Bernard offers the Japanese a banana. He takes it and sits down
to eat. Timothy points at himself.*]

Timothy: Timothy.
Bernard: Bernard.
Japanese: Ishaki.

[*Timothy offers his canteen of water to Ishaki, who takes it and
drinks. Bernard gets out a home-made flute (bamboo) and begins
to play—a soft, wistful, gentle melody.*]

Timothy: [*singing*]:
  The fish are in the water
  The birds are in the sky,
  The men are on the battlefield
  Waiting for to die.
  The owls are in the treetops
  The dolphins jumping high;
  The girls are in their lonely beds
  Waiting for to cry.

[*Timothy hums. Bernard goes on playing. Ishaki stretches out
in the sun.*]

Narrator: All that day, Timothy and Bernard played the flute and
sang for Ishaki.

[*Ishaki sits up, holds out his hand for the flute and begins to play.*]
And Ishaki played for Timothy and Bernard.

[*The music continues. The camera scrutinises the three men, the
chimp, the jungle. The music fades. The scene darkens. We hear the
cawing and screeching of the tropical night. C.U. the men's faces,
asleep.*]

That was how Timothy and Bernard and Ishaki spent the war. Until one day—

TELECINE

Film of atom bomb explosion.

Narrator: Some clever men found out how to incinerate one hundred thousand Japanese in a matter of seconds. And in case this was a language the Japanese didn't understand—

TELECINE

Film of second explosion.

Narrator: The clever men did it again.

TELECINE

Timothy and Bernard, impeccably dressed for the city walking away from a bank in the City of London.

Narrator: So Timothy and Bernard came back.

TELECINE

The twins walks faster and faster.

Narrator: Lord Fountain had obtained them sinecures in an old merchant bank, but they hated it so much they ran away.

TELECINE

They begin to run.

SCENE XI: INTERIOR TIMOTHY AND BERNARD'S ROOM

Large room—austerely comfortable. Each wall is papered with a huge blow-up of the jungle.

Narrator: They took a large room, W.C. and bathroom near Regents
Park.
  [*Cut to same room with Timothy and Bernard sitting in it.*]
And wondered what to do.
  [*Pause.*]
Whilst Lord Fountain—
  [*Still of Lord Fountain. Huge C.U. ancient and wrinkled.*]
Consulted a famous geriatrician.

SCENE XII: INTERIOR CONSULTING ROOM

*A desk with the doctor sitting at one side and Lord Fountain at the
other.*

Doctor: I can assure you, Lord Fountain, that you are not sterile.
Fountain: Then why can't I procreate, man? [*Slyly*] It's those
  women!
Doctor: Er—now—it's six marriages isn't it?
Fountain [*snappily*]: Seven.
  [*Pause.*]
Doctor: I would have thought—I mean, even from a statistical point
  of view there should have been a little toddler by now.
Fountain: We're doomed.
Doctor: I beg your pardon?
Fountain: My family, doctor, was begettin' barons when yours was
  still in burrows!
Doctor: And I've no doubt, Lord Fountain, that my family will
  continue to beget ordinary citizens when yours is extinct!
  [*Lord Fountain begins to cry. The doctor passes across a handker-
  chief.*]
Fountain: I have two bastards, y'know.
Doctor: I didn't mean to upset you.
Fountain: But they're peculiar.
Doctor: What?
Fountain: I think it's their mother.
  [*Pause.*]

They're not real. Not human.
[*Pause.*]
They're spiritually deformed.
Doctor: In what way?
Fountain: They don't *do* anything.

SCENE XIII: INTERIOR TIMOTHY AND BERNARD'S ROOM

Timothy and Bernard's room. Bernard is sitting on one of two beds, dressed in a shirt only. On the other side is a girl (Poppy) in a slip. The bedclothes are rumpled. Both look gloomy.

Poppy: That was miz—wasn't it?
Bernard: I'm sorry!
Poppy: Are you sure it isn't because you. . .?
Bernard: Positive.
Poppy: Then you don't like me!
Bernard: I do like you, Poppy. I even love you.
Poppy: Even!
Bernard: What about Timothy and Laura then?
Poppy: Where *is* Timothy, anyway?
Bernard: Gone to the pictures.
Poppy: Something nice?
Bernard: It's to do with the Amazon, I think.
Poppy: Oh God! You two!
Bernard: It has an armadillo in it. Tim specially wanted to see the armadillo.
    [*He begins to get dressed, climbing into a zoo keeper's uniform which is on a hanger behind the door.*]
Poppy: I'm quite willing to keep on trying, Bernard—
Bernard: It's no use Poppy.
Poppy: You look silly in that uniform. Tim does as well. What do you both want to work in a zoo for?

Bernard: It's a complete enigma.

Poppy: And what you got to go there at this time of night for?

Bernard: One of my elephants is sick. It's got a tumour in its trunk, I believe.

Poppy: All that way out of London. Why can't you work in a proper zoo?

Bernard: It *is* a proper zoo. It's very small, but it's very proper.

Poppy: Time you got your weight down as well.

Bernard: I was born fat, Poppy. It's the metabolism. I don't seem to be able to intervene.

[*Poppy gets up, looks round.*]

Poppy: This room gives me the creeps.

Bernard: We like it.

Poppy: My last boy friend had a flat in Chelsea. Just think, if you and Tim hadn't caught me and Laura feeding those ducks—I might still be with him.

Bernard: Yes. It's a sombre thought.

Poppy: Might still have been happy!

Bernard: My mother's boy friend has a flat in Chelsea—

Poppy: I'd have thought she'd be too old for boy friends.

Bernard: Oh well. They're a sort of bohemian Darby and Joan, you know.

Poppy: I told my mum you went to Oxford and were a lieutenant during the war. She was ever so impressed.

[*Pause.*]

She asked me if we was thinking of getting married.

[*Bernard is now in full uniform, including peaked cap. He looks absolutely hopeless. His eyes roll with helpless despair at the last remark.*]

Bernard: I'm moving into the aquarium next week. I've been trying to get into the aquarium for months.

Poppy: What's that got to do with it?

Bernard: Nothing.

Poppy: You'll have to learn to overcome your handicap sometime.

Bernard: It isn't a handicap. It's more of a . . . more of a symbolic incapacity.

Poppy: Which in plain language—

Bernard: Means I'm not cut out for loving people.

Poppy: What are you then, a flipping pervert?

Bernard: Don't be superficial.

Poppy: I think you're very evasive on that subject.

Bernard: Not on that subject. I'm evasive altogether.

Poppy: Oh, go and stick a thermometer in your elephant.

Bernard: You'll have me crying in a minute. I cry very easily.

Poppy [*sulkily*]: *I* love *you* Bernard.

Bernard: I didn't say I don't love you. I said I'm not cut out for it. Dammit, it isn't five minutes since I said I do love you!

[*Poppy stalks into the kitchen.*]

Poppy: I'll wash the dinner things. And you can meet me from the office tomorrow.

[*Bernard stands looking at the crumpled bed. Dabs away a tear with his handkerchief. Straightens the bedclothes. He moves to the centre of the room.*]

Bernard: Alas. *Alles ist kaput*—as General Remnitz said at Nuremberg.

Poppy [*from the kitchen:*] What's that?

Bernard: Poor General Remnitz! It wasn't his fault—

Poppy [*from the doorway*]: What wasn't whose fault?

Bernard [*declaims*]:
The lungfish has a stately mien,
It's eyes are like two spoons.
And everywhere the lungfish goes
It writes its name in runes.

Poppy [*softly*]: What am I going to do with you?

Bernard: What am I going to do with myself? Did my father ask himself that? Twirling his moustachios over mummy's navel, did he ask himself? *Niet!*

Poppy: I saw his picture in the paper the other day. All bandaged up. It said he'd been thrown at a point-to-point. If you and Tim were to make it up with him—

Bernard: One of these days they'll have farms on the sea bed. Won't that be lovely? I'll go down and never come up again. Imagine. Mowing the seaweed. Milking the whales—

Poppy: I don't know what you've got against your father.

Bernard: And I'm tired of bicycling to the zoo. I keep getting punctures at Elephant and Castle.

Poppy: You could take the tube—

Bernard: Couldn't bear that, Poppy.

Poppy: You and Tim could afford a Rolls Royce each, if you wanted.

Bernard: My father gives us all that money because he's a sadist. If people are determined to give you money, it's very hard to stop them—did you know that?

Poppy: Catch me stopping them!

Bernard [*going to door*]: Well. Bye-bye, Poppy. Have a banana. There's a bunch in the kitchen.

Poppy: Aren't we going to—try again?

Bernard: I doubt it. This was my hundred and eighteenth fiasco since V-J day.

[*Poppy turns away. Bernard goes out, sad and ponderous. Poppy goes into the kitchen. Takes a banana from the bunch, peels it, bites the end off.*]

TELECINE

A pet food commercial. Narrator's voice over.

Narrator: In the meantime Lord Fountain has been advised to expand and modernise his investments. He put half a million into pet food: Fountain Fresh. The food that dogs dig. By a sad oversight, however, it was unclear whether the food was *for* animals or *from* animals. And the day after Timothy and Bernard saw the adverts—

SCENE XIV: INTERIOR THE CAT HOUSE

The cat house at Timothy and Bernard's zoo. All the cage doors are open, and the place in a state of terrible disorder. Straw littered about, bones, bits of meat etc. We hear the wailing sirens of police cars. Timothy and Bernard sit on a bench crying. The Director of the zoo comes in followed by a police constable. The Director is a big, ruddy, irritable man. He stands looking down at Timothy and Bernard.

Director: Is that all you can do? Sit and blubber?

Timothy: Well, since we let them out, it'd be inconsistent to help to catch them again.

Director: All I want to know is why? God dammit, why?
[*Looking at the constable.*]
Before I hand you over to the police that is. Constable, give these two maniacs the latest—
[*The constable lugubriously disinters a notebook and reads out.*]

Constable: One wombat in Tunbridge Wells; a cheeta at Headcorn; two tigers and an elephant on the A20; three wolves sighted near Ashford; gorilla heading for Canterbury.
[*Stops, looks unbelievingly from Timothy to Bernard.*]
In fact, sir, [*to the Director*] the country's swarming with all sorts of ferocious animals.
[*Pause.*]

Director: Well?

Timothy and Bernard [*together*]: We couldn't stand it any more.

Director: And what about all those women and children out there in mortal fear of their lives?

Timothy: Yes. And men too.

Director [*bellowing*]: Of course men too, you cretinous nincompoops!

SCENE XV: INTERIOR A CELL

Shot of Timothy and Bernard's faces behind bars, with loud clanging of cell door.

SCENE XVI: INTERIOR TOWSER GRIDDLE'S STUDIO

Newspaper behind bars with huge black headline: 'ZOO KEEPERS— WE DIDN'T MEAN ANY HARM' The paper is held by Maggie, who sits in her cage in Towser's studio. She peers bleakly out over the paper at Lord Fountain, who, mounted on a saddle placed on a vaulting horse, is being painted by Towser. Fountain's latest wife, a plump, dressy young blonde, sits submissively watching the others.

Fountain: I'll have them whipped!
    [*Maggie looking at Lady Fountain.*]
Maggie: You see, Lady Fountain, Timothy and Bernard—
Fountain: Don't talk to her! She's barren.
Lady Fountain: Oh, Jeremy!
    [*She begins to sniff.*]
Fountain: They're horrid. Horrid. I never liked them.
Maggie [*reproachfully*]: Your own flesh and blood, Jeremy.
Fountain: Towser, can I dismount?
Towser: If you like. It's time for my egg.
    [*Fountain tottering down.*]
Fountain: Flesh and blood!
    [*Goes to Lady Fountain.*]
Is there any flesh and blood left in the world? Look at her! What's the matter with them all!
    [*Pinches Lady Fountain's arm.*]
If you don't come up with something soon, dammit if I don't bequeath everything to those two lunatics, just out of spite. When you get to my age, there's precious little fun in anything but spite—
Lady Fountain [*getting up*]: I shall divorce you. I shall! For cruelty!
Fountain: Good! Splendid! Get on with it—leave me without an heir to my name.
Fountain [*swinging to face Maggie*]: Have you noticed how selfish everyone's getting, Maggie?
Maggie: P'raps you ought to get yourself examined—
Fountain [*shouting*]: I've been examined woman! I'm as sound as a bell. I'm vigorous.
    [*Stomping over to Lady Fountain.*]
They cheat me, that's what it is. That, and those bastards of mine have put the blight on me. I've tried to be rational. Is there any use for uselessness? If there is—where? I offered them something in the Foreign Office, I've still got me influence, y'know. They turned it down. My family's put its idiots into the Foreign Office for generations. What did I get? A telegram. A telegram which informed me that diplomacy is for squares. Square what? Square

who? Is there even a conspiracy to befoul the withering language?

Towser: If you want to shout and be paranoid and all that Fountain, I wish you'd go somewhere else to do it.

Fountain: You see! *He's* crippled with guilt as well.

　　[*Begins to cry.*]

He took my Maggie Pooh!

　　[*Towser throws up his arms in resignation. Sits down and stares moodily at Maggie. Lady Fountain goes to Fountain.*]

Lady Fountain: There, there, Jeremy. Come along. I'll give you one more chance—

　　[*Fountain is led out, blubbering. Maggie comes out of the cage, sets a pan on the cooker, puts an egg to boil.*]

SCENE XVII: INTERIOR TIM AND BERNARD'S ROOM. NIGHT

Timothy and Laura are lying on one of the beds.

Laura: Isn't Bernard coming back?

Timothy: Not till Monday. A friend of his in Berkshire's got some dolphins. Bernard's down there observing—

Laura: Dolphins—in Berkshire?

Timothy: In a pool.

Laura: Poppy's very miz. Without Bernard.

Timothy: Yes.

　　[*Pause.*]

Laura: Was it awful in prison?

Timothy: Yes. Ssssh!

Laura: Why?

Timothy: I've had an idea.

　　[*Pause.*]

Laura: Are you really never going to see me again? [*Pause*] I don't dig you and Bernard.

Timothy: Something hurts.

Laura: Where, love?

Timothy: Inside, of course.

Laura: Go and see your doctor then!

Timothy: It isn't that kind of hurt.

Laura: Well, go and see the other kind of doctor—

Timothy: It isn't that, either.

Laura: You don't half exasperate me.

Timothy [*getting up*]*:* I'm the bright one. Bernard isn't very bright. He's the sensitive one. I'm more—cerebral. That's it. Bernard was very unhappy in prison, though they did let him keep a goldfish. I was more . . . sort of stunned than unhappy. After all, those animals we let out didn't hurt anybody, did they?

Laura: Except for that wolf eating some poor old lady's pekinese! You ought to be ashamed. Both of you. Served you right being sent to prison.

Timothy: I'd be all right if it wasn't for this pain—

Laura: There's got to be an explanation. [*Truculently*] For every-thing! Pains and all.

Timothy: I quite agree. But what *is* the explanation? Every morning when I open my eyes, I feel as if I've just arrived. But where from? [*Pause*] And everything's new and mysterious. [*Pause*] At one time it was very serious. I had to go round at bedtime putting cards on things with their names on. Chair, bed, lamp, Bernard. Bernard looked quite odd, with a card pinned to his pyjamas with 'Bernard' written on it. [*Pause*] It helped, though, in the mornings. It made for re-orientation. Otherwise, panic. I woke up once, there was a funny smell in the room. I couldn't quite put a name to it. You know what it was?

Laura: What?

Timothy: Air.

> [*Laura gets up. Like Poppy in the other scene, she is wearing a slip. Her dress is on the floor. She goes quietly into the kitchen. Comes back with a basin, smashes it on the floor.*]

Poor Laura.

Laura [*dressing*]*:* I'm *fine*, thank you. Swinging.

Timothy: You must have a theory. How can you not have a theory?

Laura: About what?

Timothy: About me and Bernard.

Laura: I used to think just because you were strange, it made you interesting. It doesn't. And I'm clearing out. You haven't got enough to occupy your minds, that's what it is.

Timothy: Have you?

Laura: My mind's . . . my mind's . . . *buzzing*.

Timothy: Funny. All I've got is a large blue space with a little silver bell chiming somewhere at the back.

Laura: Sounds lovely!

Timothy: Sometimes it isn't a bell. It's a little bell-shaped man. And he sings. [*Singing*]

Ding dong, ding dong
It won't be long
Before you hear
A louder gong.
Ding dong, dong ding—
That'll be death,
Pealing in.

[*Laura stands looking at him. His face is quite expressionless. She shivers.*]

Laura: Have you ever loved *anybody*?

Timothy [*sadly*]: I loved our bailiff's daughter when I was eleven. Nothing's been quite the same since. [*Pause*] I love Bernard though.

Laura: Not me?

Timothy: I was all right till this thing started hurting. It makes me egocentric. I can't concentrate on anything except how hurt I am.

[*Laura gets her coat. Goes to the door.*]

Laura: I hate you.

Timothy: I wish you wouldn't. It makes this hurting thing hurt harder.

Laura: I could kill you.

Timothy: Well at least—that's human.

[*Laura goes out, slamming the door.*]

TELECINE

Exterior a divorce court, in the Strand Palace of Justice. (Note: the following scene is mimed without words by the actors, and described by the narrator.) Lord Fountain comes out of the court looking very pleased with himself.

Narrator: The following week, just as Lord Fountain was hobbling

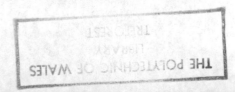
THE POLYTECHNIC OF WALES

triumphantly out of the Divorce Court and humming gleefully to
himself [*Pause*].

TELECINE

*Laura and Poppy approach Lord Fountain. They begin to tell him
some long story.*

Narrator: Poppy and Laura hunted him down threatening to sue
Timothy and Bernard for breach of promise. Lord Fountain's
mind said to Lord Fountain:

Fountain's Voice: Ha, ha, me pretties!
Narrator: They all decided they hated Timothy and Bernard.

TELECINE

*Three quick close-ups of Lord Fountain, Poppy and Laura making
'hate' faces.*

And they went to the nearest espresso to concoct a letter.

SCENE XVIII: INTERIOR TIM AND BERNARD'S ROOM

*Bernard is in bed, his face drenched in sweat, his eyes closed. A doctor
is examining him. Timothy sits dejectedly nearby. The letter, signed
by Fountain, Poppy and Laura, is on the bedside table.*

Narrator: When they read the letter, Bernard fell ill and went into
a coma. Timothy's hurting thing got worse, too. But he had to
keep a hold on himself in order to look after Bernard.
   [*The doctor puts his things back in his case. Goes to Timothy.*]
Doctor: He's grotesquely overweight, you know.
Timothy: But that isn't what it is. Is it? If you see what I mean—
Doctor: Frankly, I don't know what it is. Some sort of fever. Has
he ever been in the tropics?
Timothy: We once got lost in a jungle—
Doctor: Hum—

Timothy: Is that the nearest you can get to a diagnosis? Hum?
　[*Pause.*]
Doctor: Yes.
Timothy: And we're illegitimate, and our father and our girl friends all hate us.
Doctor: Look, old man, don't let's start careering down one of those Freudian side-tracks eh? Are you given that way?
Timothy: No.
Doctor: Well then. Plenty of cool drinks, quiet, and when he comes round—if you could have something nice for him to look forward to. Back tomorrow.
　[*The doctor leaves. Timothy goes to the bed, stands looking down at Bernard. C.U. Bernard.*]
Narrator: No one knew what was going on inside Bernard's head. [*Pause*] But this is what was going on:

TELECINE
Porpoises leaping and swimming—sunny, glittering weather.

Narrator: Whilst Lord Fountain—

SCENE XIX: INTERIOR FOUNTAIN'S BEDROOM

Lord Fountain in bed. One leg is in a plaster cast and is suspended by block and tackle.

Narrator: Recovering from a riding accident in the country—plotted revenge most foul.
　[*Lord Fountain, who is reading, suddenly bursts out cackling and flings the book to the floor. Shouts.*]
Fountain: Got it! Nannie . . . Nannie!
　[*Nannie, grown old and wizened, comes gliding in in a wheel-chair which she propels herself. Lord Fountain is beside himself with glee.*]
See that book, Nannie?

Nannie: Yes, sir.

Fountain: Know what it is?

Nannie: I don't think anyone can accuse me of prying, sir.

Fountain: Mimsy old devil! It contains the secret, Nannie. The light.

Nannie: What's it called, sir?

Fountain: Oedipus Rex.

Nannie: Sounds like some kind of dog, sir.

Fountain: You're an old ninny, Nannie. The import of this tome is that [*shouting*] I've got to get *them* before they get me!

   [*Close-up Lord Fountain's face, apoplectic.*]

Narrator: And as Lord Fountain grew angrier and angrier—

TELECINE

Perfectly calm sea. No porpoises.

There was a distinct improvement in Bernard's condition.

TELECINE

Open lorry driving through London with Maggie in her cage on the back.

And he asked to see his mother.

SCENE XX: INTERIOR TIM AND BERNARD'S ROOM

Maggie, in her cage, in the centre: Towser broods by the window. Timothy, now cheerful, is spooning soup into Bernard's mouth.

Towser: It was damned embarrassing getting your mother here, I can tell you.

Maggie: But I had a lovely time, dear. Hasn't everything changed?

Towser: It's enough to make any humanist weep. You put somebody in a cage. No harm meant. All very jocular. And before you know where you are, they begin to *like* it!

   [*He looks wistfully at Maggie.*]

She carried it off with quite a bit of panache, in the thirties. It's just a gimmick, now. And a very worn old gimmick, if I may say so. Look at her expression! She looks as if she's just had a prefrontal leucotomy—

Maggie: Never mind, darling. It's Bernard we've got to think about now.

Towser: How are you, Bernard?

Bernard: I had a lovely coma. It was all sort of—porpoises.

Maggie [sadly]: I do *love* you and Timothy. I get butterflies in my tum-tum when I think I actually carried you both inside me.

Towser [eyeing Bernard]: It must have been bloody cramped!

[*Timothy stands, puts down bowl and spoon.*]

Timothy: As a matter of fact, it was snug. Not cramped. Bernard occupied more than his fair share of the space. Naturally. But then I needed less than the average.

Towser: Average what?

Timothy: Foetus.

Towser: How can *you* know when you weren't conscious!

[*Pause.*]

Timothy: I have . . . a kind of memory. There we were. Floating between mother's hips. With our arms round each other.

[*Maggie beady-eyed with sentiment.*]

Maggie: Isn't that lovely Towser?

Towser: I think it's rather disgusting. *And* untrue.

Timothy: I think the outside didn't come up to our expectations at all—

Towser: What outside?

Bernard: The outside of mother.

Timothy: And when they cut that cord—

Bernard: And tied those little knots—

Timothy: We knew we were in for it.

Bernard: It's no coincidence father's letter made me ill. He had every right to expect two real people to pop out of mother. But can we help it if we're a disappointment?

Maggie: My poor little Bernie! But Tim says he's got a wonderful surprise for you to help you get better.

Towser: Dammit, we're *all* going round with our cords cut and little knots tied on us. Do we make a fuss? Do we spend *our* time crying and letting people's tigers out of their cages?

Maggie: It's all right for you, Towser. You have your painting—

Towser: They should have stayed in the Army! Not that they'd have been allowed to. Not those two.

Bernard: I think art's had it. I think everything everybody's doing is

extremely useless. And what's more, they've been trying to kill
me ever since I was born.

Maggie: Who has, lovey?

Timothy: All of them. I came to the same conclusion as Bernard.

Bernard [*to Maggie*]*:* As soon as we dropped into this world, what
happened? Noise. Light. Bacteria. [*Pause*] Every time you stuck
your little fist out it got burned, bitten, fouled. You just got used
to daytime and then it was night. Same with summer and winter.
The whole thing goes churning on like some bloody great machine.
What do they mean by cutting my cord? How dared they?

Towser: The feller's drowning in self-pity!

> [*He goes to Bernard.*]

You've never done a hand's stroke. That's what's wrong. [*To
Timothy*] And you!

Timothy: Oh? And what do you think we did at the zoo?

Towser: I'll tell you what you did. You sat mooning over those
filthy animals all the time. Tunny Crook took his nippers there
one day, and said he caught *you* ... [*He prods Timothy in the chest*]
... singing to a giraffe. Do you deny it?

Timothy [*bashfully*]*:* No.

> [*Towser steps back, oozing pompous complacency.*]

Towser: Need I ... [*He turns to Maggie*] ... say more? [*Pause*]
Need you?

Timothy [*to Maggie*]*:* We've had an eviction order. Father's bought
this house.

Maggie: Why?

Timothy: He's going to have it torn down.

> [*Towser goes to the door, flings it open. Two men are waiting out-
> side. Towser waves them in.*]

Towser: Time to break camp—

> [*The men hoist Maggie's cage out of the room. Towser, with a
> final contemptuous look, flings out after them slamming the door.
> Timothy and Bernard stare at one another.*]

Timothy: I refuse to cry.

Bernard: So do I.

Timothy: Want any more soup?

Bernard: No thanks. I feel rather well, actually.

> [*Timothy sits down.*]

Timothy: What a pity mother ever left Barnsley. If she hadn't,

we might have had one of those archetypal working class dads,
all love and pigeons.

Bernard: Beer and braces.

Timothy: And you know what he'd have done?

　　[*They sing together in comic bravura style:*]

Bernard and *Timothy* [*together*]*:* Sent us to Oxford, Oxfor-hord . . .

　　[*Pause.*]

Bernard: Does it still hurt?

　　[*Pause.*]

Timothy [*cautiously*]*:* A bit—

Bernard: Tell you what—

Timothy: What?

Bernard [*timidly*]*:* My surprise. Wouldn't it cheer us both up?

Timothy: It will. [*Pause*] But it's a place. [*Pause*] When you're
really better, we'll go there.

　　[*Bernard closes his eyes.*]

Bernard: I'm getting drowsy—

Timothy: Any porpoises?

Bernard: One.

Timothy: What's it doing?

Bernard: Grinning.

　　[*Pause.*]

Timothy: Do you think we'll survive?

　　[*Bernard snores gently. Timothy tucks him up. Ambles round,
　　begins to take his tie off. Stops in front of a mirror. Looks at
　　himself. Turns to face the camera.*]

Down in Edgecombe Bassett
Where the forms of love are tacit,
There lived a man in a bowler hat
Who wondered what they were laughing at.
It wasn't the hat, or the brow beneath
But his lonely face hung there like a wreath.
He had no one to love
Or cherish
And wept at the thought
That man must perish;
His days were stolen
By the office grind;
At night he pondered

The concept of mind—
Until one sunny afternoon—
Bernard [*plaintively*]: Tim—
Timothy: I thought you were asleep.
Bernard: They've turned into sharks.
Timothy: The porpoises?
Bernard: Yes.
  [*Timothy goes and sits on the bed. Timothy puts his hand on Bernard's forehead.*]
Timothy: What are the sharks doing?
  [*Pause.*]
Bernard: Eating some people—
Timothy: Who?
Bernard: Father, and Poppy . . . and Laura.
Timothy: Open your eyes—
  [*Bernard opens his eyes. He is shivering and sweating.*]
  Listen—
Bernard: What?
Timothy: What can you hear?
Bernard: Traffic.
Timothy: What else?
Bernard: Jazz. [*Pause*] Somewhere—
Timothy: Bessie Smith.
  [*Pause.*]
Bernard: It's hot. Isn't it?
  [*Timothy puts out the light. Goes to the window, draws the curtains and opens the window. There is street lighting in the room now, and we hear the Bessie Smith record, very lonely and sad.*]
Timothy: The sharks have gone now—
Bernard: Yes.
  [*Pause.*]
Timothy: I was writing a poem. [*Pause*] A sort of poem. In my head. When I thought you were asleep.
  [*Bernard suddenly hurls himself out of bed and across the room. He grabs Timothy by the shoulders, shouting.*]
Bernard: What's wrong with us?
  [*He subsides, trembling. Steps back a little.*]
Timothy: Go back to bed—

Bernard: What happened one sunny afternoon?

Timothy: How do you mean?

Bernard: I heard the last line. You said: until one sunny afternoon—

Timothy: Get back into bed and I'll tell you.

   [*Bernard gets back into bed. There is a long pause. The Bessie Smith dies away.*]

   Until one sunny afternoon

   The light went dark

   And there was no moon.

   [*Pause.*]

Bernard: Dead?

   [*Pause.*]

Timothy: Yes.

Bernard: I think I have a great capacity for happiness.

Timothy: I know.

Bernard: And you—

Timothy: Yes. Me too.

Bernard: So—

Timothy: Go to sleep.

Bernard: All right. But I'd like some warm milk with rum and honey in it.

Timothy: All right.

Bernard: And Tim. Would you run my bit of film through? You know the bit—

Timothy: Yes. If you'll go to sleep.

Bernard: And we'll . . . go to that place soon—

   [*Timothy goes into the kitchen, sets a pan of milk on the stove to boil. Goes back into the other room. They have a projector and a screen set up permanently. Timothy feeds a reel of film into the projector. Turns out the lights. Bernard settles down. The film is of Timothy at the zoo singing to the giraffe. Film back-projected on screen in room.*]

Timothy:

   Who was it thought of you?

   What a funny thing to do;

   Your molecules break all the rules

   More than the kangaroo.

   [*The film cuts to a hippo afloat in its tank. Bernard leans over a railing staring at it, and sings.*]

Bernard:
   Oh plump and muddy hippo
   I'm very fond of you!
   You blow nice bubbles and
   You have no troubles,
   But I hate you in the zoo.
      [*Now the film cuts to Bernard and Timothy riding an elephant.
      Both singing.*]
Timothy and *Bernard* [*together*]:
   They think we're too eccentric—
   We'll surely get the sack;
   Because junior grade zoo keepers
   Aren't allowed on the elephant's back.
      [*Timothy brings the milk. Bernard is asleep. Timothy (now in
      dressing gown and pyjamas) takes off his dressing gown and gets
      into the other bed. Bernard opens his eyes. Cut from Bernard's
      eyes to Timothy's eyes. Bernard puts his hand out between the
      beds. Timothy takes it. Holding hands, they close their eyes.*]

SCENE XXI: INTERIOR LORD FOUNTAIN'S DREAM

*Lord Fountain, in full coronation dress, sits on a high stool surrounded
by darkness. A spotlight picks him out. He is blinking.*

Narrator: That night, Lord Fountain dreamt he was being inter-
   rogated by God. Fountain was dyspeptic and God was invisible.
      [*God speaks in Fountain's own voice.*]
God: You're managing to hang on a long time, Fountain—
Fountain: I'm sorry, God.
God: You've got a face like a mouldy washleather.
Fountain: It's worry. Anxiety. Where are you, by the way?
God: Everywhere.
Fountain: Are you—going to hurt me?
God: I thought we'd just have a chat. That's all. [*Pause*] Hurting
   you isn't my job.

Fountain: Damn it all man, you talk like a gas-meter inspector.

God: Somebody has to inspect the gas-meters—

Fountain: Well you might as well know. I've got it in for Timothy and Bernard. It's their birthday next Saturday. I'm going to invite them down to a party and wreak me vengeance.

God: I see. Vengeance. Now—that *is* my province.

Fountain: Stuff and nonsense. [*Pause*] What do *you* make of them?

God: They're very good at singing.

Fountain: They're very good at everything useless!

God: They're gentle and kind. They do their best.

Fountain: Let me put it another way. What do you think of them sub-specie aeternitatis? Eh? Couple of drivelling nits from that angle, aren't they?

God: Have you got a pain anywhere?

Fountain: Never had a pain in me life.

God: No lumps? Contusions? Lesions? Bruises?

Fountain: You see that woman there. Asleep beside me—that blonde.

God: I can just make her out.

Fountain: She's barren. You want to put your silly questions to *her*.

God: You're a very old man. You should have more dignity—

Fountain: Why did I learn Greek and Latin? I've forgotten it, but why did I learn it? A civilisation founded on antiquity, blessed by the Church, grazing harmlessly off its colonies—what was wrong with all that? Damn and wither it, we've only had the fag-end in my lifetime. Those boys won't adapt. If only they'd adapt. They're knocking forty. We've still got a grip you know. Still got a firm grip. What were those statistics?

God: Quote. The top one per cent of British adults owns forty-three per cent of total net capital. Twenty thousand own more than one hundred thousand pounds each. Sixteen million, on the other hand, have less than one hundred pounds each—

[*Pause.*]

Fountain: Swinging!

God: Unquote.

Fountain: You'll forgive me if I grin—

[*Pause.*]

God: Why not? It's your dream.

Fountain: I have those boys followed you know. I have detectives on them. I know who they see and where they go. I've been allowing them five thousand a year tax paid since they went to Oxford, and do you know how much they had when I checked their bank balance last week?

God: How much?

Fountain: Six pounds fourteen and ninepence.

God: Perhaps profligacy goes hand in hand with bastardy—?

Fountain: Profligacy my foot. They keep giving it away. They don't like it. They've had the insolence to donate it all to saving animals from the Kariba dam project!

    [*Pause.*]

God: I will say, I'm on your side, Fountain. I'm with you.

Fountain: But me dear feller—you always have been, haven't you?

God: That's the formula—

Fountain: Bully for God!

God: Shall we stop dreaming then?

Fountain: Might as well.

God: You old scoundrel!

Fountain: A nation without some kind of hierarchy, my dear God, is like a body without a skeleton.

God: Well said.

    [*Fountain gets off his stool—shuffles away into the darkness. As he does so, Music: 'Comfort Ye My People' from the Messiah.*]

TELECINE

Fountain on horseback, galloping.

Narrator: The next day, whilst Lord Fountain was riding to hounds and the present Lady Fountain was writing invitations to the party—

TELECINE: ENTIRE SWIMMING BATHS SCENE

Timothy and Bernard in swim trunks, stand at the deep end.

Narrator: Timothy was showing Bernard his surprise. [*Pause*] Bernard has passed the night without a single shark and woken up completely better.

Timothy: Do you like it?

Bernard: It's just what I wanted—

Timothy: I thought with our birthday coming up . . . and look—

TELECINE

Timothy walks down the bath side opening the cubicle doors. From each cubicle he takes an inflated rubber animal and throws it into the water. Pointing up Timothy says:

Timothy: I've had trapezes fitted, as well.
Bernard: We could live here—
Timothy: We're going to!
Bernard: A cubicle each—
Timothy: As many as you like—
Bernard: We could have a baths-warming party.
Timothy: Did you know we're being followed?
Bernard: It's only Fountain's private detectives.
Timothy: I thought they'd stopped—
Bernard: I think he must still love us, really.
Timothy: Father?
Bernard: Mother does. Even Towser isn't actively hostile like he used to be.
Timothy: But Father doesn't.
Bernard: The world's swarming with people who don't love us.
    [*Timothy looks round.*]
Timothy: We'll be all right here—
Bernard: How did you . . . manage to—?
    [*Pause.*]
Timothy: It's condemned.
Bernard: But—the water, and all that?
Timothy: I got us the full use of the place . . . Unless Father . . .?
    [*Pause.*]
Bernard: What's to become of us?
    [*Pause.*]
Timothy: Race you to the shallow end—
    [*Timothy and Bernard poise on the bathside, then dive in and swim furiously between the bobbing rubber animals.*]

SCENE XXII: EXTERIOR BATHS DOORS. NIGHT

Poppy tries the doors—they are open. She looks over her shoulder once, then goes in.

INTERIOR BATHS

Bernard creeps out of his cubicle. The baths are lit by scores of candles placed at random. Bernard climbs up the steps to the top diving board. He is in swim trunks. One of the trapezes can be reached from the diving board. Bernard stands a moment, then reaches for the trapeze. He climbs on it and begins to swing gently. Round Bernard— the flickering light and darkness, the echoes, the glint of the candles, the animals in the still water. Poppy comes into the baths without being seen by Bernard. She is frightened. Huddles in the upturned collar of her coat.

   CUT TO: *Timothy's cubicle. He is asleep. He jerks awake, listens to the music. Gets up, reaches for his swim trunks.*

   CUT TO: *Bernard on the trapeze, it is as if he is floating in a darkness which quivers with the light of the candles. When Bernard and Poppy speak, their voices echo as if in a cathedral.*

Bernard: Poppy? How did you—?

Poppy: What's the matter with the lights?

Bernard: Fused.

   [*Pause.*]

Poppy: Laura's coming. Why wouldn't you marry us? What's wrong with us?

Bernard: We live here now. Do you like it?

   [*Pause.*]

Poppy: He ought to have you two put away.

Bernard: Who?

Poppy: Your dad. He's a nice old man. He's nice.

Bernard: Come up on the balcony.

   [*Poppy hesitates, then goes up to the balcony. Bernard now catches the second trapeze and climbs on to it, letting the first one swing back to the diving board. Timothy comes out of his cubicle, goes up to the diving board, gets on the trapeze abandoned by Bernard*].

   CUT: *Doors. Laura comes in.*

   CUT: *Interior. Timothy and Bernard are now swinging backwards and forwards each in a long slow pendulum. Laura enters. Timothy and Bernard wave to her. She leans against one of the cubicle doors, laughing—a jeering almost hysterical laughter, which slowly dies away.*

Timothy: Would you like a swim?

Poppy: Laura—I'm up here.

    [*Laura joins Poppy on the balcony.*]

Timothy: It's stopped hurting, Laura—

Poppy: What's he talking about?

Laura: Don't you start getting at Tim. Look at that fat thing of yours, anyway.

Poppy: He may be fat, but he's got beautiful eyes. I've missed him. Have you? Tim I mean?

    [*Pause.*]

Laura: I'm scared—

Bernard: I'm very solid. I'm very well made. Fat men needn't be graceless. There's a grace of the spirit. Of the soul, if you don't hold that concept to be a laughing matter. I've seen fat trees and thin trees. Fat warthogs and thin warthogs. [*Pause*] A man's weight should be a matter of indifference to a woman.

Poppy: It isn't because you're fat, Bernard. Honest.

Bernard: What I want to know is—what isn't?

Poppy: What isn't what?

Bernard: What isn't because I'm fat?

Poppy: Oh he's droll!

Bernard: It's very nice on this trapeze. All we need is some fireworks· I'd like a few Roman candles popping off here and there. And rockets—

Laura: How do you think *we* feel?

Timothy: First of all, I'd like to demolish any suspicions in your mind that we have a phoney respect for the primitive. Isn't that so Bernard?

Bernard: I came across a tiger in the jungle one day. Walked up to it. Walked round it. Examined it. A lovely piece of design. [*Pause*] It was purring. [*Pause*] Then it yawned. It was a hot day. I expect it was sleepy. [*Pause*] I yawned, the way you do when other people yawn. Made my jaws ache. Well. We sized each other up. It struck me as ludicrous that the damn thing wouldn't talk to me. It looked as though it'd have plenty to say, if only it had the power of speech. [*Pause*] Gave me a funny feeling. Right in the pit of the stomach. I began to sweat. Why can't we all talk? Birds, tigers, wallabies, people? What's the matter? What's gone wrong? [*Pause*] That tiger was—I believe replete is the correct expression. Chocker block with meat and suchlike. It didn't care. Didn't want to know. I began to wonder why *I* care. Why should I wish to communicate with a lump of mobile fur, however beautiful? [*Pause*] It turned round and stalked away. Didn't give a damn. Didn't even want to eat me!

Timothy: It seems to me that the arrangements are inadequate. You begin with a ball of burning gas. Before you know where you are, you have a bewildered fat man gaping at an indifferent tiger. [*Pause*] If *that's* the best that cause and effect can do for creation!

Bernard: It was whilst all those English and Germans and Japanese were killing each other. I suppose you girls are too young to remember.

Timothy: It isn't that we haven't tried to get on with people—

Bernard: He's right. We've done our stint there. Before we went to the Far East, I had two rainbow fish in a little tank. Somebody poured a bottle of ink in. That's the sort of behaviour I've encountered all my life. Nothing happens to some people, and everything happens to some of the others. I don't expect to get through without inconvenience. All I can say is there's been a funny edge on things since nineteen thirty-nine. It was bad enough, before then, admitted—but it's got worse. It's got—well, menacing I'd say.

Timothy: I used to be hopeful, Laura. I should say by the summer of nineteen thirty-nine I was familiar with all the best visions.

   [*Timothy snaps his fingers.*]

Timothy: Bernard—

Bernard: Saint Augustine—

Timothy: Give me chastity and continence—but not yet.

Bernard: Aristotle—

Timothy: Plato is dear to me, but dearer still is truth.

Bernard: Cervantes—

Timothy: Fear has many eyes, and can see things underground.

Bernard: Cromwell—

Timothy: The State, in choosing men to serve it, takes no notice of their opinions.

Bernard: Feuerbach—

Timothy: A man is what he eats.

Bernard: Kant—

Timothy: The starry heavens above me and the moral law within me.

Bernard: Tolstoy—

Timothy: All, everything that I understand I understand only because I love.

Bernard: Upanishads—

Timothy: This earth is the honey of all beings; all beings the honey of this earth.

Poppy: Get stuffed!
[*Pause.*]

Bernard: Taxidermy?

Timothy: Wouldn't you like to come here and live with us? And Poppy? [*Pause*] We might get better—

Poppy: He's off his tod!

Laura: I want a nice house.

Poppy: Babies.

Laura: A garden.

Poppy: Security.

Laura: Silver.

Poppy: Furs.

Laura: They can afford it.

Timothy: That all sounds very sane and reasonable to me.

Poppy: Is it off or on? That's what I want to know.

Laura: Lord Fountain says you two's derelict.

Poppy: That was the word he used. Your own father. He ought to know you—

Laura: He's going to pull this place down and build a supermarket.

Poppy: People like you ought to know better.

Timothy: Know what better?

Laura: Everything.

Timothy: Why?

Poppy: You've had all the advantages. You ought to be helping to run the country.

Bernard: Where to?

Poppy: How should I know? Nobody asks me.

Laura: Come on, Poppy. It's a bleeding madhouse.

Timothy: The arrangements have been inadequate all the time. [*Taps his head*] Don't you go imagining it was Lord Fountain shaped this bony-pot. The contents were mere tissue when I was born, all pink and quiet and nice. Then what? If there's a God, I know what he is. He's a chuckling idiot with a tape recorder.

And what does he do? Plays his tapes through *my* head! Is that fair? Is that any way to treat a baby? I've never had a minute's peace. Things flashing through all the time, even when I'm asleep. [*Pause.*] *Especially* when I'm asleep. There's no such thing as madness. All it is is that bastard indulging himself in a random playback. I'm not trying to reject responsibility. What I'm grumbling at is the interference—the outrage. I don't know how I'm supposed to make sense of things when they're busy going *on* all the time.

> [*There is a moment of complete stillness—the two men swaying gently, Poppy wide-eyes and vacuous, Laura's expression jeering and angry. Laura makes a sudden dash for the stairs down from the balcony, followed by Poppy. Seeing her go, Timothy dives into the water, followed by Bernard. The men swim for the bath side. As they reach it, the girls come up to them. Timothy and Bernard cling to the side. The girls stand over them. Laura crouches, staring at Timothy.*]

Laura: I could curse you. I ought to curse you.

Timothy: It wouldn't help.

Bernard: Poppy—

Poppy: You got us under false pretences.

Laura: Where's your ambition?

Timothy: Our mother's background was ideologically impeccable. Daughter, grand-daughter and great grand-daughter of servants. But in my opinion she acquired a dubious admiration for the aristocracy. She dreamed of mansions, jewels and endless supplies of port wine. Fountain was her apotheosis, and I can only assume that some kind of death wish took her in the direction of Towser Griddle. Those whom ambition raises, perversity brings low.

> [*Having delivered this last speech in tones of saddened irony, Timothy begins to heave himself on to the bath side. Laura calmly and gently boots him back into the water, and walks out.*]

Poppy: See what you've done now. You've upset her. And what was all that about God? I thought you two was atheists—

Bernard: Agnostics.

Poppy: Well then. It's all blasphemy.

Bernard: I didn't know you were religious, Poppy—

Poppy: You've got to have something to hang on to. What else have I got besides nine pounds a week and a bedroom overlooking the railway at Clapham?

[*Timothy has climbed out again and sits crying dejectedly on the bathside. Poppy eyes him caustically.*]

Poppy: And what's *he* got to cry about?

Bernard: He really likes Laura. Underneath.

Poppy: I suppose you like *me* underneath?

Bernard: I suppose so.

Poppy: Well, what about a bit of on top for a change?

Bernard: Is it rough in Clapham?

Poppy: It's bloody awful. My dad wheezes down his nose when he eats his dinner. And my mother's false teeth click. That's Clapham for you—all wheezing and clicking.

Bernard: Why don't you go home and get your toothbrush and your bikini and come and live here?

Poppy: Then what?

Bernard: We'll play water-polo.

Poppy: For ever?

[*Pause.*]

Bernard: I've ordered a sea-lion. It can sing carols—

Poppy: And I suppose it can balance you on its nose!

Bernard: Don't be nasty, Poppy.

Poppy: What's your brother *mean* when he talks about 'the arrangements'?

Bernard: The cosmic amenities. The furniture of the space-time continuum.

Poppy: You're nothing but a pair of snobs, when it comes to the crunch.

[*Bernard clambers out, stands facing Poppy with a kind of sly hauteur.*]

Bernard: If that sea lion can honk its way through Ding Dong Merrily on High, then as far as I'm concerned, life has meaning.

Poppy: Can't you stop him crying?

[*Bernard hams it, with one hand on his chest.*]

Bernard: Our tears are all we have to offer.

Poppy: You can keep them.

Bernard: You're very grim, Poppy. Very bleak.

[*Timothy glumly shuffles his way between them, heading for his cubicle.*]

Poppy: Tim—

[*Timothy stops and turns to face them.*]
Timothy: Yes?
Poppy: You want a bit of advice?
Timothy: What?
Poppy: Why don't you shoot yourselves?
　　[*Poppy hisses into Bernard's face.*]
Poppy: Both of you.
　　[*Poppy stalks out.*]
Timothy: Why don't we?
　　[*Bernard dashes into his cubicle, comes out with a revolver. Spins the chamber, hands it to Timothy. Timothy puts it to his head and fires. A click. He hands it to Bernard who does the same, again spinning the chamber. Another click. The gun is handed backwards and forwards at ever-increasing speed, but does not fire.*]
Timothy: Did you put the bullet in?
Bernard: No.
Timothy: Why? We had the bullet in last time.
Bernard: It makes me too nervous.
Timothy: It doesn't make sense, without the bullet—
Bernard: If you're going to start wanting things to make sense—
Timothy: I don't want things to make nonsense. They already do that.
　　[*Timothy aims the gun at one of the rubber animals and fires. This time it shoots and the rubber animal explodes. Timothy turns on Bernard with the look of a detective who has finally extorted the truth.*]
Bernard: You're going to get me killed one of these days, trying to make sense. [*Pause.*]
Timothy: Or me—[*Pause.*]
Bernard: Do we love Poppy and Laura, or don't we?
Timothy: We love them.
Bernard: And all the others?
Timothy: Yes.
Bernard: The animals, fish, etcetera?
Timothy: Yes.
Bernard: And all those trees, and blades of grass and so on?
Timothy: Yes.
Bernard: The total set-up, in fact.
Timothy: The total set-up. [*Pause.*]

Bernard: Then why the hell can't we get started in life?

[*Timothy suddenly yelps and bends double.*]

Bernard: Now what's the matter?

Timothy: You've brought my pain on.

Bernard: You know, you're getting to be quite whimsical. It embarrasses me.

Timothy [*straightening up*]: *I* am! What about you? What could be more whimsical than buying a sea lion just to teach it songs out of The Threepenny Opera?

Bernard: I suppose you'd actually *prefer* it to go on braying away at all that Christian mythology!

Timothy: I hold no brief for Jesus.

Bernard: One, two, three—

[*They sing in chorus.*]

Bernard and *Timothy* [*together*]:

A ball of burning gas
Cooled into a curious mass;
Earth and air and fire and water,
Man and woman, son and daughter.
Now it's here
We're full of fear
Our lives must end in darkness;
Mohammed and Buddha and Jesus too
An Arab, an Indian and a Jew
Deceived us.
Reprieved us,
Too late—
Our fate as you will see
Is to hang on the knowledge tree.

[*With their arms across each other's shoulders, they begin a slow march down the bath side. At the diving boards they stop. Timothy turns to face Bernard.*]

Timothy: Shall we survive?

Bernard: I'd like another swing before I go to bed—

Timothy: Bernard—

Bernard: Just because I'm fat you expect me to be reassuring. Why is that? Is there any valid connection between weight and optimism? Do you expect me to chuckle at the facts?

Timothy: There must be some nice facts—

Bernard: Do you expect me to wag my wattles and heave with glee just because all that stuff outside is *there*?

Timothy: No.

Bernard: Well then!

Timothy: We could be—engineers, doctors, architects, civil servants. Feed the hungry. Heal the sick. House the homeless. Build things. Change things. [*Pause*] Modify the environment, so to speak. Serve our fellow men with passion and compassion. Have we gone off the tracks? Do we live in mutual and reciprocal futility?

Bernard: Those girls are beginning to corrupt you!

Timothy: My toes go numb sometimes. Do you ever get that? And my fingers. I wait for it to spread. Through the hands and feet, the arms and legs, until everything's gone numb. There I shall be, hanging inside my head, at an uncertain distance from eyes, ears, nose and mouth—and the work of my own body will be like the murmuring of voices in a distant room. I shall be reduced to my recollections. The bailiff's daughter lying like a crumpled swan in a green field in my mind. Towser Griddle's choleric inanities. Mother's doltish face . . . Ishaki's flute . . . Laura's body twitching with frustration. [*Pause*] And nothing done . . .

[*Pause. Bernard begins to go up the ladder on the diving boards.*]

Bernard: Come on—let's have a swing.

Timothy: We can't even deceive anybody into thinking we're all right.

Bernard: Up to the trapeze. That'll make you feel better—

[*Bernard gets on to his trapeze. Timothy begins to climb up.*]

Bernard: We could do with a few palm trees in this place. And a bit of sand. [*Pause*] Maybe the odd parrot—

[*Timothy has reached the top diving board. Now he transfers to the trapeze.*]

Timothy: Otherwise, you realise, we're heading for extinction.

Bernard: We could phase out the rubber animals and phase in real ones. Let's swing, then—

[*Narrator's voice over Timothy and Bernard swinging.*]

Narrator: So Timothy and Bernard swung nearly all night. [*Pause*] And made up poems. [*Pause*] And sang to each other.

[*Quick close-ups as they swing.*]

Bernard: Oh Darwin—

Timothy: —Was a funny 'un—
Bernard: And Marx had a—
Timothy: —Septic bunion—
Bernard: Whilst Freud—
Timothy: —Left us in a void—
Bernard: Thinking—
Timothy and *Bernard* [*together*]: Down with the lot!
  [*The music continues. Bernard waves, then Timothy. As they do so they fall off their trapezes into the water with a great splash. Fade out on detached face of bobbing rubber crocodile.*]

SCENE XXIII: INTERIOR DINNER PARTY/
CONSERVATORY

Long dinner table—Lord Fountain's birthday party for Timothy and Bernard. There should be no set—simply the table against black drapes. Fruit, plates, flowers, glasses, candelabra, etc. The guests are seated. It is the end of the dinner: Lord Fountain, the latest Lady Fountain, Poppy, Laura, Maggie, Nannie, Towser, the Zoo Director, Ishaki, Timothy and Bernard. In the gloom behind the table, unseen until referred to, are two boxes, 6 feet × 2 feet × 2 feet standing on end. As the narrator speaks, the camera briefly focuses on each person at the table.

Narrator: On the Saturday Tim and Bernard, dinner jackets by courtesy of Foundling Bros., Saint James's, hitch-hiked to Lord Fountain's country seat for their birthday party. Fountain himself was failing. A paraboloid curve described by him from a horse galloping through Coombe Bassett had resulted in a fractured collar bone. Nannie was noticeably gaga. The incumbent Lady Fountain bemused. Conversation at dinner had been . . . desultory. Only Fountain, inwardly communicating with his macabre plans for the twins, displayed any sense of occasion. [*Pause*] We have arrived at port and nuts. The ladies have been persuaded not to withdraw.
Fountain: What's the matter with that little yellow chap, then? I

have him flown over here at enormous trouble and expense, and he keeps his damned little oriental trap shut.

[*Fountain feels for his stick, reaches down the table and pokes Ishaki in the shoulder with it.*]

You. What's-your-name. Say something.

[*Ishaki looks round him wonderingly. Feels inside his jacket, brings out his bamboo flute and puts it to his lips. As the first thin notes wail out, Fountain brings his stick crashing down on the flute and slams it to the table. Ishaki sits mute, tears rolling down his cheeks.*]

Griddle: Now look here, Fountain—

Fountain: Call this a birthday party? What's the matter with you all? [*Leaning towards Ishaki*] No offence, dear feller. Can't stand music. If you want to play that thing go into the conservatory.

[*Ishaki does not understand but smiles.*]

Lady Fountain: Jeremy—

Fountain: Quiet!

Bernard: Father—

Fountain: Stand up boy. [*Bernard stands*] Well?

[*Bernard points at Lady Fountain.*]

Bernard: This lady—

Fountain: Janine, kiss your stepson. He's just paid you a compliment. [*Janine does so*] Name of Lasso. I decided to go back to the grass roots in me old age. Like your mother, this one. Common but sturdy.

[*Lady Fountain speaks like a weighing machine.*]

Lady Fountain: I'm a fully qualified dental nurse and I won't be bullied, not even by a lord.

Fountain: She may look normal this evening, but she's usually covered from head to foot in leather. Spends half her time pestering the villagers about something called Camfam.

Lady Fountain [*reproachfully*]*:* Oxfam, Jeremy!

Fountain: I believe in the charities. Always have. The first Lady Fountain—Millicent that was, 1903/1915—used to make crab-apple jelly and send it to the hospitals during the war. A sensible woman but not exactly a breeder. Oxfam Camfam it doesn't matter, the women have always been indispensable in this country. [*Pause*] Carry on my boy. It's your day today. Let's not be hypocritical—

Bernard: I was only going to say you shouldn't speak to her so brutally. [*Sits.*]

Maggie: Hear hear . . .

Fountain: Was that Maggers? Good old Maggie Pooh. Two glasses of wine and she thinks she's the dormouse at that tea party.

Griddle: If it's a question of revolutions or charity, give me charity any day. Does she ride?

Fountain: A Japanese motorbike. [*Pokes Ishaki again with his stick*] What's the matter with these Japanese? Eh? [*Squinting shrewdly at Griddle*] He works in a golf ball factory. What do you make of that? They'll bury us, you know, these Asians!

> [*Janine pats Ishaki's hand. Overcome with gratitude, he produces his flute again and tries to play. Again Fountain knocks it down with his stick.*]

Timothy: If you do that again—

Nannie: They were lovely babies. And Miss Maggie was lovely. Everything was lovely. I strongly disapprove of the last forty years. Sir.

Fountain: Dear, wrinkled Nannie—

Maggie: She was a bitch. She wanted to run my little darlings like clockwork. Pot, bottle, bath—like clockwork. Didn't she, loves?

Fountain: And you—hated them.

> [*A curious stillness falls over the party. One of those moments when, apparently by accident, an intolerable truth is revealed to people who are aware of it but don't understand it.*]

Everybody knows they're warped. And it's your fault.

> [*Pause.*]

Timothy and *Bernard* [*together*]: Warped?

Fountain: The aristocracy of this country has always known how to enrich itself. You don't think I took her on for her intellect, do you? No by God. I wanted some of those Lumpengenes.

Maggie: You said you'd marry me—

Fountain: I might have. I might have.

Maggie: If what?

Fountain: Come come Maggie-Pooh. It's all in the past. And after all here they are, grown men. In the pink of fatness and thinness.

Griddle: Fountain, I question your right to the Pooh-suffix.

Fountain: I'm sorry Towser. You're quite right. Maggie and I are no longer really on Pooh-terms. I'm getting sentimental in me old age. [*Pause*] I think I *would* have married you Maggie—

Maggie: It was that nasty old Nannie you loved. *I* know. And she stank of gripe water and cheap talcum.

Nannie: Lord Fountain was lovely when he was a baby. Lovely, lovely, lovely. Sir.

Maggie: Then you *would* have that string of titled bints after me. I hope they taught you a lesson.

Nannie: He had lovely little biffy feet, and totty hands, and dimply-wimply cheeks, Sir.

Poppy: Nannie, you're pissed!

Zoo Director: Why is that Nip crying?

> [*Pause.*]

Timothy: He's sad.

Director: Why?

Timothy: Isn't it perfectly obvious? Because Father keeps knocking his flute out of his hands.

Griddle: Let the poor devil have his flute, Fountain.

Fountain: In the conservatory. [*Beckoning to Butler.*] Wheldon, show this—er—gentleman the way, will you?

> [*Wheldon taps Ishaki on the shoulder. Ishaki looks puzzled. Wheldon deftly whips the flute from Ishaki's inside pocket, mimes playing, and beckons Ishaki to go with him.*]

Fountain: I'd like to come to the evening's serious business, if you don't mind. [*Pause*] First, I'd like to refer to the matter of an absent friend. [*Pause*] I invited General Remnitz, whom some of you may remember, but alas, his duties as Public Prosecutor have detained him in West Germany.

Griddle: I thought Remnitz got his at Nuremberg—

> [*Pause.*]

Fountain [*with dangerous patience*]: Remnitz's case was re-investigated and the charges against him declared null and void. In fact he spent the entire war running a poultry farm near Hamburg.

Maggie: He's kept some rum company in his time, has Fountain!

Fountain: Indeed! And from one of my rummiest liaisons proceeded the issue whose birthdays we are gathered to celebrate this evening. [*Everyone claps. Timothy and Bernard look sheepish*] It is, dear friends, a moment of reconciliation. A ritual. [*Pause*] If fatherhood brings anxiety—old age brings humility. [*Pause. Nannie claps*] One has many things to cherish. In myself, at the spritely moment of their conception—I think I can claim the embodiment of that England now shattered, alas, by the puny reformers . . . the vulgar ethics of commercialism . . . the utter degradation of grace, chivalry and honour. [*Griddle thumps the table approvingly.*] In my chosen partner the vigour, loyalty, devotion to crown and country of the toiling classes—[*Maggie stands up, waves her clasped hands over her head like a victorious boxer. Towser leaps up, takes an enormous bull whip from under his chair and loudly cracks it in admonishment of Maggie. Cowed but serene, she creeps into her cage—which is standing behind her chair.*] Thank you, Towser.

Griddle: Regression.

Fountain: Quite.

[*Maggie in tones of mincing gentility.*]

Maggie: Ay was ravished when ay wasn't looking.

Nannie: Ravish is as ravish does. Sir.

[*Fountain stares pitilessly around, until all are subdued.*]

Fountain: The time was auspicious. [*Pause*] The consummation not devoid of satisfaction. [*Pause*] And yet, and yet . . . [*Fountain hams a little 'breakdown'. Dabs his eyes with a handkerchief.*] God in His infinite obscurity saw fit . . . if indeed 'fit' is the word . . . to curse the womb of Maggie-Pooh.

Griddle: Maggie *sans* Pooh.

Fountain: Of Maggie. [*A great weeping and wailing goes up around the table, and from Maggie in her cage, but not the twins—who sit with bowed heads.*] Boys—stand up. [*Timothy and Bernard stand up, heads bowed, hands slack at their sides.*] You will be given your chance to speak. But before that and before the presents— the indictments. Certain of us here this evening have prepared statements which poor Remnitz was to have read out. In the event, we shall read our own. [*Pause*] Nannie—

Nannie: Ah sir, they was always at it. Breathing, looking, chewing. They picked flowers and interfered with the bailiff's daughter. Always stroking animals and watching the maids undress. Sinful, wilful, weak and cowardly. Disobeyed the rules, stubborn as mules, wouldn't pray. Godless and lecherous from the start. *Physical*, sir. Too physical. Physical physical physical. Sir.

Fountain: The . . . er . . . Zoo Director—

Director: To my certain knowledge they fraternized with several species of fauna. Their conduct was prejudicial to good order and zoo discipline.

Fountain: Poppy—

Poppy: I loved him. The fat one. But I knew there was something wrong. You know when boys are serious. We tried intercourse but it was a flop and I began to worry. Me getting home late one night my mother asked some searching questions about Bernard. I was shocked by my own reluctant answers. I glimpsed a world of vice and shame.

[*Pause. Poppy appears to have forgotten her lines. Fountain is unctuously encouraging.*]

Fountain: Go on, Poppy. Vice and shame.

Poppy: What I mean. Don't get me wrong. [*Pause*] I've lost me place, sir—

Fountain [*grimly*]*:* The spiritual vices—

Poppy: The spiritual vices of idleness, apathy, conspicuous refusal to consume, to copulate; to inegrate, to . . . er . . . [*voice dying away*] to *venerate*.

Fountain [*clapping*]*:* Thank you Poppy—

Poppy [*crying*]*:* And then he went to live in them baths! And I've been caught on the rebound by a boxing promoter. I—

Fountain: Now, Poppy!

Poppy: All I wanted was a white wedding with cake and fizz, and a little box to live in and good clean regular habits—I don't want to make things difficult for the government, the Church, the army, the National Health Service, the Civil Service, the—

Fountain [*almost crooning*]*:* Good girl!

Poppy [*mounting hysteria*]*:* I don't want to stand in the way of more and better to bite the hand that strokes me. I don't want to be seen heard tasted or smelled. But you *got* to respect me!

[*Sobbing, Poppy sits down. There is a long silence. Towser yawns.*]

Griddle: I think she's got the hang, Fountain—

[*Timothy and Bernard turn, begin to walk away from the table.*]

Fountain: Stop! [*They stop, turn, Laura stands.*]

Laura—

[*Pause.*]

Laura: And mine was the thin one. [*Pause*] It takes all sorts, of course, can't think why it should. I'm not like her. I'm in the market but I'm not petit bourgeois I believe is the expression. [*Pause*]

Nobody takes me in. [*Pause*] These two are not persons. Not human persons, if you dig me. They're figments of *nobody's* imagination! I don't hold it against a man if he's a bastard! But we can all *learn*. They don't seem to have picked anything up, if you see what I mean. Nonentities. I like strength in a boy. Character. My dream boat'll set me up like a queen when he comes along. I love queens. I want to be a queen to my dreamboat. I've shaved off all my unsightly body hair and deodorised my nooks and crannies. I'm fragrant and exciting and . . . and . . . and [*She burst out in a shrill scream*] desirable. [*Pause. She begins to cry*] I'm [*shouting*] adorable. Delectable.

Fountain: Thank you, Laura. [*Laura sits down, crying. The twins are immobile. Nannie is asleep with her mouth wide open. Maggie has her hands over her ears.*]

All that remains is for me to sentence you to your birthday presents. Lady Fountain has the keys to those two large boxes behind you— [*Lady Fountain goes to the twins and hands each a key, kisses them on the cheek, returns to her seat. They stand holding the keys, looking at them*] One looks to one's children for hope. [*Pause*] A few great families like mine cradled the nation in their hands for centuries. [*Pause*] When the time came to relinquish, when free institutions grew sturdy . . . other hands reached out to relieve us of our burden. [*Pause*] That is good. What is good is right. What is right is . . . a fearful responsibility. [*Pause*] I hoped to survive in you. To preserve a . . . a continuity. My simple world has been obliterated. I am denied legitimate issue. There is a deadly virus in what they fatuously call the wind of change. [*Pause*] I see chaos, disintegration and madness all around. Who best fitted for a world of madness than pawky fools and amiable madmen? [*Pause*] Like yourselves. [*Pause*] And in choosing your gifts, I have tried to make the presents fit the crime!

[*He motions them towards the boxes. Slowly, Timothy and Bernard go to the boxes, put the keys into the locks. When they open, inside Bernard's is a thin lifesize doll Princess. Inside Timothy's a fat one. Like dazed children, they remove the dolls, holding them by the waists, and turn to face the others. Lord Fountain begins to cackle. Griddle joins in. One by one the others join in until there is a cacophony of jeering laughter. Timothy and Bernard stand unmoving until the sound dies away. Silence.*]

*Taking their dolls by one arm, they slowly walk out, the dolls
trailing on the floor. The camera tracks them. In the conservatory
Ishaki is waiting, huddled in an overcoat and looking miserable.
All three walk out together. As they reach the outer door, Wheldon
opens it for them with a smirk. Standing outside is a small
telegraph boy. He hands a telegram to Bernard, who absent-
mindedly opens it. It is in Japanese. He hands it to Ishaki.]*

Timothy: What is it?

Bernard: He's got the sack from his golf ball factory. Absent
without leave.

   [*Ishaki reads the telegram, starts grinning.*]

Narrator: When he read the telegram, this is what was going on
inside Ishaki's head.

TELECINE

*Standing by a flagpole, Ishaki is hauling a huge replica of his telegram
to the top. Japanese National Anthem played.*

SCENE XXIV: INTERIOR DINNER PARTY/
CONSERVATORY

*Timothy and Bernard each put an arm across Ishaki's shoulders.
With the dolls trailing on either side, the three walk out the door
closes behind them.*

Narrator: Meanwhile in the dining-room. [*Each of the characters is
immobile. Their positions are as when we last saw them, like a
stopped film. C.U. Maggie.*] Something stirs in Maggie's mind.
[*Maggie opens her handbag, takes out a large revolver. Leaves her
cage. Advances on Fountain.*]

Maggie: Can you hear the voice in my head, Jeremy?

   [*C.U. Fountain's face, terror-stricken. We hear a voice hugely
   amplified through a loudspeaker. Before each word there is a
   slow, heavy, drumbeat.*]

Voice: Kill . . . kill . . . kill. . . . kill . . .

Maggie: They're my babies. My babies.

[*She empties the revolver into Fountain, who crashes forward onto the table. Pause.*]

Lady Fountain: That was a mistake, darling—

Maggie [*vacantly*]*:* Mistake?

[*Pause.*]

Lady Fountain: The old fool made his will out in favour of the twins. Last week. [*Pause*] Course, it's the end of the title.

TELECINE

Exterior prison gates. Early morning. Tim, Bernard and Ishaki stand waiting, huddled in overcoats. The clock strikes eight.

Bernard: There goes mother—

[*Ishaki looks from one to the other, fishes in his pocket and brings out three black arm bands. They put them on and slowly walk away.*]

MIX TO: *Int. swimming baths. Daytime. Ishaki sits on the bathside dangling his feet in the water playing his flute. Timothy and Bernard are diving, swimming, splashing water at each other.*

Narrator: And inside Ishaki's head—

[*Film of man driving at a golf ball.*]

Narrator: And Bernard's—

[*Film of sea, porpoises, seals, etc.*]

Narrator: And Timothy's—

[*Film of wild animals in flight—giraffes, etc.*]

Narrator: Whilst on the balcony—

[*We see the doll princesses sitting by the balcony rail.*]

CUT TO *Timothy and Bernard on the trapezes.*

Bernard [*to the flute*]: Now mother's dead—

Timothy: And father's gone—

Together: It's up to us to carry on.

[*Suddenly there is a great throbbing roar which gets louder and louder.*]

Bernard: What's that?

[*Pause.*]

Timothy: Bulldozers—

[*Pause.*]

Bernard: The supermarket!

[*Ishaki stands listening, shivering, his silent flute rattles between his teeth. The noise stops.*]

Timothy: It was all in Father's will. [*Pause*] I didn't want to frighten you.

Bernard: I was in a supermarket once. In the food self-service. [*Pause*] It was nothing but rows and rows of tinned animals—

Timothy: Fish—

Bernard: Rabbits—

Timothy: Even bees!

Bernard: And ants—

Timothy: Time to scarper—

[*They dive into the water.*]

SCENE XXV: INTERIOR PICTURE GALLERY

Timothy and Bernard's faces spotlit in darkness.

Narrator: That night Timothy and Bernard went to Lord Fountain's house in the country to take a last look at their ancestors.

[*Timothy and Bernard each have a candle. They appear to be walking down a long gallery. On either side there are full-size portraits. They move along, holding up their candles to look at the pictures. On Timothy's side the ancestors are all extremely fat. On Bernard's side they are extremely thin. Music. Handel's Water Music.*]

And some days later—

TELECINE: INTERIOR BATHS

Deserted. The noise of the bulldozers is overpowering. The main door splinters and breaks under blows from outside. Policemen enter, with Towser Griddle. The water is quite still. On it, floating face downwards, are the two princess dolls.

Griddle: They can't have *disappeared*!

Policeman: They have, sir. No trace. [*Pause*] We're pursuing our enquiries—

Second policeman: Funny—them dolls.

Policeman: Somebody was saying them two gents'd inherited quite a bit—

[*The second policeman gets a pole and begins to recover the dolls from the water. Towser stands looking round.*]

Griddle: Country house, town house, factories in the Ruhr, two thousand acres, half a million in liquid assets. God knows what else—

Narrator: Meanwhile on the Amazon River—

TELECINE

A dug out canoe. Ishaki is paddling. Timothy and Bernard sit impassively facing up river. They are dressed in battered straw hats, greasy singlets, threadbare white denims. The jungle hums and roars and screeches on all sides.

LET'S MURDER VIVALDI

CHARACTERS

BEN
JULIE
MONICA
GERALD
A HOTEL WAITER

SCENE 1

A shabby flat in Camden Town—one very large room with a kitchen off. A few simple, second-hand pieces of furniture. A long, solid table with drawing board and instruments—a draughtsman's tools. A lot of books in stacks and rows. A woman's clothes and shoes are scattered in various places. In one corner, a small upright piano with music open on it. Near it, a music stand, a chair and a stool with a violin and bow on it. It is evening. The room is in shadow, lit only by an angle-poise lamp on the table with its shade close to the wall. BEN, *a man in his late twenties, sits hunched by the gas fire drinking whisky. His back is to the door. He gets up once, lifts the violin and bow from the stool, half begins to play. He puts it down and resumes his former position. The door opens and* JULIE *enters, a girl of twenty-five. She hesitates in the doorway looking at* BEN. *He doesn't turn round. She gropes for the light switch.*

BEN: Don't turn that bloody light on!
She closes the door and comes uncertainly into the living room.
JULIE: Ben—
BEN: Get out. Get back wherever you've been. [*turning*] With whoever you've been.
Pause.
JULIE: I haven't. You know I haven't.
BEN: Do I?
JULIE crosses to a smaller table where BEN *has recently had a meal. Stares at it.*
JULIE: I'm hungry.
With a sudden quick movement BEN *goes to the cupboard where* JULIE *keeps her clothes. He piles some of them into the middle of the floor. She watches, impassive.*
BEN: Come on. Get your stuff and get out.
He takes a suitcase off the cupboard top and throws it among the clothes.
JULIE: I didn't finish work till seven.

143

He goes to a record rack, starts pulling out the records and throwing them onto the floor.

BEN: Which are yours? I don't know. Take the lot. [*he seems to suddenly weary of his own mood and speaks gently*] I'm tone deaf. I like a good brass band. [*pause*] Don't I?

JULIE *turns away, crosses to a chair, sits down.*

JULIE: A man was pushing against me in the tube. [*pause*] I stood on his foot. He just stared at me and went on writhing about. [*pause*] Why can't I ever say anything to them? Something loud and rude. [*pause*] I never can.

Pause.

BEN: Poor sod.

Pause.

JULIE: Him or me?

BEN *goes to his work table and picks up a pair of shear-like scissors.*

BEN: Him.

Pause.

JULIE: He had bad breath as well.

BEN: What you need for the tube love is a pair of scissors. A pair of big sharp scissors.

He snaps the scissors and throws them back on the table.

BEN: Chop their cobblers off. Serve them right. Those nasty men. Aren't they nasty men? Fancying you like that? [*pause*] It's notorious, is the Northern Line. [*pause*] Bakerloo's a runner-up. [*pause*] Where've you really been?

JULIE: They do it to ugly girls as well.

BEN: Where've you been?

JULIE: If you really want me to leave—

BEN: *raging*] *Naturally* I want you to leave! I'm tired of you. Bored with you. [*pause*] I never *see* you, do I?

JULIE: I'd bought a joint. I was going to make you a nice supper.

BEN: What—to *placate* me?

JULIE: I swore if you threw my clothes out once more—I'd go.

BEN: Well then.

JULIE: You're always so *angry. Is* it me? Do I make you like that?

BEN: I've been bad tempered ever since I was old enough to throw a rattle.

JULIE: Well look. I mean, just look. What you've done with my things.

Decisively, she gets up, takes a carrier which she had brought in with her and goes into the kitchen.

JULIE: *I'm* not going to hang them up again.

She unpacks the carrier, putting various things away. Unwraps the joint, puts it on a plate. BEN *comes to the doorway.*

BEN: If you'd only admit you don't want to go on. Just *admit* it.

JULIE: Are people bad tempered for no reason? All their lives? [*she goes up to him quizzically*] Were you breast fed?

BEN: How the hell do I know?

JULIE: Ask your mother. Ask her.

She tumbles some potatoes into the bowl and starts peeling.

JULIE: And pick my things up.

BEN: You aren't bad tempered are you? Certainly not. I *will* admit. [*pause*] You're bloody *passive*. No wonder you went into the Civil Service—

JULIE: I don't see the connection—

BEN: Where does he live? What's he like? What *are* senior civil servants like? [*pause*] He's married. He's got children. He lives in Potter's Bar.

JULIE *turns to him stonily.*

JULIE: He lives in St. John's Wood—and I'm *not* having an affair with him.

BEN: Potter's Bar.

JULIE: St. John's *Wood*!

BEN: You've been there. Met his wife. Patted his kids. She's fair-haired. In a bun. Going a bit grey. A bit heavy. Fleshy. She's very quiet and she just sits there placidly after the pair of you've washed up. Whilst *he* plays that bloody Bartok record he got in Budapest when he was sniffing round their town planning department. [*pause*] I'm on to the lot of you.

JULIE: Ben—

BEN: What?

JULIE: *Stop* it. Please.

Pause.

BEN: I hate you.

He goes back into the sitting room. JULIE *goes on peeling potatoes.*

BEN: I'll bet she's called Alice. And she knows he knocks off girls at the office. But she's *sensible* about it. [*picks up a newspaper*] They have more enduring things in common than sex. What about gardening? I'll bet they spend Sundays burrowing about like a couple of bloody moles. [*pause*] They'll be experts. Know all the different flowers . . . contact with nature in the midst of urban squalor . . . to say nothing of well-organised dinner parties.

With a crunch, a potato rips the newspaper from his fingers. JULIE *stands in the kitchen doorway looking pleased with herself.* BEN *picks the potato from his lap and holds it up.*

BEN: You've slept with him.

JULIE: I haven't.

BEN: You've been out with him.

JULIE: Once or twice for a drink. That's all.

BEN: And in the office? In the evenings? When the rats have abandoned the sinking ship of state for the night?

JULIE: In the *office*?

BEN: On the floor. They get carpets at his rank don't they? [*pause*] On the floor. [*pause*] I'll bet he's had a few of you down on that floor. [*pause*] Murmuring bits of Rimbaud as the twilight falls over Horse Guards Parade—

JULIE: He hasn't even *touched* me.

Pause.

BEN: Shall we start a kid tonight?

Pause.

JULIE: I've told you. You're completely unrealistic about it.

BEN: *Why* am I?

JULIE: Because look at us. Listen to us.

BEN *dives for the pile of clothing, grabs two or three dresses and makes for the window. As he reaches it and heaves at the sash:*

BEN: This bloody lot's going out—

JULIE: If you do that—*I* shall go.

Very deliberately, BEN *lifts the sash and hurls out the dresses. Pulls the window down. Turns to her.*

BEN: Blow, then—

He picks up the suitcase and throws it at her. It crashes at her feet. She stands looking at it.

JULIE: I haven't slept with him. You know you trust me. Why

do you [*pointing at the mess on the floor*] need all this?

BEN: *Need* it? *Me*? *Need* it? You're the one that needs it. The only form of communication you can understand is emotional extravagance. It's *you* needs it love! I suppose you *were* breast fed? Well. If you're a living example of what breasts can *do* for somebody—

JULIE: If I slept with another man, you'd be relieved—wouldn't you? You're *desperate* for it. Why does my not wanting somebody else *frustrate* you so much?

BEN: You know what? You live in a fog of self-deception.

Pause.

JULIE: I wouldn't mind being married.

BEN: Not *that* again. Please. I mean—you're the one that thinks being married or not married is an irrelevance!

JULIE: Yes. That's what I think.

BEN: Yes. Well, It's bloody well what *I* think.

JULIE: I just thought maybe we ought to get married.

BEN: I suppose it's one way of expressing a sense of total failure.

JULIE *kneels and begins to bundle her remaining dresses into her case.*

JULIE: I see. That's it then. So I'll go. [*pause*] You'd better turn the oven off.

BEN: Go where?

JULIE: Anywhere.

BEN: *Where?*

JULIE: Off you go again! Irritation posing as concern. That's you.

BEN *sits down and watches her fumbling with the clothes.*

BEN: I might *not* turn the oven off. I might put me head in it.

JULIE: With the jets lit?

BEN: There's nothing makes me feel more vicious than watching you pack.

JULIE: It's quite simple. The only times I pack—I'm grovelling about on the floor with stuff you've chucked down. It makes you feel guilty. [*she kneels back a moment, looking at him*] I know every phase you go through on these occasions. Only one thing. This time I *am* going, and this time we can do without the knife bit.

She is folding a skirt with her head bent low. BEN *leaps for her, grabs a handful of her hair . . . wraps it round his hand . . . raises her head with it.*

BEN: Can we?
Pause.
JULIE: If you *believe* I'm going—you won't start on that.
He lets go of her hair, rushes into the kitchen—comes back with a thin sharp butcher's knife.
JULIE: I'm not frightened, Ben. This time you look—silly.
BEN: You're not going—
Pause.
JULIE: I'm really tired of it. That's all I can say.
BEN: I wish you were ugly—
JULIE: If I was . . . and you loved me . . . it'd still be the same. [*pause*] I know you love me. [*pause*] But you choke the life out of me. [*pause*] Living with you . . . I just seem to be a kind of endless provocation to you. I don't know how . . . or why. I just know that's what I am. [*pause*] I don't think anybody's ever made me feel so helpless.
BEN *fingers the knife blade. He is almost trembling.*
BEN: You think I wouldn't mark you?
She closes the case and stands up facing him.
JULIE: Go on, then—
BEN: I look silly, do I?
Pause.
JULIE: No.
BEN: You'll say anything to calm me down, won't you?
JULIE: I doubt if I *can* calm you—
BEN: Do you lie to me?
JULIE: Never over anything important.
BEN: It depends what you mean important, doesn't it?
Pause.
JULIE: I mean, I wouldn't ever lie about something where you needed the truth.
BEN: You sanctimonious twat!
Pause.
JULIE: I suppose so.
BEN: You're not going.
JULIE: I think—I am.
BEN: You don't give me a single thing I want.
Pause.

JULIE: No.

BEN: What do we live together *for*?

JULIE: If you want to buy a house. And put a woman in it. And get her pregnant. [*pause*] Get on with it.

    BEN *is rigid, holding the knife.* JULIE *backs away. She finds her coat, picks up the case. He is completely immobile. She goes to the door.*

BEN: Julie—

JULIE: I'm off, Ben.

BEN: Julie—

    Pause.

JULIE: You can't believe it, can you? It isn't me, is it? I never *do* go do I? [*pause*] *I* don't bloody well exist—do I?

    She reaches for the doorknob and opens the door. As she does so, BEN *hurtles across the room and pulls her back by one arm. She turns to him. He rakes the knife down one side of her face. The shock even prevents her screaming. She touches her face. Her hand comes away wet with blood. She rushes out leaving her case, the door open—*BEN *looking at the knife. He goes onto the landing—looks downstairs. We hear a door slam. He goes back in. The door closes quietly behind him.*

SCENE 2

A comfortable, smart flat in St. John's Wood. Off the large main room, a dining section at right angles. GERALD, *a thin rather tired looking man in his mid-forties, and his wife* MONICA, *are having coffee after dinner. She is pouring herself a brandy. She is about his age—dark, vivid, a bony attractive face and a forceful, intelligent presence. She pushes the brandy bottle across to him and lights a cigarette.*

MONICA: What's *he* like?

GERALD: I've never met him. He sounds rather hysterical.

MONICA: *She* makes him sound hysterical.

GERALD: I mean—that's the impression I have.

    Pause.

MONICA: Shall we not talk about it?

GERALD: It's a form of self-indulgence you don't *usually* spare yourself.

MONICA: What does he do?

GERALD: I believe he's a draughtsman.

MONICA: You "believe"!

GERALD: He's a draughtsman.

MONICA: Whenever you start saying "I believe" or "I imagine" or "there's some possibility" or "it could be likely"—it always means that you *know*. Definitely.

GERALD: He's twenty-eight. Born in Hull, like Julie. Wanted to be a violinist. Didn't. And I assure you she *is* evasive on that subject. [*pause*] Father a drayman for a brewery . . . now let me think. Is there anything else? [*pause*] Yes. [*pause*] She says he's violent.

MONICA: Which means *she's* a masochist.

GERALD: Does it?

MONICA: I imagine there's some possibility.

Pause.

GERALD: If you think I'm having an affair with Julie—

MONICA: What's his name?

GERALD: Ben.

MONICA: Ben.

GERALD: Yes. Do you like that as a name?

MONICA: I can't say I like Julie.

GERALD: But you like *her*—

MONICA: Oh yes. I like *her*. The ones you bring here are always nice. [*pause*] She's perhaps a shade . . . dissociated.

GERALD: Eh?

MONICA: Isn't that a good word?

GERALD: I do know it.

MONICA: Yes. I know it too. Incoherent girls always like you best. I mean—fragmented ones. A bit for you. A bit for me. A bit for them. [*pause*] A bit for Ben?

GERALD: I see. Dissociated.

MONICA: Women who are all of a piece know that you know they're the most troublesome. It makes them realistic. Besides, I think your *particular* kind of charm thrives on muddleheadedness.

GERALD: Why does it do that?

MONICA: I don't want you to think I underestimate Julie.

GERALD: I don't really mind. If I *were* having an affaire with her I might get tetchy on that score.

MONICA: I can see that you have to love them to make it work. You must have loved an extraordinary number of girls by now.

GERALD: To make what work?

MONICA: To justify the consequences to yourself of having an affaire. [*pause*] And the imagined consequences for me. [*pause*] But I think I've always been rather cheerful, haven't I?

GERALD: Indefatigably.

Pause.

MONICA: Makes you suspicious.

GERALD: Naturally.

MONICA: You can't bear me taking you in my stride.

Pause.

GERALD: I think it's a devious form of aggression.

Pause.

MONICA: But you can't bear me taking you in your stride either.

GERALD: I don't think I quite . . . follow that.

MONICA: I don't know whether I do. [*pause*] It sounded perspicacious when I said it. [*pause*] Witty, even.

GERALD: I *always* find wit enigmatic.

MONICA: Julie isn't witty. But she's—acute. Yes. Odd. Being both acute *and* muddleheaded.

GERALD: I think wit is a dangerous form of self-congratulation.

MONICA: Perhaps Ben is very simple. Simple people do develop hysteria in relation to a certain *type*.

GERALD: Is Julie that type?

MONICA: Is Ben hysterical?

GERALD: He throws things at her. Locks her out. Gets drunk and smashes the furniture. Always bursting into tears on those occasions.

MONICA: And you think his motivations for all that are obscure?

GERALD: Well—

MONICA: What if he's simply damned, bloody, annoyed with her most of the time? What I mean. What if she's simply damned, bloody, annoying most of the time?

Pause.

GERALD: She's a rather placid person.

MONICA: Could you imagine anything more damned bloody annoying than *that*?

GERALD: Aren't I placid? Do I annoy you?

MONICA: People do different things with their annoyance. It would bore me to cry, and smash furniture. And if I threw things at you, I'd miss. Which wouldn't be satisfactory. [*pause*] When I was sixteen, my gym mistress said: your physical co-ordination is not of the best, Monica. [*pause*] I couldn't hit balls, and things like that. Couldn't get them through hoops, and those funny dangling sort of baskets. As for vaulting horses . . .

GERALD: Bad at that too?

MONICA: I used to wonder quite a lot how *boys* dared—

GERALD: Yes. It's not so bad for girls if they land on the crutch. [*pause*] Yes. [*pause*] *I* was frightened of vaulting horses, I'll admit.

MONICA: I wasn't *frightened* of anything—

GERALD: More—inadequate.

MONICA: No-o—

GERALD: Incompetent—

MONICA: Definitely not.

GERALD: Can't think of any other words.

MONICA: I can. I was disdainful.

GERALD: That makes sense. In the context.

MONICA: Shall we get divorced?

GERALD: I think I've always been intimidated by your disdain.

MONICA: For you?

GERALD: It in general. I can cope with it specifically. But not in general. It's a question of your behaviour versus your character.

MONICA: If only we didn't discuss getting divorced so *often*! [*pause*] The children don't give a damn. Judged by the way they conduct *their* lives, divorce is practically an act of saintly penitence.

GERALD: Did Clarry ring today?

MONICA: Yes. The man aborted her, took his money, then got her a taxi. [*pause*] Take it easy for a few days, he said.

Pause.

GERALD: And Tom?

MONICA: He flounced out at seven, looking very Carnaby Street and sulky. [*pause*] For someone who *isn't* queer, he gives a very dodgy impression that boy.

Pause.

GERALD: He probably is.

Pause.

MONICA: Queer?

GERALD: Mmm.

MONICA: He's capable of going that way out of sheer spite.

Pause.

GERALD: Do you think we despise Clarry and Tom?

MONICA: Not at all. It's resentment. And *that's* because they've turned out badly and we feel guilty.

GERALD: Wouldn't say Clarry's turned out *badly*.

MONICA: Messily. A bit like your Julie.

GERALD: What it is—Julie makes me feel nostalgic.

MONICA: Jesus wept!

GERALD: She wouldn't go in for abortions, either.

MONICA: Now if you're going to start getting at Clarry—

GERALD: I've nothing *against* abortions. Bloody hell. I paid for it didn't I?

MONICA: Yes. And I thought you were curiously eager to do so. Something nasty *there*, Gerald.

GERALD: She wanted it didn't she? You accepted her point of view. *I* did. [*pause*] You're beginning to make me feel as if I aborted her myself!

Pause.

MONICA: I'm glad you see what I mean.

GERALD: If I paid Tom's gambling debts would that turn me into a roulette wheel?

MONICA: I've *always* thought your devotion to Clarry a bit nasty. Still. I can see how you've tried to cope.

GERALD: How?

MONICA: By bedding that succession of girls in your department.

GERALD: I do loathe that expression "bedding". If you're going to be crude—be cruder. What's more, I wish the idea of the unconscious mind had never been thought of. I'm not interested in any sort of casual relationship between my feelings for Clarry and my feelings for—other people. I don't deny the existence of things like that—it's simply that I don't feel illuminated by it. I also "bed" girls because I just like it. Enjoy it. Positively revel in it. [*pause*] But haven't yet with Julie.

MONICA: We really must get divorced.

Pause.

GERALD: One thing I will say for divorce, it's as cheap as an abortion.

MONICA: You're so immature, Gerald!

GERALD: Do you know what maturity is?

MONICA: What?

GERALD: It's behaviour determined by the plans other people have in mind for you.

MONICA: Ho ho.

GERALD: Ho ho.

Pause.

MONICA: There's always the possibility that you're seriously interested in her. I think I'm still attractive, but it'd be a pretty good swap all the same for somebody of your age.

Pause.

GERALD: Have *you* got your eye on anyone?

MONICA: My eye tends to . . . flit about. But unlike you, I have the disadvantage of being fastidious.

Pause.

GERALD: Monica—

MONICA: What?

GERALD: How *many* years have we been talking to each other like this?

MONICA: Years and years. Ever since you had your first chick, or dolly, or whatever they call them nowadays.

GERALD: I wonder what the masculine of chick and dolly is?

MONICA: I don't hate you or anything. I don't even dislike you. I don't even not love you. It's just that you've become . . . microscopic to me. D'you see what I mean darling? Lots and lots of tiny details. I've got you *terrifically* in focus—

Pause.

GERALD: Mmm.

Pause.

MONICA: Oddly enough, you still amaze me. Like things do, when you see them through a microscope. [*pause*] I suppose amazement is as good a basis for marriage as any—
Pause.

GERALD: I can't see you *at all*.

MONICA: On the other hand, when one adds your details *up*—the effect is rather depressing. Sort of anonymous.

GERALD: I don't mean anything obvious, like familiarity. But I just can't see you.

MONICA: What a pity. I'm still quite vivid, after my fashion. *I* think I'm *very visible*. It's you. You've acquired a blind spot. A bloody big one, too. [*pause*] Do you think it could be something superficial? Like say your being very preoccupied with Julie?

GERALD: 'Fraid not. No. Logically impossible.

MONICA: *Logically?*

GERALD: What I mean—the condition antedates Julie. Anyway she doesn't preoccupy me. She obsesses me. I think. [*pause*] Yes. [*pause*] That's why I haven't actually done anything with her if you see what I mean. I'm so *obsessed*—that I can't come to terms with the actual person. [*pause*] Poor old Julie.

MONICA: Do you think she'd agree to be—what do they call it?—the Named Woman?

GERALD: Might. If we'd had—what do they call it?—sexual intercourse.

MONICA: Well. That *is* something you can do. Isn't it. Up to a point.

GERALD: Don't be sly, Monica.

MONICA: Of course, I could name her couldn't I, with or without her agreement? That's what I like about divorces. You can ignore people's *wills* with them.

GERALD: I will not have you imply that I'm losing my sexual piquancy! [*pause*] It isn't that the implication makes me feel angry, or anxious, or threatened. No. It's simply a position I have adopted, that I won't have you imply it.

MONICA: Unconscious fears of castration.

GERALD: No one could define their attitude to the unconscious more clearly than I have. I'm dug in there, and you can't undermine me. [*pause*] I believe Jean-Paul Sartre is of the same opinion. [*pause*] I am a kind of *machine*. Complicated—I'll give you that. But still a *mechanism*. If we hadn't had to invent the unconscious, we wouldn't have needed it.

MONICA: Let me see. If we're going to get divorced, could you move out of the flat by Thursday? [GERALD *merely stares*] Could *she* ditch *Ben* by Thursday?

GERALD: She can't ditch him at all. He's too violent. [*pause*] He might kill me. [*pause*] I hear I'm down for a C.B.E., by the way.

MONICA: You don't love her at all. It's that she puzzles you. You're a sucker for women who puzzle you. [*pause*] The irony of it is —she isn't *puzzling*. [*pause*] But I don't think I can take more than a few more days of you. I'm glad she's brought things to a head. [*pause*] I'll tell you what. We'll make it a *week* on Thursday, and this weekend you can take her off somewhere and *try* her. If she doesn't work, I promise I won't throw you out lightly. All right?

GERALD: All right.

MONICA: Not that I want you to be calculating about her. I don't want you to let either of you down, Gerald. That sort of thing can be very binding when people aren't married.

GERALD: I realise that.

Pause.

MONICA: Does she know how peculiar you are?

GERALD: I believe I do intrigue her a little.

MONICA: But is it because of your *peculiarities*?

GERALD: Julie is profoundly attracted by things she doesn't understand. She identifies incomprehensibility with stature, one might say.

MONICA: *rising*] A week on Thursday then?

GERALD: Right.

Pause.

MONICA: Goodnight.

GERALD: Goodnight.

MONICA *exits.*

SCENE 3

*A hotel bedroom with an adjoining bathroom. The door opens—*GERALD *and* JULIE *are ushered in by a porter carrying two small cases. He puts them down and goes out.* JULIE *stands looking steadily at* GERALD *for a moment.*

JULIE: I'm sorry about my face.

GERALD: I'm sorry *for* your face.

JULIE: They say there won't be a scar.

GERALD: Hasn't Ben tried to get in touch with you somehow?

JULIE: At the office. [*crosses to bed and sits down*] He cries and says how sorry he is. Says he nearly killed himself that night. [*pause*] He didn't know where I went or anything. Says he wants me to go back. [*pause*] Where did you tell Monica you were going this weekend?

GERALD: With you.

JULIE: Honestly?

GERALD: Honestly.

JULIE: Thank God Ben doesn't know where *I* am. [*pause*] Ben can do something like that . . . with the knife . . . then what he needs most of all is to be punished for it. Well. There he is alone, and I'm not there to punish him. [*pause*] It'll be quite frustrating, don't you think? [*she smiles*]

GERALD: *Very* frustrating.

JULIE: *touches her wounded cheek*] He's more upset about this than I am. Does Monica think you and I've already been to bed together?

GERALD: She assumed it. I denied it. For once, I think, she didn't know what to believe. Monica's not so much interested in the truth, as in what she's decided to believe.

JULIE: What happens when she decides wrong and finds out?

GERALD: She feels that whoever was involved has been obscurely cheating her.

JULIE: That's what I'd feel.

GERALD *looks at her and laughs. She laughs.*

GERALD: Are you hungry?

JULIE: Yes. I'm sorry.

GERALD: Sorry why?

JULIE: That was an enormous dinner we had. [*pause*] I feel sort of sick and hungry at the same time.

GERALD: To do with being here with me?

JULIE: Yes.

GERALD: Is it a good idea to eat then?

JULIE: Yes. That's how I work.

GERALD: Coffee and sandwiches?

JULIE: Yes, please.

GERALD *takes his top coat off, picks up the phone and orders coffee and sandwiches.* JULIE *stands up and slowly unbuttons her coat. She doesn't remove it.*

GERALD: Aren't you going to take it off?

JULIE: I've stayed in hotels with Ben. We always called ourselves Mr. and Mrs. Whittaker. You can't do it abroad though because of the passports.

GERALD: Which bit do you mean you can't do?

JULIE: The Whittaker bit. Nobody ever tried to make us have separate rooms.

Pause.

GERALD: Why Whittaker?

JULIE: I don't know. Ben's idea. He said it sounds more like us than either of our own names. He thinks you should always lie about anything even remotely official. [*removes her coat*] He's a kind of anarchist.

GERALD: He would be, wouldn't he?

JULIE: I see what you mean.

GERALD: What are you?

JULIE: Something like confused communist but no illusions. I think that covers it.

GERALD: Party member?

JULIE: I'm not interested in the communist *party*. Anyway, joining things isn't my temperament. [*pause*] It's too unequivocal. [*pause*] I'm muddled, you see. I wish I was Vietnamese. I think I'd know where I stood then.

GERALD: I signed us in here under my own name.

JULIE: On principle?

GERALD: I don't think I've *got* any principles.

JULIE: People in the department think you have. You're regarded as having very *stern* ones. Incorruptible. They say it's your principles and your brilliant mind have got you to the top. [*pause*] At the same time, they think you're a self-interested *bastard*. What do you make of that?

Pause.

GERALD: I've got convictions.

JULIE: It'll take us an extremely long time to get to know each other. Properly.

GERALD: And I've got twenty more years to communicate than you have.

JULIE: But you've had some practice, haven't you?

GERALD: What do you mean?

JULIE: Well. You've had quite a few young women, haven't you? So you must be quite experienced at getting yourself across.

GERALD: Oh.

JULIE: Whereas, I've only had Ben and he's only three years older than me. I know two of the girls you've had, and—

GERALD: *cuts in*] I do wish you wouldn't keep saying "had" and "have". It makes me feel squalid.

JULIE: It's vernacular English.

GERALD: I'm talking about the *effect* on me.

JULIE: I don't mind using a swear-word expression if you'd prefer that. I tend to sound priggish occasionally, but I'm not.

A waiter enters with the coffee and sandwiches. Puts them on a table. Exits. GERALD *takes off his jacket.* JULIE *takes a sandwich, bites at it and pours the coffee.*

JULIE: I like hotel sandwiches.

GERALD: Do you think we're quite ourselves this evening?

JULIE: How d'you mean?

GERALD: I mean, do you think we're like what we've been like together before? [*pause*] What a bloody ramshackle sentence!

JULIE: We've never been in a private place before.

GERALD: So you do think we're a' bit different!

JULIE: Are you nervous?

GERALD: No.

JULIE: I'm not either. I've noticed before. I can get to feel quite business-like about emotional things.

GERALD: Is that what you feel now? Businesslike?

JULIE: My mouth's full of bread and ham. I'm not sure *what* I feel.

GERALD: Well swallow it down then.

JULIE: That's what I'm trying to do. That's what eating *is*, isn't it?
    Pause.

GERALD: I'm beginning to feel tetchy.

JULIE: Have a sandwich.

GERALD: No thanks.

JULIE: I've poured you some coffee.
    GERALD *takes his coffee and goes to the window.*

GERALD: I like the Suffolk coast.

JULIE: What you're thinking is that I could be pretty maddening—
    aren't you?
    Pause.

GERALD: The notion drifted across my mind. But it wasn't a
    discovery. I've realised it for some time. [*pause*] Weeks ago.

JULIE: So it hasn't put you off, then?

GERALD: Hardly, when I'm leaving Monica for you.

JULIE: You make it sound sacrificial.

GERALD: You didn't leave Ben for me.

JULIE: I would have. Ben and I lived in a chronic process of leaving
    each other. I suppose I needed something outside us to help me
    do it. Him as well. [*pause*] I *would* have left him for you Gerald.

GERALD: I think you're picking up nuances of resentment that I'm
    not experiencing.
    Pause.

JULIE: Oh.
    Pause.

GERALD: What's known as projection.

JULIE: I know.

GERALD: The unconscious works in mysterious ways, etcetera.
    [*pause*] It's wonders to perform.

JULIE: Yes.

GERALD: I think I shall get ready for bed.

JULIE: So will I.
    Pause.

GERALD: Does your face hurt?

JULIE: No, but I have to sleep on my back or the other side. And when I sleep on my back, I grind my teeth all night. [*pause*] Ben says it's my aggressions coming out. *I* think it's something to do with the angle of my jaws when I'm lying on my back. The bottom one's bound to hang, isn't it? So my unconscious grinds them together to stop them falling apart.

Pause.

GERALD: Very logical.

JULIE: If it wakes you up, what you have to do is punch me on the shoulder.

GERALD: Right.

He opens his case, throws pyjamas on the bed, and goes into the bathroom with his wash pack leaving the door partly open.

JULIE: I don't suppose you shave at night?

GERALD *puts his head round the bathroom door.*

GERALD: Why?

JULIE: I like to watch people shaving.

Pause.

GERALD: Ben?

JULIE: Yes. I used to sit and have a pee and watch him shave.

GERALD *comes into the room.*

GERALD: I've often wished Monica needed to shave. That's something *I'd* like to watch.

And he goes back into the bathroom. Turns on the taps loudly. JULIE *wanders round the room, examining everything very carefully. She goes to the window and looks out. Sits on the bed—slowly pushes off one shoe against the other, then scrapes off the remaining shoe along the floor. She plays with the shoes with her feet.* GERALD *enters.*

GERALD: Pyjamas—

JULIE: Where?

GERALD: You're sitting on them.

She tugs them from underneath her and hands them over.

JULIE: Nice pyjamas.

GERALD: *You* don't seem to be making much progress.

JULIE: I've got my shoes off.

GERALD: Yes. *Very* sexy.

JULIE: Do you know why I took to you in the first place?

GERALD: I've speculated in vain.

JULIE: It was that article you published about socialism and town planning. Then I read your books. Then I tried to fit all that with what I'd seen and heard of you. Not that I'd *seen* much. The remote boss, and all that.

GERALD: *Did* it fit?

JULIE: You were rotten to me at my promotion board.

GERALD: You do sort of *glare* in those situations Julie.

JULIE: I glare because I'm frightened. I mean *when* I'm frightened.

GERALD: I wish I had the knack of being demonstrative.

JULIE: Why?

GERALD: Because I sniff an incipient quarrel.

JULIE: *I'm* not feeling quarrelsome—

GERALD: Neither am I.

JULIE: Well then.

GERALD: But we *are* under a strain.

JULIE: Are we? We must have put in scores of talking-hours. It isn't as if we didn't know each other at all. Or as if it was an impulse. Or just having a bit of sex. [*pause*] Is it?

GERALD: Curious thing is—I don't feel very much like *myself*. I'm watching my behaviour for signs I can recognise, and I don't think I'm seeing any. Mind you I feel precarious about this at the best of times. [*pause*] I have a suspicion that Monica and I have somehow evacuated each other's personalities.

JULIE: Where to?

GERALD: *Eh?*

JULIE: Well—*evacuated* you said. Where has it gone? What you were before you did it. If you see what I mean.

Pause.

GERALD: I don't know.

Pause.

JULIE: I *always* feel like myself.

GERALD: That must be very reassuring.

JULIE: Don't be mean.

GERALD: You know—I think I *am* mean. I've *grown* mean. I'm practically a work of art in that respect.

JULIE: And Monica's the artist!

GERALD: Ho ho.

JULIE: Ho ho.

GERALD: I wouldn't dream of saying she's responsible.

JULIE: Would you dream of thinking it?

Pause.

GERALD: I told you there was a quarrel in the air!

He makes for the bathroom door.

JULIE: Gerald—[*he turns*] Maybe we should have . . . er . . . slept together right from the start.

GERALD: I do detest that expression "sleeping together". It's worse than the other. It's nauseating.

JULIE: *tentatively*] Made love?

GERALD: Even worse.

Pause.

JULIE: There's no expression sort of . . . neutral. Is there?

GERALD: I wish you'd get undressed!

JULIE: D'you mean because you want to look at me.

GERALD: No. It's just that it would constitute—in my eyes, that is —a kind of progress.

JULIE: There you are, you see! "In my eyes". There's your unconscious giving the show away.

GERALD: I haven't *got* a bloody unconscious!

And he stalks into the bathroom, closing the door. JULIE *stands up and takes her blouse off. She is wearing a slip underneath. Goes to the telephone and lifts the receiver.*

Pause.

JULIE: Would it be possible to send up a bottle of whisky. Yes. [*pause*] Yes. A *bottle.* [*pause*] Thank you very much.

GERALD's *head appears round the door.*

GERALD: Were you on the phone?

JULIE: I've ordered some glug.

GERALD: What kind of glug.

JULIE: Whisky.

GERALD: Anybody'd think you were a bloody virgin!

JULIE: There's no connection in *me* between whisky and sexual anxiety. Maybe you're projecting.

GERALD: It was you ordered the booze.

Pause.

JULIE: I take your point.

GERALD: *Good.*

He withdraws. JULIE *goes to the bed, sits down and begins to take off her stockings. A waiter enters with the whisky—*JULIE *pulls her skirt down. He eyes her impassively—and she him. In silence, he puts down the whisky and two glasses—takes away the coffee things. As the door closes behind him:*

JULIE: Good night.

She awkwardly gets off one stocking and sits staring at her bare leg. GERALD *enters in pyjamas. He goes to the other side of the bed and gets in.*

JULIE: I'm sorry you're uneasy.

GERALD: I didn't say so.

JULIE: You got undressed [*pointing*] in *there.*

GERALD: I'm *not* uneasy.

JULIE: *I* feel as if we've been married about ten years.

GERALD: Was it a successful marriage?

JULIE: *turns, smiling*] Very.

Pause.

GERALD: Such anxieties as I have centre round my paunch, really. It's not much—but enough to be a source of shame. Intellectually, I've destroyed the problem. But emotionally, it refuses to wither away.

JULIE: Why don't you wither the paunch away.

GERALD: Can't be bothered.

Pause.

JULIE: Anyway, I like them.

GERALD: Why are you staring at your leg?

JULIE: It suddenly seemed to me a most improbable object.

GERALD: They are. The arms as well. [*pause*] The lot.

JULIE: At least my legs aren't hairy. [*pause*] Monica's are. [*pause*] You could have got her to shave *them.*

GERALD: I did get her to shave them. Quite often. [*pause*] And watched. [*pause*] I believe she thought I was afflicted with some minor perversion about it.

JULIE *removes her other stocking.*

JULIE: Do you think I'll get on with your children?

GERALD: Fortunately, my children regard "getting on" as something entirely superfluous to human relationships.

JULIE: You do talk about them disparagingly.

GERALD: Yes. I know. It's a way of not acknowledging that I'm quite fond of them.

JULIE: Why *not* acknowledge it?

GERALD: They've conditioned me over the years to regard my affection for them as a particularly noxious form of sentimentality. [*pause*] One can't rebel against one's *children*.

JULIE *continues to sit, rather vacantly staring in front of her.*

GERALD: Would you mind passing me that book out of my case?

JULIE: Your *book*?

GERALD: It's clear you're one of those people who can only get to bed in stages. I'm not criticising you. On the other hand, if I read it might make you feel uncomfortable. And when that sensation gets really acute, you might finish undressing and get into bed.

JULIE *gets his book and gives it to him.*

JULIE: I don't like her novels.

GERALD: Neither do I. But if my criterion for what I read were my enjoyment, I'd be a moron.

JULIE *stands, and takes off her skirt.*

JULIE: Have you ever had a girl on the carpet in your office?

GERALD: Several times. Not "had". Cohabited with.

JULIE: "Cohabited's" worse than any of the others!

GERALD: I was being wry. Unfortunately, wryness is a brand of humour which depends utterly upon the other person's mental agility. Wryness has the disadvantage of not having punch lines.

JULIE: Are you feeling more like you yet?

Pause.

GERALD: I suddenly feel depressingly like me.

JULIE *takes her slip off. Underneath, she is wearing a two-piece bathing costume.* GERALD *sits up, staring in disbelief.* JULIE *turns.*

JULIE: What's the matter?

GERALD: Is that a bathing costume?

JULIE: Yes.

GERALD: Are we going swimming?

JULIE: I know it seems eccentric. But—

Pause.

GERALD: But?

Pause.

JULIE: Well it *is* one of my eccentricities. [*pause*] Every now and then, I put a swimming suit on instead of underwear.

Pause.

GERALD: *Why?*

JULIE: If I had a reason, it wouldn't be eccentric. Would it?

GERALD: I think there's a tenable case either way.

Pause.

JULIE: That was why I was so slow getting undressed. You see. Because I had *this* on underneath. [*pause*] And I didn't know what you'd make of it.

Pause.

GERALD: Why didn't *you* go in the bathroom.

JULIE: I decided that would be dishonest.

GERALD: Isn't it rather uncomfortable? I mean, with clothes?

JULIE: Yes.

Pause.

GERALD: How did . . . how did *Ben* used to react?

JULIE: Quaintly, is the word I'd use to describe his reaction. He said it was an inverted form of whorishness in me. Then he'd get really worked up about whorishness in women in general. Then he'd lose his temper. And *then* he'd throw something at me.

Pause.

GERALD: I see.

Pause.

JULIE: There's quite a lot of things about me that I don't understand, and irritate other people. I know what they all are. I'm as bewildered and irritated as any of you. [*pause*] But *I'm* quite adjusted to them. They're what help me to feel like me all the time, like I said. [*pause*] I'm very stubborn about them.

Pause.

GERALD: I think it's charming.

JULIE *begins putting on her slip.*

GERALD: What are you doing?

JULIE: Getting dressed.

GERALD: You mean, you're going to come to bed *dressed.*

JULIE: I'm not *that* eccentric.

GERALD: And when you've got dressed?

JULIE: I don't know yet. I had one of my mental flashes.

GERALD: Mental flashes—

JULIE: Insights. [pause] It's all to do with the unconscious.

GERALD: So I've heard.

She puts her blouse on, then her skirt. GERALD *watches fascinatedly.*

JULIE: I try never to act inconsistently with my insights. I trust them. [pause] Other people often find it very inconvenient of me.

GERALD: Well I expect it very often *is* inconvenient. [pause] Like now.

JULIE: It's no good my apologising, because I don't feel apologetic.

GERALD: Yes. I think I can follow that.

JULIE *completes her dressing. She touches her cheek.*

JULIE: My cut started to hurt.

GERALD: And it reminded you of dear old Ben, and the happy days together.

JULIE: That's cheap, Gerald.

GERALD: Extremely. It's because I'm very angry. And whenever I have a genuine emotion, I tend to disfigure it with cheapness. [pause] That's partly what I meant about being mean. [pause] I'm mean spirited. [pause] Is that what was in your mental flash? *Pause.*

JULIE: Yes.

GERALD: I thought so. All that's left of me is posthumous remains of what once might have been a genuine identity. [pause] A complementary process has taken place in my wife.

JULIE: Are you being self-pitying?

GERALD: Not at all. Monica and I are quite fascinating, and complex —in our withered fashion. [pause] You can't play *my* games. [pause] I wondered if you'd catch on.

ULIE: Are you hurt?

GERALD: Of course I'm hurt. I love you and I want to live with you. *Pause.*

JULIE: I love you, too.

GERALD: Then what do you suggest? For the time being?

JULIE: What do *you* suggest?

GERALD *swings his legs out of bed, onto the floor. Looks at his watch.*

GERALD: *I* rather fancy a midnight drive. [pause] Back to London.

SCENE 4

GERALD *and* MONICA'S *flat. They sit at breakfast. A bright, sunny morning.*

MONICA: You do look grey, Gerald.

GERALD: No sleep. Couldn't, in the armchair. And didn't want to wake you.

MONICA: A sort of muddy colour. And you need a shave. Little black prickles all over. [*pause*] There are flecks of mucous in the corners of your mouth.

GERALD: I'm sure there are.

MONICA: Drink your orange juice, then—

He does so. MONICA *is sipping black coffee.*

GERALD: You look very well.

Pause.

MONICA: I had a good night. I was half expecting you back, as a matter of fact.

GERALD: Did you have an insight about it?

MONICA: I think it might have been an insight. [*pause*] Something to do with being quite well aware that you've always been faithful to me. [*pause*] I've never *seriously* thought otherwise, you know.

GERALD: I know.

Pause.

MONICA: My anxieties haven't been about whether—but why not.

GERALD: I see.

MONICA: Clarry's last man but one had me [*pointing*] over there. On the couch. [*pause*] When we'd finished, he said: by the way, have you had the menopause?

GERALD: Cheek.

MONICA: I've been unfaithful on and off, for years. [*pause*] How things went round and round in my little head! Wondering if you sort of *knew*, you see. And wondering whether you were

doing the same and were wondering whether *I* knew. [*pause*]
But I knew you weren't.

Pause.

GERALD: How?

MONICA: I know you too well, Gerald.

GERALD: Ah!

MONICA: I'll admit *this* time you had me worried. By actually
going off, I mean.

GERALD: Still. You knew it would turn out all right.

MONICA: I *think* so.

Pause.

GERALD: Why didn't you have one of yours in last night?

MONICA: I thought about it. Then I realised that knowing you
were with Julie, I wanted to feel above it for a day or two.

GERALD: To feel chaste, as it were.

MONICA: As it were.

Pause.

GERALD: About *your* infidelities—

MONICA: Quaint word—

GERALD: You are lying.

MONICA: I'm not, darling. [*pause*] I used our infighting about
yours as a kind of cover. Didn't I encourage you, after all, to
bring that series of girls here from the Ministry? Those poor
little girls you said lived in bed-sitters and didn't eat well enough.
[*pause*] For roast leg of lamb, strawberries and Bartok. [*pause*]
Talking of Bartok—when you were in Hungary, I had a
Hungarian. Isn't that a coincidence?

GERALD: *Had?*

MONICA: Sorry. Copulated with.

Pause.

GERALD: I was quite sincere about those girls.

MONICA: Consciously!

Pause.

GERALD: *I* might have had a Hungarian when I was in Hungary—

MONICA: But you didn't.

GERALD: I nearly did.

MONICA: There you are. That's what I *mean* about you Gerald.

GERALD: What is?

MONICA: There aren't any rules in sex. You're a bad case of *rules*.

GERALD: I have no moral positions vis-a-vis sex *whatsoever*.

MONICA: Not in theory, I'll grant you. But in practice—

GERALD: Don't you want to know why Julie and I came back?

MONICA: Would it be interesting?

Pause.

GERALD: Her part of it is complicated, I think. Mine is very simple.

MONICA: A lack of lust—

Pause.

GERALD: *Eh?*

MONICA: You lack *lust*, Gerald.

GERALD: I think I can say that's something I have more than anybody's fair share of.

MONICA: Then where do you keep it all the time?

Pause.

GERALD: Inside.

MONICA: Why?

GERALD: I've no option. It doesn't seem to be able to get out. [*pause*] But it's *there*.

MONICA: Where?

Pause.

GERALD: It's very hard to convey to someone the *topography* of an emotion.

Pause.

MONICA: But it nearly popped out when you were in Hungary.

GERALD: Very nearly.

MONICA: What was she like?

Pause.

GERALD: Huge. [*pause*] Attractive though.

MONICA: You see. Those girls you brought here—I'm afraid you *didn't* lust after them.

GERALD: How do you know?

MONICA: I can tell.

GERALD: How can you know what goes on with me *inside*?

MONICA: Because I know you inside out.

GERALD: They did live in bed-sitters. They didn't eat properly. They were charming—each and every one of them. [*pause*] Sensitive. Educated. Good looking.

MONICA: They hated Bartok. Each and every one of them.

GERALD: *I* hate Bartok.

MONICA: No. I'm sorry. They were a wretched lot, Gerald. Neurotic . . . frigid—

GERALD: *Frigid?*

MONICA: You have an unconscious preference for frigid women. It works both ways. *They* don't threaten your fears of impotence, and *you* don't threaten their fears of defloration.
Pause.

GERALD: Were they virgins then?

MONICA: How should I know?

GERALD: Well I mean. They'd need to be, wouldn't they? In order to have fears about def—

MONICA: I assure you an experienced woman can have those fears. You will be so *literal* Gerald!

GERALD: Yes. All it is—it's just me picking at the *logic* of the thing.

MONICA: Anyway. Hah!
Pause.

GERALD: Try to be explicit. For God's sake, *try!*

MONICA: You soon came scuttling back from Suffolk last night!

GERALD: Look at your face!

MONICA: What?

GERALD: I've just seen it.

MONICA: *What?*

GERALD: It looks to me like a face that's been gloating for a very long time—then suddenly given up for sinister reasons it won't let on.

MONICA: I've never done any of my gloating on my *face!*
Pause.

GERALD: *Where*, then?

MONICA: Nor inside neither.
Pause.

GERALD: The curious thing is—I don't feel betrayed because of your betrayals. I feel betrayed because of not knowing.

MONICA: Nonsense. People always know. Somewhere.

GERALD: There you go again! *Where?*

MONICA: What about inside, love?

GERALD: How can I not know something I'm supposed to know

inside? It doesn't make sense.
Pause.

MONICA: If only, like the rest of the world, you'd take into account one's unconscious!

GERALD: Not the rest of the world. Half the world's communist. And *they* wouldn't have the unconscious if you threw it at them. No. And what's more—

MONICA: Gerald—

GERALD: What?

MONICA: You look quite demented.

GERALD: Lack of sleep.

MONICA: That girl must be a fool.

GERALD: She's certainly very odd.

MONICA: I loathe teasers!

GERALD: She didn't tease me. She just changed her mind, for reasons which I could follow without any trouble.
Pause.

MONICA: Well? Go on.

GERALD: There was something about me that disturbed her.

MONICA: That sounds plausible enough!

GERALD: It transcends plausibility. It's a fact.

MONICA: I hope you escaped without humiliation? Don't you want any of your ginger marmalade?

GERALD: I'm not having ginger marmalade this morning.

MONICA: Anyone who knows you *at all* can see there's something disturbing about you. You're a bewildered, desiccated wreck with pathetic sexual fantasies that paralyse you out of your wits.
Pause.

GERALD: I think—taking things by and large, as they say—I am of that opinion myself.

MONICA: I'm sure you are. No one's accusing you of any lack of self-awareness.

She gets up and begins to gather things together on the table ready to clear it. On the corner by GERALD's *elbow there is a breadboard with bread and a long, slender carving knife which they use as a breadknife.* GERALD's *glance rests on it for a moment.*

GERALD: The question is—
Pause.

MONICA: What's the question?
Pause.
GERALD: Am I entirely a self-made product in those respects you mentioned?
MONICA: What do you think?
Pause.
GERALD: I'm sadly of another opinion. Which is that I can't evade responsibility for what I am. There may be an objective case for such an evasion, but I'm hardly in a position to make it. Am I?
MONICA: *comes close to him*] For a minute, I thought you were going to say what you are is *my* fault!
GERALD: Nothing of the kind.
MONICA: Well. At least you're not a hypocrite. [*looks at his plate*] Have you finished?
GERALD: Yes.
She leans across him to take his plate. As she does so, GERALD *takes the breadknife and neatly thrusts it into her. She collapses across him. He picks her up and takes her to the couch—puts her down. She is dead. He goes to the telephone and dials.*
GERALD: I want the police, if I may—

SCENE 5

Fade in JULIE *and* BEN'S *room. Evening.* JULIE *sits by the fire, huddled in her outdoor coat.* BEN *enters, carrying his violin case. He shuts the door behind him and leans against it. After a moment, when she does not turn to face him, he puts the case down and goes to her.*

BEN: Julie—
Pause.
JULIE: Yes. I'm back. You can start throwing things. [*turning*] Knife's in the kitchen drawer.
He puts his hand out and touches her face where the cut is. She sits frozen.

JULIE: Been for your violin lesson?

BEN: Yes.

   Pause.

JULIE: I've been on a dirty weekend.

   BEN *jerks his hand away. Steps back.*

BEN: With Gerald?

JULIE: Yes.

   Pause.

BEN: So you thought you'd just pop in and let me know!

JULIE: If you'll not lose your temper for a minute—

BEN: What do you *expect* me to do? Ask you if you enjoyed yourself?

   Pause.

JULIE: I didn't sleep with him—

BEN: What did you do? Play Bartok records?

JULIE: I was going to. I mean sleep with him.

BEN: It's quite usual to do that, when you go away with somebody.

JULIE: It was horrible.

BEN: *Intending* to was?

JULIE: Being with him.

   Pause.

BEN: Are you visiting, or what?

JULIE: I'd like to come back. [*pause*] You said on the phone you wanted me to come back.

BEN: And you said it was no use.

JULIE: *pointing at her cheek*] They had to put *stitches* in that!

BEN: Not many, by the look of it.

JULIE: We went to Suffolk. On the coast. To a hotel. [*pause*] He's a very intelligent man. [*pause*] Well. We had dinner on the way. It's a funny thing, when he'd had a few glasses of wine his breath smelt like metal. Sort of gusts of metal smell blowing across the table when he talked. And when he eats, his cheeks cave in. Don't you think that's peculiar? You'd think with food in them they'd sort of be full, at least. But they cave in.

BEN: Swallows without chewing!

JULIE: He has dandruff, as well. I saw these little flakes drifting down into his soup. *He* saw them. He gave me quite a defiant stare. [*pause*] I didn't refer to them.

BEN: Really flakes? Or just little bits?

JULIE: Flakes.

BEN: Then he'll have eczema of the ears as well. Inside, you know. It can result in a chronic discharge.

JULIE: I thought his ears looked his healthiest bit.

BEN: Do you expect me to calmly stand here talking about it?

JULIE: No.

BEN *takes his coat off.*

BEN: I've been managing very well on me own.

JULIE: I'll try to be more submissive.

BEN: Look. I never *wanted* to brutalise you! There's just something about you that asks for it.

JULIE: And there's something about you that wants me to ask for it! *She gets up and goes to look in the cupboard where she kept her clothes. It is empty.*

JULIE: Where's the rest of my clothes?

BEN: Burnt them.

JULIE: *closing cupboard*] I suppose that was to be expected.

BEN: Listen. When *I* start up with another woman, you can bloody burn mine. You won't get *me* complaining. If there's one thing I do understand, it's human aggressiveness. What's more—

JULIE: I don't think I'd mind if you had somebody else.

BEN: Oh? How would *you* react?

JULIE: I'd ignore it.

BEN: You don't seriously think I can believe that!

JULIE: I'd ignore it.

BEN: You'd *seethe*, mate! I know you. You're one of those people that's adjusted to a personality they haven't got. I suppose when you went off with Gerald you really believed you were going to sleep with him?

JULIE: *You* thought I was doing it *anyway*!

BEN: I'm talking about your lack of realism about your chronic behaviour patterns.

JULIE: I may be unrealistic about them but I do try to overcome them. Which is more than you do.

BEN: Fists came before thoughts.

JULIE: And how long did it take to evolve *knives*?

BEN: I don't *want* you back.

JULIE: Hah! After all that histrionics on the telephone!

BEN: Next time I might kill you.

JULIE: Well that's my risk isn't it?

BEN: It'd be me would do the life sentence.

Pause.

JULIE: I liked him. But he made me feel suicidal. [*pause*] He undressed in the bathroom.

BEN: So you did get as far as undressing!

JULIE: He did.

BEN: Not you, of course. You went down in full battle kit, I suppose?

JULIE: You've already implied that I *couldn't* have believed I was going to sleep with him. Looked at in purely rational terms, I can't make your position out at all. Was I or wasn't I going to?

BEN: If *you* look at anything about me in rational terms, it just makes me want to punch you.

Pause.

JULIE: I'm sorry for his wife.

BEN: Why?

JULIE: She must feel so *guilty*.

BEN: Why?

JULIE: When she sees what their marriage has turned him into.

BEN: *What* has it turned him into?

JULIE: It's deformed him.

BEN: Physically, I hope.

JULIE: Now listen—

BEN: And the usual thing? He turned to you because she doesn't understand him?

Pause.

JULIE: He turned to me . . . because he understands himself.

BEN: What did he look like undressed? Sickening?

JULIE: I only saw him with his pyjamas on.

BEN: With his pyjamas on then—

Pause.

JULIE: Like a sort of—striped hen. [*pause*] A *donnish* striped hen. And when I started getting undressed—

BEN: How far did you get?

JULIE: Blouse, skirt, slip, stockings.

BEN: So you were in your bloody underwear then!

Pause.

JULIE: I had my swimming costume on.

BEN: Was the man visibly shaken? Did he scream? Try to get away?

JULIE: I'm trying to be serious, Ben—

BEN: Despite the facetious tone, I'm bloody serious.

JULIE: The thing is, I got dressed again almost straight away. [*pause*] And we came back to London.

Pause.

BEN: So. You stood in front of him half naked then!

JULIE: If I'd been on a beach or somewhere—

BEN: You *weren't* on a beach, were you?

JULIE: Don't be so petty!

BEN: Is that petty?

JULIE: Well isn't it?

BEN: *Objectively* it's petty. *Subjectively* I've got some very nasty feelings coagulating round it.

JULIE: Ben we didn't *do* anything—

BEN: I'm obsessed with the intention—

JULIE: I could see afterwards I hadn't intended.

BEN: But you couldn't see it at the time?

JULIE: No.

BEN: Then as far as I'm concerned you were intending. Now get out—

JULIE: Please, Ben—

He rushes into the kitchen, grabs three cups and stands in the doorway with them.

BEN: Are you getting out?

JULIE: Do you want me to?

BEN: If you provoke me any more I shall feel ludicrous. And you know what happens then!

JULIE: If you hadn't cut me, I'd never have gone—

BEN: *Right!*

One after the other he hurls the three cups at her—they all miss, and break on the wall. They stand facing each other in silence for a long time, immobile.

BEN: *quietly*] I *am* ludicrous. [*pause*] Aren't I? [*pause*] Why is that? I can *see* I'm ludicrous. [*pause*] Why should genuine feelings come out ludicrous?

There is another long silence.

JULIE: *turning to the piano*] We never got started on that violin piano sonata—

Pause.

BEN: I promised myself—that if you came back, I'd control myself.

JULIE *sits down and tries a few bars of the Vivaldi violin piano sonata on the piano.*

Pause.

BEN: Gerald gone back to his wife?

JULIE: Yes. [*pause*] Come on. Shall we try it?

BEN: The Vivaldi?

JULIE: Yes.

Pause.

BEN: All right.

He gets out his violin, sets up his music stand and sits down ready to play. Tunes the violin.

BEN: Give me A then—

She gives him the note.

BEN: Right. Come on then. Let's murder Vivaldi.

They continue to play.

End

IN TWO MINDS

CHARACTERS

KATE WINTER
MRS. WINTER
MR. WINTER
MARY WINTER
TV INTERVIEWERS
JAKE MORRISON
ANNIE ROWAN
TV DIRECTOR
HAIRDRESSER
CONSULTANT
YOUNG DOCTOR
MENTAL HEALTH OFFICER
NURSES
YOUNG MAN

SCENE 1

Int. Suburban House. North London.
Camera tracks down the long hall to a sitting room at the end.
The door is open—the room in semi darkness.
A TV in one corner is turned on.
KATE *sits rigidly on a chair facing the screen. Her arms are folded, her head thrown back, face expressionless. She is in her twenties—a rather rough, plain face, but she could be very attractive.*
Int. T.V. screen
An interviewer is interviewing two men.

INTERVIEWER: But in the last resort sir, *would* our troops be used?
FIRST MAN: I think we've defined the circumstances in which that might be necessary.
INTERVIEWER: Then you do concede such a situation might arise?
SECOND MAN: If we were faced with such a situation, then naturally we should have to rethink our position and take whatever steps might be appropriate.
INTERVIEWER: Many people think the government has been ambiguous, to say the least, on this question.
FIRST MAN: I can think of no crisis in which any government has set out its intentions more clearly.

Int. sitting room
KATE *is crying.*

SCENE 2

Int. dining room.
KATE's *father,* GERALD WINTER, *is being interviewed, as it were, by camera. Camera's* "VOICE" *is that of investigating doctor.*

VOICE: Well. What do you feel about Kate then, Mr. Winter?
WINTER: Well I mean. She's sick. Isn't she?
VOICE: Sick.

181

WINTER: What else is it then? You tell me. I don't think we . . .
I don't think you can say we—
Pause.
VOICE: That you what?
Pause.
WINTER: That we haven't done everything we could for her.
Pause.
VOICE: Can you tell me why you think she's sick?
WINTER: I'm trying to say. You've only got to look at her. Haven't
you?
VOICE: Look at her?
WINTER: I mean, listen to her. Listen to her to what she says.
What she does. [*pause*] She's killing her mother.
VOICE: One of Kate's . . . delusions . . . you see . . . isn't it?
is that her mother is killing *her*.
WINTER: That's plain nonsense, isn't it? You can see. You're a
doctor. We've tried to tell everything what we know. [*pause*]
Her drinking, and that.

SCENE 3

Int. hairdresser.
KATE *is seated waiting for the* HAIRDRESSER *to come to her. She eyes
herself in the mirror. Lifts up her long hair and lets it fall into place
again. The* HAIRDRESSER *comes up behind her.*

HAIRDRESSER: Can I help you?
KATE: How d'you mean?
HAIRDRESSER: Any particular style?
KATE: I want it all off.
Pause.
HAIRDRESSER: *All?*
KATE: Yes.
HAIRDRESSER: Are you sure?
KATE: Yes.
HAIRDRESSER: It's a lovely head of hair.
KATE: All off.
Uncertainly the HAIRDRESSER *steps back, and turning, calls one of
his girl assistants.*

HAIRDRESSER: Vivienne—here next, please—
He goes to talk to Vivienne. KATE *gets up and walks out.*

SCENE 4

Int. sitting room.
MRS. WINTER *sits squarely facing camera. She is a confident, upright woman in her fifties.*

VOICE: So then. Kate drinks, Mrs. Winter?

MRS. WINTER: Well. Not what you could call drink.

VOICE: But your husband says she drinks.

MRS. WINTER: Gerry's very hard on drinking. He doesn't like it. And in a young girl either, it isn't . . . well it's not our way. Is it?

VOICE: What I'm trying to get at. How much does she drink? Does she get drunk?

MRS. WINTER: *Drunk?* Our Katie? What's Gerry been saying to you? What I mean—are we trying to get it all out in the open or aren't we?

VOICE: So Katie drinks, but she doesn't get drunk?

MRS. WINTER: I think I can say we've brought that girl up to know how to behave. But she goes in these pubs, you know. With all sorts. Talks to them. It's her illness.

VOICE: You think her illness makes her talk to people that she shouldn't talk to?

MRS. WINTER: She's brought shame to this house. To me and her father. And all we want to do is help her. To do what's best for her. She *defies* us.

VOICE: Does Mr. Winter go to the pub?

MRS. WINTER: What are you suggesting, young man?

VOICE: I was suggesting nothing, Mrs. Winter. I asked if—

MRS. WINTER: He's a man and he's entitled to his drink if he wants one. [*pause*] He has his drink, and that's that.

VOICE: But he doesn't get drunk?

MRS. WINTER: *Nobody* in this house gets drunk, doctor.

VOICE: Including Kate?

MRS. WINTER: *Nobody*. We're respectable people, and we know what's what. And that's how we've brought up our Katie. [*pause*] You don't want to go listening to *her*!
Pause.

VOICE: Do you listen to her, Mrs. Winter?

MRS. WINTER: Do *I* listen! Do I do anything else? She's my girl and I love her, and all I want is . . . all I want—
Pause.

VOICE: What do you want?

MRS. WINTER: I want her to get *well*, don't I?
Pause.

VOICE: Does Mr. Winter talk to people in pubs?

MRS. WINTER: He's got his friends, hasn't he? A man usually has his drinking acquaintances at the pub, hasn't he?

VOICE: But as far as Kate's concerned?

MRS. WINTER: I'm trying to tell you the truth as best I can.

SCENE 5

Int. sitting room.
KATE *is sitting facing camera, upright on her chair. She is bewildered, potentially co-operative, slightly afraid.*

VOICE: Kate?

KATE: Don't bother about her!

VOICE: About Kate?

KATE: What's the point? Asking about a corpse?

VOICE: Kate?

KATE: Kate is a corpse. Been killed. By *her*—

VOICE: By—?

KATE: I'm lying. I don't want to lie. But she wants me to be dead. You've only got to look at her.

VOICE: To see that she wants you to be dead?

Pause.

KATE: Yes.

Pause.

VOICE: She hates Kate?

Pause.

KATE: Yes.

VOICE: Why is that?

Pause.

KATE: Doctor?

VOICE: Yes?

KATE: Do you love me?

Pause.

VOICE: What do *you* think?

KATE: Do you fancy me?

VOICE: Why have you been crying?

KATE: You're the same as the rest! You won't just *answer*. Will you?

VOICE: Are you alive?

KATE: *I* am. *She* isn't.

VOICE: Because your mother—

KATE: She doesn't want me to live.

VOICE: Why is that?

Pause.

KATE: She'd go mad—if I lived.

VOICE: If you lived . . . how?

KATE: Like me.

VOICE: How is that?

KATE: You're a bleeding rotten bitch and you hate me.

VOICE: Why do I hate you?

KATE: She hates sex. She thinks I'm a whore.

VOICE: Have you any boy friends Kate?

KATE: I did have. Before I got ill. [*pause*] I don't do anything right. I get—lost. I stay in bed half the day. Sometimes I can't move. I mean I really can't move my body. Can't make my limbs work. She's good to me, then—

VOICE: Your mother?

KATE: Yes. She brings meals up to me in bed. [*pause*] I want to get better. For their sakes.

VOICE: You mean you want to be what they want you to be?

KATE: Well that's it, isn't it? Like I am, I hurt them. I worry them. She worries. She's losing weight. And then—I've had all those jobs. [*pause*] I had an abortion. [*pause*] I *am* bad.

VOICE: Did you have a special boy friend?

KATE: Jake Morrison. He's an actor. Mum and dad are very suspicious of people like that. Well *I* am. Half of them's queer, aren't they? But not Jake. Only I wouldn't bring him here. We went dancing. And in pubs. I like those pubs by the river at Hammersmith. Nothing like that round here. Do you like my hair? I like it long. My mother says I should have it cut. Says I look like a beatnik. [*pause*] Maybe I'll have it cut.
Pause.

VOICE: Was it Jake's child you aborted?
Pause.

KATE: No. She had it by another man. She's *wicked*. *I'm* not like that! I'm going to have my hair cut. I'm going to get up in the mornings. I might try another job—I won't use bad language. *She* uses bad language—

SCENE 6

Int. rehearsal room.

A DIRECTOR *and two actors—*JAKE MORRISON *and* ANNIE ROWAN *are working on a scene.*

The actors are sitting on chairs facing each other.

The DIRECTOR *stands watching them.*

JAKE *rises and goes to the* DIRECTOR, *grinning.*

JAKE: I warn you—I might put that nasty word in when we can it.

DIRECTOR: You do, and they'll have my nipples for press-studs!

JAKE: Bloody censorship. *That* word in *that* context is exactly what he'd say. Bloody dirty-minded censors.

DIRECTOR: All right Jake, let's just take the last page shall we?
JAKE *comes close to camera.*

JAKE: What do you think of *that*, doctor?
   Pause.
VOICE: I agree with you.
JAKE: *to* DIRECTOR] There you are, you see—
DIRECTOR: Oh come *on*, Jake!
JAKE: *to camera*] Ten minutes? And we'll go round to the pub.

SCENE 7

Int. pub.
Camera is, as it were, at a table. We see JAKE *at the bar. He comes*
over with two pints and a plate of sandwiches. Puts them down. Sits
down.

JAKE: What do you think of the play then?
   Pause.
VOICE: It's about Kate, isn't it?
JAKE: She was the author's bird for two or three months. He's a
   real bastard. And *I* introduced them!
   Pause.
VOICE: It was good of you to see me.
JAKE: Don't be daft. If it'll help Kate—
VOICE: Were you in love with her?
   Pause.
JAKE: I wouldn't say that.
   Pause.
VOICE: Fond then.
JAKE: Yes I was fond. I was fond all right. But what do you do
   when you wake up with a girl beside you and she suddenly
   starts saying her mother's shouting at her? I mean she meant it
   literally. Her mother was screaming at her . . . calling her
   names . . . filthy little tart, things like that. Wow! And she'd
   go into these trances. Sort of trances, you know what I mean?
VOICE: Not yet.
JAKE: Look. We'd be at a party or somewhere. And she'd be

sitting there. And she'd go stiff. Dead stiff. [*pause*] Then afterwards she'd cry. Couldn't explain it. She once said—Christ!
She said her mother could sit at home, and watch Kate wherever
she was, whatever she was doing . . . on the *telly*! Said her
mother could watch her and me in bed. [*pause*] I don't want
to give the wrong impression. I *cared*. But what could I do?
God, that family of hers! Wouldn't be surprised if her mother
had got a private telly network!

VOICE: Well. It makes sense as a joke then. Doesn't it?

Pause.

JAKE: I see what you mean.

VOICE: Do you?

JAKE: Look. *I'm* not a psychiatrist!

VOICE: She told me she felt "out of her depth" in your world.

JAKE: She came across as kooky as hell. And some bastards go for
that. I don't think I did her any harm, and when I realised she
was ill—

VOICE: You dropped her.

JAKE: Oh god! You're not a moralist as well, are you?

VOICE: No, I'm not. I mean it strictly as a factual question.

Pause.

JAKE: All right. I stopped seeing her.

VOICE: Did you tell her why?

JAKE: Not really.

VOICE: What did you tell her?

JAKE: You don't say: look, darling—I don't dig schizophrenics.

VOICE: Is that what she is then?

JAKE: How the hell should I know?

Pause.

VOICE: You used the word.

JAKE: You're beginning to piss me off!

VOICE: I'm sorry.

JAKE: Has your Ma got a telly screen watching *you*?

VOICE: If Kate *feels* she's being watched—then for her, she *is*
being watched.

Pause.

JAKE: I told her I'd got a small part in a film abroad. I told her she
needed help. She knew that. She was *getting* help—wasn't she?

I mean professional help.
VOICE: Yes. She was.
JAKE: Well then?

SCENE 8

Ext. Hampstead Heath.
KATE *is walking, her hands thrust into her pockets. Camera films her from the side. She keeps looking sideways into camera, then away.*

KATE: I know people don't lie to me. I *think* they do. Then I accuse them of lying. And I know it's all me, really. It's something in my head. I get so frightened. I was frightened of Jake leaving me. I *knew* he had this film. But I said he was lying. [*pause*] And when you're frightened, you frighten people away. Don't you? [*pause*] So I suppose when he got back he thought: no more of *her*. Well. I never saw him again. I can see what it is. That I don't *please* people. They know I'm different in a bad way. And there's nothing I can do about it. [*pause*] Is there?
VOICE: When did they begin to notice this about you Kate?
KATE: I was all right when I was little. Mum says I was perfect when I was little. I wish we'd gone to Regents Park. There's boats there—

SCENE 9

Int. sitting room.
Interviewing MRS. WINTER.

MRS. WINTER: She was as near perfection as a little girl could be!
VOICE: You noticed nothing?
MRS. WINTER: She was obedient. Clean. She always had a lovely

little smile for you. Never a tantrum. Never a sign of temper. A sweet child. We never had a minute's trouble from her. What's more, she's still our Katie. Still the same girl. All this going on now . . . well she can't help herself? Can she?

VOICE: Would it have upset you if she'd been troublesome as a little girl?

MRS. WINTER: Well you expect it, don't you? You *expect* children . . . I mean I think any mother . . . nobody thinks they've brought an angel into the world. Children get naughty, and then they learn. Don't they? It's growing up. That's what *I'd* say by growing up.

VOICE: But you had none of this with Kate—
Pause.

MRS. WINTER: Nothing what I'd say, out of the ordinary. Her grandma says the same about me. I often used to think there was a lot of me in Kate. Well I still do. What I mean, when she's being *herself.*
Pause.

VOICE: Then you'd say you did have some of the ordinary problems with her? As you would with any child—

MRS. WINTER: Only the little things, you know. The kind of thing that's soon over and forgotten. [*pause*] I think . . . looking back . . . I can say there wasn't *anything*, really. [*pause*] P'raps she wasn't all she might have been with her father.

SCENE 10

Int. consulting room.
Camera behind desk. The door opens. MR. WINTER *comes hesitantly in.*

VOICE: Good afternoon, Mister Winter. Come in—
WINTER: Afternoon—
VOICE: It's good of you to see me here—do sit down.
WINTER: *sitting*] Dolly doesn't like it. Doesn't like the idea of me seeing you on me own.

VOICE: Why do you think that is?

WINTER: She's a good woman, Dolly.

VOICE: Yes, but—

WINTER: She's doted on that girl. I've often said . . . I mean when Katie was younger . . . I said you ought to be a bit more selfish Dolly. Get out a bit. The girl's old enough. [pause] We've only got one life, haven't we?

VOICE: How have you always got on with Kate?

WINTER: Well. I've never been allowed, have I? Never been let in on it, you might say.

VOICE: I don't quite follow.

WINTER: I've always felt Dolly stood between me and Katie, somehow.

VOICE: You mean that Mrs. Winter prevented you?

WINTER: Prevented? Dolly wouldn't prevent nobody doing nothing! It's not in her nature. No. It's more like . . . well, she's Katie's *mother* after all. Isn't she? It's just sometimes . . . well when she was a kid, I'd take her on me knee. Give her a cuddle. Bounce her up and down a bit. I used to make her laugh, see? I don't think Mrs. Winter cared for that.

VOICE: Why not, do you think?

WINTER: I don't know. Seemed to irritate her. Frankly, doctor, I wasn't much cop for Dolly. A cut below her, as you might say. Didn't get on with her family. She had her own little business, Dolly. And I think they thought I was after it. Her mother, you see—she had her own idea who Dolly'd marry. [pause] Well I can understand it. If we can see Kate through this bit of trouble alright, she'll have her chance. With the right kind of feller I mean. [pause] Her mother'll see to that.

VOICE: Supposing Kate just married someone then told you and Mrs. Winter afterwards?

WINTER: I can't see there's any need for that. She can marry who she likes, can't she? That's her own business, so long as she's happy. [pause] But I think we have *some* rights. It's natural for parents to think that.

VOICE: When do you think Kate's trouble started?

WINTER: If you ask me, it was when she started running round with them actors and people.

VOICE: So she told you about Jake?

WINTER: Oh, she told us. She's always been a very open girl. That's what we've tried to encourage, you see. [*pause*] But you can't have that sort of thing going on. When they come in late . . . you don't know where they are . . . who they're with.

VOICE: Perhaps you didn't like Jake?

WINTER: Well. I'd never met him. I didn't like the *sound* of him. I didn't like what he was doing to our Kate.

Pause.

VOICE: What was he doing, Mister Winter?

Pause.

WINTER: Making her ill, wasn't he?

SCENE 11

Ext. the Winters' garden.
KATE *sits very still in a canvas chair with her hands folded in her lap.*

KATE: Do you really want me to go through all that again? I've told it so many times. To different people. Our doctor. And at the hospital. [*pause*] I get confused. Sometimes I ask myself: am I telling the truth? And the way people look at you. Once I thought I was made of glass. [*pause*] There's nothing interesting to say. I'm very ordinary. A bit stupid. Well, I never got to the grammar—and then you think you've had it. You lose interest. You don't know what's going on. What does it matter? You could see some of the teachers *tried*. [*pause*] I think we tired them out. [*pause*] I really let Mum and Dad down about the grammar. [*pause*] It isn't as if I didn't want a good education, neither. I did. [*pause*] Everybody wants to be something, don't they? [*pause*] To do something. [*pause*] What do you do if there's nothing exceptional about you? You know? Nothing to convince anybody with. [*pause*] You haven't been to see me for a week. Have you?

VOICE: No.

KATE: You've been talking to all the others—

VOICE: Some of them.

KATE: I'll bet they've told you some stuff! When it comes down to it, they're ashamed of me. I don't blame them. [*pause*] People round here, they're kind and all that. [*pause*]. But they're nervous when they meet me. They've got this special manner: Oh, if it isn't *Katie*! How are you then dear? Isn't it lovely weather? How's your Mum and Dad keeping? [*pause*]. And I think . . . all the time . . . they're expecting me to do them in, or go for them or something. They're nice to me—but they sort of can't see me. Can't see *me*, you know, for what's been happening to me. That's what they can't get out of their minds. Somebody's little kid . . . one of the neighbours . . . brought me a kitten. And her mother came with her. Well, she couldn't wait to get the kid away. [*pause*] Course, I was pretty bad just then. People couldn't get through to me at all, Mum says. She says I just stared at them, like they weren't there. [*pause*] That's a bit back, now. [*pause*] Before I went to hospital. [*pause*] Did you see Jake?

VOICE: Yes.

KATE: Is he working?

VOICE: He's in a television play. [*pause*] Written by Peter.
  Pause.

KATE: I expect he told you about Peter—

VOICE: Not very much.

KATE: I couldn't *believe* I was going round with a real writer! Me!

VOICE: Why not?

KATE: It's not my world, after all. Is it?

VOICE: What's your world?

KATE: You can ask me *that* one again!

VOICE: What would you like to do? Where would you like to be?
  Pause.

KATE: I don't know what I am. Or what I want.

VOICE: But if you tried to imagine it—?

KATE: My sister Mary got her own flat, and a job. She works as a secretary. [*pause*] She ran away from here when she was seventeen. [*pause*] *She* got away!

VOICE: Why didn't you go away?

KATE: I couldn't very well, could I?

VOICE: Why?

KATE: I just couldn't.

VOICE: Was there someone actually stopping you?

KATE: No. I mean they couldn't stop me by force, could they? [*pause*] But I *felt* I couldn't leave.

VOICE: Before you were ill—

KATE: Yes.

VOICE: What was it you felt, then? Can you tell me?

KATE: Mary going really cut them up, you know. And I was still there. My mother seemed to depend on me, somehow.

VOICE: She depended on you not to leave home?

KATE: I once got a job I thought I'd like, and a girl offered to have me with her to share her flat. Well. My mother nearly had a fit. She went on and on about Mary leaving. [*pause*] I just gave up.

VOICE: Now, it's nearly a year since you went into hospital isn't it?

KATE: Yes.

VOICE: When do you think . . . can you remember how it happened . . . ? When you began to get ill?

KATE: They've told you.

VOICE: I want you to.

KATE: I went for her with the breadknife, didn't I?

VOICE: It's what your parents say, certainly—

KATE: If they say it, it must be true. [*pause*] My mother locked me out the night before.

VOICE: You haven't got a key of your own, then?

KATE: Oh, she offered me one. But she said I didn't need it. What did I want to bother with a key for? She'd never lock the door before I came in, and she trusted me she said—to come home at a reasonable time. [*pause*] I think she was right. It's right to trust somebody. Well. I got back very late this night, it was about two o'clock. And the door was locked. She put her head out the bedroom window and said I could do what I liked— she wasn't going to let me in. [*pause*] I got in an awful temper and went off. Went to a girl friend's. [*pause*] It turned out she

came down a few minutes later to open the door and I'd gone.
So then, she and dad—well they were awake all night worrying.
[*pause*] I should have known she wouldn't lock me out. I mean,
I didn't think—I was so worked up. [*pause*] So—well, at breakfast, you see I came back at breakfast time—

SCENE 12

Int. the Winter's sitting room.

MR. *and* MRS. WINTER *sit facing each other in chairs by the fireplace.*

MRS. WINTER: It was the Friday, wasn't it?

WINTER: Yes. The Friday.

MRS. WINTER: No wait a minute. It was the Saturday. Saturday
because I told her, it doesn't matter if you're on the late side.
Not on a weekend, when it's Sunday then, and you don't
have to get up.

WINTER: That's right. It was the Saturday.

MRS. WINTER: I had no *intention* of locking her out, did I?

WINTER: We'd hardly lock our own daughter out.

   Pause.

VOICE: But you told her you would—

MRS. WINTER: I will admit, I wanted to shake her up. Give her a
bit of a fright. How did *we* know where she'd been?

   Pause.

VOICE: *neutrally*] But you didn't ask her.

MRS. WINTER: I didn't have time, did I? She'd gone, when I came
down. Off. In a temper. [*pause*] She's a grown girl and her
life's her own, but they've got to consider you haven't they?
Shouldn't they? Just think a minute, you know, and take others
into account. [*pause*] I tossed and turned all night.

WINTER: Your mother wouldn't have taken it from you, Dolly.

MRS. WINTER: Well. Thank goodness times have changed and we
live in a different world now. Children's more free, and they
expect it as well. What's more, they've a right to it. [*pause*]

But she's been in trouble once, as you know.

VOICE: Yes. The abortion—

MRS. WINTER: Don't! I can't even bear to hear the word!

VOICE: You're against abortion?

MRS. WINTER: I think it's wicked. They should give life sentences to people that do them.

Pause.

VOICE: *tentatively*] But you did help Kate—

Pause.

MRS. WINTER: I stood by my daughter, doctor. When the harm's done, it's done.

WINTER: She was peculiar round about that time, was Kate. She *wanted* it—

VOICE: The baby?

WINTER: That's right. The baby. [*pause*] *We'd* have looked alright, wouldn't we?

MRS. WINTER: She didn't want it. She *said* she wanted it. [*pause*] But I knew different.

VOICE: How did you know?

MRS. WINTER: I've carried two, and I know the moods a woman can have when she's pregnant. And pregnant with a husband, let alone somebody she won't even say who it is. Or anything about him.

WINTER: That's one I'd like to lay my hands on!

MRS. WINTER: She wouldn't even tell him.

VOICE: So he knows nothing about it?

WINTER: I'd just like to put my bloody hands on him, that's all.

MRS. WINTER: She talked herself into having the baby.

VOICE: Then, how did she come round to the abortion?

MRS. WINTER: I pointed out. I knew how it would end up. It'd have been *my* baby after she'd got over it, and wanted to work and start going out again, and all that. I'd be the one stuck with it, do you see? [*pause*] For one thing, she's not fit. Is she?

VOICE: But wasn't that before she—

MRS. WINTER: Oh yes, before she was ill. But she hadn't been herself, not for some time.

VOICE: So, well in the end you persuaded her not to have the child—

MRS. WINTER: Persuaded her nothing! I got her round to seeing what she knew very well in her own mind, at bottom.

Pause.

VOICE: Can we come back to—Sunday morning, the Sunday morning it would be then, after Kate was away for the night?

WINTER: Came slinking in here—

MRS. WINTER: Well. She was frightened of you, wasn't she? Frightened of what you'd say to her.

WINTER: Of *me*?

MRS. WINTER: He was proper worked up, I can tell you. [*pause*] When it's too late, oh he can open his mouth *then*!

WINTER: I never said a word to her!

Pause.

MRS. WINTER: It's more a matter of what she was *expecting*. Isn't it?

WINTER: I've *never* been one to crack down on her!

MRS. WINTER: She'd gone too far that time, you can say what you like.

WINTER: As long as the girl's under my roof, she—

MRS. WINTER: You've got your bigoted side—

WINTER: Now listen, Dolly—

MRS. WINTER: He's got his bigoted side. Some times he can't see anything right in her, going on and going on. Her hair, her clothes . . . one thing and another. [*pause*] It's no good not being frank with the doctor. [*pause*] Admit, you wanted a son. And—

WINTER: But I loved Katie from the minute she was born—

MRS. WINTER: A right tomboy she'd have been, if you'd had your way.

Pause.

VOICE: The Sunday morning, then—

Pause.

MRS. WINTER: She was mistaken in one thing. There was no row. No recriminations. We behaved as if she wasn't there. [*pause*] I put the breakfast on the table. She was looking from one to the other. She couldn't get over it, see, that we weren't *angry*! [*pause*] I gave her the bread and the knife, to cut some. She's cutting the slices, and crying over it. [*pause*] Well it was up to her to say the first word. And when she did, it gave me a chill

I can tell you.

VOICE: What was that?

MRS. WINTER: She said: "You got rid of my baby"—

WINTER: And she takes the breadknife and goes for Dolly—

MRS. WINTER: What happened actually, she threw it at me.

VOICE: She missed you completely, though—

MRS. WINTER: Well, it fell on the floor in front of me.

WINTER: Yes. But there's no mistake Katie threw it *at* her.

Pause.

VOICE: What did you do then?

Pause.

WINTER: Katie run upstairs. Dolly burst into tears. And in the end, well—I got our doctor over. [*pause*] That was the first time Katie had one of her fits.

VOICE: Fits?

WINTER: Well. Fits. I don't know what you call them. When the doctor got upstairs, she was sitting as stiff as a poker on her bed. Wouldn't move or speak. [*pause*] I told him she'd attacked her mother. We had a terrible day of it. A terrible day.

VOICE: You and Mrs. Winter did?

WINTER: Yes.

MRS. WINTER: Since you're taking it all down on that tape recorder thing, I just want to say this: I know my Katie wasn't in her right mind. She musn't be judged the wrong way. If she hadn't been getting ill, that with the breadknife couldn't have happened. [*pause*] I want you to know I've not blamed Katie—it's something in her poor mind made her do it. It wasn't *her*, doctor.

Pause.

VOICE: Something that made her act in a contradictory way to the girl you know?

MRS. WINTER: That's right. That's what I mean.

SCENE 13

Ext. street.

KATE *and* MRS. WINTER *are pushing their way through a busy street on the way to the doctor's. Their talk is broken and fragmented as they are separated, people come between them, sometimes they are trying to talk from different sides of the pavement.*

KATE: I don't want to go to the doctor—

MRS. WINTER: It was your idea—

KATE: *You* suggested it!

MRS. WINTER: *I* said: maybe you ought to see the doctor. And you agreed. If you hadn't agreed, then we wouldn't be—would we?

KATE: I mean, what does *he* know about it?

MRS. WINTER: He's a *doctor.*

KATE: What does he know about it?

MRS. WINTER: You said yourself you haven't been feeling well—

KATE: *I* said—

MRS. WINTER: *You* said: maybe I ought to see the doctor.

　KATE *stops and faces her mother truculently.*

KATE: You just admitted it was you!

MRS. WINTER: What I mean Katie—you were thinking the same—

KATE: How do you know what I was thinking?

MRS. WINTER: We'll go straight back home.

　MRS. WINTER *turns and walks away. After a moment,* KATE *follows her.*

KATE: Mum—

　MRS. WINTER *stops and turns.*

MRS. WINTER: I really don't know what to do with you. What to say—

　Pause.

　KATE *turns back towards the doctor's.*

KATE: Come on then Mum . . . come on—

　They set off together.

SCENE 14

Int. consulting room.
KATE *sits by the window, looking out.*

KATE: The following week, I went into the mental hospital. I was feeling better. I—well they talked it over with me, you see. I thought it the best thing to do.

VOICE: Who was "they" Kate?

KATE: Oh, our doctor you know. And the Mental Health Officer. And my parents. [*pause*] Another doctor from the hospital came to see me as well.

Pause.

VOICE: Why do you say "best" thing to do?

KATE: After I'd attacked my mother—well, I'm confused about that day. I remember sitting on the bed. My limbs were all cold and stiff. And I heard these voices. They shouted and screamed all these accusing things.

VOICE: Do you think you *did* attack her?

KATE: What else is it, throwing a knife at somebody? [*pause*] *I* think, it was like . . . like somebody else inside me chucked that knife.

VOICE: Who would that somebody be?

Pause.

KATE: I'll never know that, will I?

VOICE: Why not?

KATE: Well. What I want is to get better. And times when I'm better, I don't have that feeling of somebody else. It's a—what do you call it? Delusion. Yes I think so. Normal people don't have those feelings. And when I'm better, I can tell because I can see it in my mother. She gets happy. We go out and shop together. There's no conflicts between us at all. That's how I can recognise when I'm improving.

Pause.

VOICE: What do the voices say?

KATE: They shout I've been turned to stone. For my sins. And this stone me, it'll be put in a coffin and buried. But I shall still be able to look out at the world. And that'll be my punishment, for ever and ever.

Pause.

VOICE: What do you think about the idea of sin?

Pause.

KATE: It's hurting other people, isn't it?

VOICE: And when other people hurt you?

KATE: No. I'm lucky. Nobody's tried to hurt me, not really. It's the other way round. They're probably too lenient. What I mean, If I feel hurt—I can't overcome the idea it's my own fault. It's not the other person. [*pause*] People always seem to be living by rules I can't quite grasp. But I know they're right. Without laws and rules, where would we be?

VOICE: This other person inside you then, you're sure it's a bad you?

KATE: *thoughtfully*] I'd say I've *learned* that. It's something I've had to learn, and I can see other people do it and they're normal responsible people, and I'm *not*. [*pause*] There's another Kate who *won't* learn. Only, when I'm on drugs . . . tranquillisers . . . she's quiet.

VOICE: One evening when I came to your house, you'd seen something on television that upset you. You talked about your other Kate then—

KATE: Yes. They haven't got rid of her.

VOICE: You mean the hospital?

KATE: Yes.

VOICE: Is that what you want them to do?

KATE: I don't want to be *mad*! I want it to be like now, when I can talk. To you, anyway. [*pause*] And think . . . not be awful. [*pause*] But if I have to go back into hospital—I shall stay there.

VOICE: Why?

KATE: Well. For one thing, they know what you are there, don't they? [*pause*] That way, it's a relief being in hospital. [*pause*] If you manage to behave, you're not interfered with. [*pause*] Once you're in hospital, people . . . they sort of . . . they know where they are, don't they? Know where they stand with you. [*pause*] Things are—regulated.

VOICE: And that gives you some relief—

KATE: It's like being a kid again, I suppose. You fall over, you hurt yourself. Somebody picks you up and takes care of you. I don't know how to put it. They can get on with looking after you, and you can get on with feeling whatever it is . . . pain—

VOICE: And—where's the pain when you are on tranquillisers, Kate?

Pause.

KATE: A long way away. And I don't feel unreal. I don't feel much at all.

VOICE: Can you tell me about this feeling unreal?

Pause.

KATE: I seem to myself like a piece of machinery. All the bits whirring and ticking, but it's not me. It's a *thing*. And I'm outside this machine. Only the "I" that's outside, it's not a person either. [*she laughs*] Sometimes I think I'm operated by remote control. Like a robot. [*pause*] I get dizzy thinking about it, because my mind, it won't . . . it can't . . . you can't properly describe it. You can only feel it.

She turns away, resting her head on her arms on the back of the chair.

SCENE 15

Int. Winters' sitting room.
MR. *and* MRS. WINTER, KATE, *and* KATE'S *sister* MARY. *They are standing in a self-conscious group, like a posed photograph.*

MRS. WINTER: This is Katie's sister Mary—

MARY: How do you do.

VOICE: How do you do.

Pause.

MRS. WINTER: I suppose we'd better get on with it, then.

*She sits down. One by one the others sit down—*KATE *somewhat apart.*

Mary's got a good job in a big firm. She's doing very well.

MARY: *turns to mother*] I wrote and told you six months ago! I gave up the job and I'm trying to do modelling. [*turning to camera*] That's what I wanted to do, and I saved up to do it.

MRS. WINTER: That's right. Well. You're between jobs is what I meant. [*pause*] Like I said—

MARY: I don't see what this has to do with Kate.

MRS. WINTER: She's got plenty of character, has Mary. [*turning to* MARY] Too much, some might say.

MARY: I didn't come here to bicker with *you*, mother!

WINTER: Do you want to help your sister or don't you? That's what we're here for.

MRS. WINTER: You'll gather she's risen above us in the world, has Mary!

MARY: I wouldn't have to get very far up to do that—would I?

WINTER: *rising*] I won't have you talking of your mother like that—

MRS. WINTER: Gerald, sit down. The doctor's got a mind of his own.

MARY: I just don't see what the point is of having us all together.

VOICE: You agreed to come, though—

MARY: Yes. And I'm here. [*pause*] So?

WINTER: You can't exactly say *you've* set your sister a good example!

MARY: Dad—you resented my leaving home for just one reason. It meant there was one less person to draw my mother's fire. What's more, Katie should have got out as well and left the two of you to get to know each other!

KATE: *timidly*] You musn't talk like that Mary—

MARY: I don't think you're ill at all. You're weak. I'm sorry Katie. If I'm supposed to speak my mind—that's what I'll do, then.

WINTER: Would somebody not ill attack their mother with a knife?

Pause. MARY *turns slowly to her mother. The two women stare at each other.*

MARY: Did she attack you mother? Really?

MRS. WINTER: I've told you.

MARY: She wasn't just waving it about? You know, angry? And

threw it on the floor?

MRS. WINTER: Are you doubting my word?

MARY *gets up and lights a cigarette—paces up and down. She stops and stares into camera.*

MARY: It's like being with a bloody detective.

Pause.

VOICE: Very like that.

MARY: Well I'm no witness. I left here years ago. It seemed to me I'd been in trouble from the minute I was born, and as soon as I could thumb my nose at them I did.

MRS. WINTER: Mary!

MARY: Look, Katie—you can come and live with me, you know. I've kept writing to you about it.

MRS. WINTER: She doesn't want to!

MARY: How do you know?

MRS. WINTER: Ask her.

MARY: Well, Katie?

Pause.

KATE: You don't want somebody like me on your hands.

MRS. WINTER: Can't you get it into your head she's a sick girl?

MARY *comes into close-up.*

MARY: Something called—schizophrenia?

VOICE: That's the hospital's diagnosis.

MARY: What are you messing about in all this for then?

VOICE: Kate's case was referred to me by a friend at the hospital. And Kate herself came to see me.

MARY: Then what are you doing about it?

MRS. WINTER *rises and goes to* MARY.

MRS. WINTER: I knew it. I shouldn't have allowed you back in this house—

MARY *comes further into close-up.*

MARY: I love my sister and I want to know.

Pause.

VOICE: What did you mean when you spoke of Kate being weak, Mary?

MRS. WINTER: I can tell you! Katie respected her mother. Which is what *Mary'd* call weak.

MARY: She's weak because she won't leave this house. She broods, and starts fancying things. I've always fought her battles for her—

VOICE: Why did you do that?

MARY: She wouldn't fight them herself. She's dreamy, and indifferent. Let's people walk over her. [*crosses to* KATE] It's time you learned to spit in a few people's faces!

Pause.

KATE: *Why* should I? When I don't want to—

MARY: *to camera*] She sleeps around, she nearly had a kid, she gets sacked from all her jobs; then when the chickens come home to roost—what do we get? She pretends to be mentally unbalanced. Isn't that what half mental illness is? People won't face *up* to life.

MARY *suddenly realises that she is shouting. Her voice is ringing in the room.*

She stops, looks round her. Sits down. She starts sobbing.

No one moves, for a moment. Then KATE *goes and puts her arm round her sister.*

SCENE 16

Ext. the Winters' garden.
KATE *is being interviewed.*

VOICE: Your mother says you've been feeling unwell again, and you want to go back into hospital.

KATE: Yes. I told her.

VOICE: You don't think you can manage outside?

KATE: Oh, manage! What's that?

VOICE: Did Mary upset you?

KATE: I think there was a lot in what Mary said.

VOICE: How?

KATE: I've brought it all on myself. [*pause*] I'm getting what I deserve. [*pause*] All that with Jake. I just got myself picked up, didn't I? I was silly and romantic about him being an actor, about meeting those people he knew. Such different people. Still, no better or worse than anybody else. I'm immoral. Can people be sort of born immoral?

VOICE: What's immoral?

KATE: Well. Not living by standards, you know—

VOICE: Whose standards?

KATE: Well you're brought up with it aren't you? Everybody knows what's right and wrong. There's the church . . . and your parents . . . the whole world really . . . you can't set yourself against things. I mean, you shouldn't.

VOICE: Why not?

Pause.

KATE: All I know is that if I *do*—I suffer for it.

VOICE: What if the things you set yourself against *are* wrong?

KATE: Seems to me, if I'm wrong I'm just wrong, and there's no way out of it. If I think there's something wrong outside me, it gets explained away you know—special circumstances, or— oh I don't know. I get mixed up. [*pause*] There's a boy I know, well I knew at school, he's really brutal and violent. He bashed an old man at a garage with a bit of pipe, to get into the till. If he'd killed somebody abroad somewhere, in the army during a war—well, he'd be a bloody hero, wouldn't he? [*pause*] I know it's not the same thing. [*pause*] But if it's not the same thing, exactly what *is* the difference? People end up dead, either way. [*pause*] I don't understand.

Pause.

VOICE: But coming back to standards—isn't it that you want to arrive at your own?

KATE: I must be too weak, like Mary said. [*pause*] I was crazy about Peter, but—

VOICE: Your writer friend—

KATE: Yes. But I could see my mother was sensible about it. I couldn't go back to a man I'd had to have an abortion for. [*pause*] I gave that up—

VOICE: Only—I believe you never told them who Peter was, or told him about the child?

KATE: That's right.

VOICE: So you assumed he wouldn't want it—

KATE: In the end, I didn't know what I believed. [*pause*] It's unlikely he'd have wanted it, isn't it?

VOICE: What I'm getting at Kate, if you'd told Peter—you'd have known what he felt, one way or the other.

KATE: Yes. [*pause*] But my mother *is* shrewd. I think I'm a bit simple-minded.

VOICE: I'm not saying your mother's opinion of Peter was wrong. But it *was* an opinion, you see. And you knew him and she didn't. But you took your lead from her—
Pause.

KATE: I can't go on—
Pause.

VOICE: So you'll ask to go back into hospital—
Pause.

KATE: I'm hearing things again. And seeing things—

VOICE: What did you see?
Pause.

KATE: I went for a walk yesterday evening. When this thing happens . . . it has once or twice before, at dusk. The sky seems to light up and I want to scream. I think it's nuclear war, or something. And then everything goes very still. The air, it's like glass. And I feel if I screamed, everything'd shiver to bits and break. [*pause*] In a second or two, it's over. My legs are shaking. I want to cling to somebody. But it happens when I'm on my own. [*pause*] I can't go on.

VOICE: When you have this experience, do you feel these things are actually happening?

KATE: I sort of know they aren't. And yet they are. Well they happen to *me*—don't they? [*pause*] That's why I'm mad, I can't think who'd call it sane! [*pause, she laughs*] The explosion's in *me*!

VOICE: Yes. Well that's a perfectly sane and intelligible idea—

KATE: Is it?

VOICE: A way of expressing something real to you, I mean—
Pause.

KATE: The sky *doesn't* light up like I said. Things don't go still and quiet. The world won't break into bits if I scream. [*pause*] So to have these thoughts . . . these feelings , . . well then you *are* abnormal, and you can't expect to be taken any other way. [*pause*] Leave me alone, please.

VOICE: You think then . . . you think, Kate, that you're . . . how shall I put it? Not entitled to be yourself. Why is that?
Pause.

KATE: Because if I am—if I'm myself, well that leads straight back to the hospital, don't you see?
Pause.

VOICE: I see.
Pause.

KATE: So leave me alone, then. [*pause*] I *am* alone. No. I mean, I don't exist. *She* exists. I don't. I don't know if that's right either. I mean, she wants to be in me. To take me over. [*pause*] She'll kill me. [*pause*] Let her. [*pause*] Leave me alone—
Camera tracks back towards the house. At the door, a long pan round to KATE.
Pan back to the door.
The door opens.
Track through into the house.
We hear the door close behind.
As it does so, close-up KATE.

SCENE 17

Int. hospital. Long corridor.
Now the camera is KATE, *and we hear her speech and her interior thoughts as* KATE *and* VOICE.
MR. *and* MRS. WINTER *are slowly walking down the corridor.*
"KATE" *is tracking them.*
They stop.

MRS. WINTER *turns.*
MRS. WINTER: Come along, darling—
KATE: You want me in here, don't you?
WINTER: Katie, it's you wants to be in here. Isn't it? Didn't you

say so? Where you'll be safe, and looked after.
Pause.
KATE: Yes. I said so.
WINTER: And you'll be better in no time—
MRS. WINTER: *Don't* trail on behind us love—
But instead of waiting for her, they turn and continue walking down the long corridor.
Pause.
VOICE: Safe and looked after. Yes. I *want* it. To be in here—
[*cont. . . .*]
KATE stops and stares at the corridor wall.
We see KATE'S hands come up, and rest splayed out on the wall.
VOICE: *cont.*] I could pass through this. It isn't really solid. Swim through it like a goldfish in a tank.
MRS. WINTER'S VOICE: *pleading and exasperated*] Kate!
The hands disappear from the wall.
KATE continues after her parents.
They stop and wait for her. Now she is between them, a little to the rear.
MRS. WINTER: *We* didn't want you to come. I pride myself I know how to look after my own daughter. It was your idea, Kate. You're a free girl. We can turn round and go back home this minute.
KATE: You look peculiar, mother—
MRS. WINTER: *I* do?
KATE: Like somebody I've never seen before.
MRS. WINTER: *false humour*] Well, you've seen me before!
KATE: Dad—
WINTER: What?
KATE: Who is she?
WINTER and his wife stop.
MRS. WINTER looks away.
WINTER can hardly face the situation.
WINTER: It's your mother. Don't you know your mother?
Long pause.
Uncomfortable, they walk on.
VOICE: I don't know. Why should I know? What does he *mean*?
[*pause*] What's all this, then? Whoever she is, her bottom's

spreading. Ugly. I think it's really ugly. Fancies herself, too.
Look at that fat arse on her!

KATE: We didn't bring my bag—

WINTER *holds up* KATE's *travelling bag.*

MRS. WINTER: There it is. I put in everything you need. There's
all you'll need. [*pause*] You can have anything you want. Only
got to say.

Pause.

KATE: *I'll* carry it.

WINTER: No Katie—let me.

KATE: Put it down. I'll take it. [*he hesitates, looking at his wife.
She nods*] What are you nodding at him for? What's going on
between you? [*pause*] What are you *planning* now?

Pause.

MRS. WINTER: *quietly*] It's all in your imagination Katie. You're
tired. Let's get you in—

KATE: Leave my bag. I'll follow you.

They leave the bag.

Camera tracks towards it and stops.

Close-up the bag.

SCENE 18

Int. ward.

KATE *is in bed.*

A battered old doll lies on the cover. A NURSE *approaches with a glass
and two pills.*

NURSE: Now then, Kate—

KATE: Yes?

NURSE: Just these, and a glass of water. We want a good night's
sleep, don't we?

KATE: What are they?

NURSE: Just to make you sleep.

KATE: That doesn't say what they *are.*

NURSE: Well lovey, it would be one of those long chemical names
  —wouldn't it?

KATE: Do you know it?

NURSE: Of course I know it.

KATE: What is it then?

NURSE: Now that doesn't concern you, so long as we're doing
  our best.
  Pause.

KATE: Who does it concern?

NURSE: That your doll, then?

KATE: It was in my bag.

NURSE: Funny how you young grown-up girls—you will have
  your dolls, won't you?

KATE: It wasn't me. I didn't bring it.

NURSE: Something to cuddle while the sleepy-man comes—
  Pause.

KATE: Why do you talk in that silly way?

NURSE: Now we mustn't get rude, must we?
  Pause.

KATE: No.

NURSE: That's right. I shall be back to see if you've taken your
  pills. [*pause*] That's a good girl.

KATE: I'm not good.

NURSE: *leaving*] That's a good girl.
  We see KATE's *hand pick up the doll and toss it out onto the floor.*

SCENE 19

Int. shop.
KATE *and her mother are in a small shop—*KATE *trying to buy a dress.*
They are looking at one particular model, which KATE *is wearing.*

KATE: I like this—

MRS. WINTER: Oh, you don't like that.

KATE: Why not?

MRS. WINTER: Well, it's—it's on the short side, isn't it? And that material. Cheap stuff.

Pause.

KATE: This is exactly what I wanted.

MRS. WINTER: You've got some funny ideas on clothes, I will say.

Pause.

KATE: All right then. So *you* don't like it.

MRS. WINTER: I'm not saying that.

KATE: I don't know what you *are* saying.

MRS. WINTER: Look, Katie—it's your choice and your dress. If you want to wear *that*—

KATE: What's wrong with it?

MRS. WINTER: Not exactly *wrong*—

KATE: Oh, Mum!

MRS. WINTER: But I don't think . . . I mean to me, it's not quite you, I'd say. [*pause*] I don't think I like what they're wearing nowadays. Showing themselves off. [*pause*] It's all sex, that's what they rely on when they make them.

Pause.

KATE: I think I want it, though—

MRS. WINTER: Go on then. Buy it. Don't trust *my* taste. I know *I* haven't got taste. I think you ought just . . . you know, to get something you think is right. After all, you've got to wear it—

Pause.

KATE: Does it really look awful then?

MRS. WINTER: It's quite pretty, in a way. Yes.

The assistant approaches.

KATE: *to assistant*] No, I won't take it. Thank you. But I don't think it's right for me.

SCENE 20

Int. hospital room.

KATE *is being interviewed by a* YOUNG DOCTOR *and a* CONSULTANT.
A MENTAL HEALTH OFFICER *is also present.*

CONSULTANT: You've come back to us for a little while then
    Kate?

KATE: I hate you all.

M.H.O.: You want to get better Kate, don't you?

KATE: I've forgotten. I don't know. I've forgotten. [*pause*] She
    tried to get in, last night. Tried to get inside me and kill me.

YOUNG DOCTOR: Who did?

    Pause.

KATE: Kate. Dolly.

CONSULTANT: Dolly is your mother—yes?

KATE: No, it was Kate. She takes after Dolly. Dolly always said:
    Kate takes after her, I'm getting fat. Putting on weight, aren't I?
    My arse—

    The CONSULTANT *and the* YOUNG DOCTOR *have a whispered
    consultation.*

    The M.H.O. *smiles at* KATE.

VOICE: How did she get inside? In those pills? Those torpedoes.
    I've seen that in a film, they cut through the water. Then an
    explosion. Some old film. [*pause*] She got into my stomach.
    With a knife.

KATE: She got into my stomach with a knife.

    The others watch her impassively for a moment.

    The CONSULTANT *looks through some papers.*

M.H.O.: You'll be well looked after, Kate. [*pause*] You want to
    be able to go home, don't you? And to work. Back to your
    normal life—your parents.

KATE: I've been ungrateful, stubborn, independent in a bad way.
    I can see that—

M.H.O.: And your mother and' father, they've been distressed
    haven't they? Naturally, they've been concerned. Which is
    why we all agreed, well when you and they came to see me the
    other day—we agreed with you. [*pause*] I think you can see

we're on your side, Kate. Or we wouldn't have agreed that you should come back for a while, would we?
Pause.

KATE: What do you want out of me?

M.H.O.: Nothing out of you. Only to help you.
The CONSULTANT *and* YOUNG DOCTOR *are whispering again.*
KATE *rises and goes to them.*

KATE: What are you saying about me? What are you doing to me? Interfering—
The CONSULTANT *speaks but we don't hear him—instead,* KATE'S *interior monologue.*

VOICE: I did something. The shouting. When was it? I'd *done* something.

SCENE 21

Int. Winter's sitting room.
MR. *and* MRS. WINTER *are shouting at each other.*

MRS. WINTER: She's disgusting. I tell you. She's going out with men, and she's letting them have her!

WINTER: Oh, now—Dolly!

KATE: I'm not. I'm not. I'm bloody *not*!

MRS. WINTER: And don't you swear at me, my girl!

KATE: I *shall* let somebody have me—that's what I *do* swear. I promise you. What's wrong with going out with somebody.

MRS. WINTER: Nothing. There's nothing wrong with that.

KATE: Well then—

MRS. WINTER: It's what you *do*. Letting them interfere. You're turning into a loose girl. *I* know what you're doing. I know what you all do nowadays. And don't come to me when you've got something inside you!

KATE: And if I had—is it wrong? Is sex wrong then, or something?

MRS. WINTER: It's right and natural in its proper place.

KATE: And where's *that*, mother—?

MRS. WINTER: In marriage. That's what you want to be—married.
You find the right man, girl—then you get married.

KATE: I've told you, I'm a virgin. By why does it matter so much?
Why does it mean so much? Why does it mean *so much* to you?
My—my sex is my own isn't it? *Mine*. Not yours. It's you two
that's disgusting.

MRS. WINTER: *rising*] Wash your dirty mouth out!

KATE: I'll do something. I will. I'll go out and pick a man up on
the street!

WINTER *hurls himself at her.*

WINTER: You're a whore! A tart. You're a bloody little whore—

SCENE 22

Int. hospital room.

CONSULTANT: And so I think, Kate—well, rest and quiet. You need
plenty of that. And Doctor Garfield will see you in the ward
tomorrow.

KATE: I've had hundreds of men. I've had some very well known
people. [*pause*] She's a whore. You want to stop her, you want
to watch her. Don't let her. *I* can see through her. I think you
can see into me can't you? [*points at her belly*] In there? See
what she's doing? [*pause*] *You* can have me if you want. But it
doesn't really matter. You can't get at me when I don't exist—
can you? Not *me*. You can't really have *me*, you see—so it
doesn't matter what you do. You can even kill her. I'd like
that. I want that. When you do away with her, that leaves
me—will it? I mean, if you want me to exist—

YOUNG DOCTOR: Yes. We want you to exist, Kate—

KATE: I don't know what it is—

DOCTOR: It's being able to take your place in the world, isn't it?
To have relationships . . . marry . . . have children. You'd
like a house, and friends, and your own life. [*pause*] You want
these things, Kate. I think we know what you want—what's
best for you. And we're here to help you—

KATE: It all sounds—foreign.

DOCTOR: It does now. It's bound to. Until you find yourself,
  I think—
  Pause.
KATE: I'm mad then.
  Pause.
DOCTOR: You *are ill*—
  Pause.
KATE: When I was talking just now—it isn't that I don't know it.
  But it's hard to explain. It's like somebody else speaking out of
  my mouth. And I'm somewhere a long way away—sort of
  hypnotized. Listening. [*pause*] I know I'm ill.
DOCTOR: And you're going to get better.
  Pause.
KATE: But when I'm well—I almost feel worse.
DOCTOR: Perhaps you haven't been really well, yet?
  Pause.
KATE: I can't have been, can I?

SCENE 23

Ext. hospital grounds.
An ageing woman patient sits on a bench, restlessly picking at the
shoulders of her dress. KATE's *point of view from nearby, watching the*
woman, perhaps under a tree.

VOICE: Somewhere far away. Foreign. An empty place. Maybe
  one of those long beaches, and the sea. Where there's no people.
  [*pause*] She walks down the beach . . . she walks down the
  beach . . . and . . . [*pause*] What am I like? From the outside?
  What am I really like? [*pause*] Because inside, there's nothing.
  KATE *walks away. A little further on, she sees a* YOUNG MAN *painting*
  a tool shed. She stops quite near. After a moment he turns.
YOUNG MAN: Hello—
KATE: Hello.
  Pause.

YOUNG MAN: I'm just—doing a bit of painting.

KATE: Really?

He laughs. She laughs.

YOUNG MAN: I was going to have a cigarette—

KATE: Go on, then—

YOUNG MAN: Do you want one?

KATE: I don't smoke.

YOUNG MAN: I wish I didn't.

KATE: I think though—I'll try one. [*they smoke*] Are you—in here?

YOUNG MAN: Yes.

KATE: Nobody at home stopped me smoking—

YOUNG MAN: Well that's all right then.

KATE: Only it made my mother sneeze. And her eyes water.

YOUNG MAN: I expect you could in your own room.

KATE: Not in the *bedroom*. [*he laughs*] Anyway, I don't like it—

YOUNG MAN: Here, let me nip it out. Don't throw it away. [*she hands him the cigarette*] You in here as well, then—

KATE: Yes. I came in of my own accord—

YOUNG MAN: I was brought in. A bit since. [*pause*] I'm better now—

KATE: How does that feel?

YOUNG MAN: I've got rid of it all, you know. Managed to cut it out. [*pause*] You've got to have discipline, haven't you? Letting your thoughts run away with you, and that. I think they're good here—they bring you back to things.

KATE: What things?

YOUNG MAN: Well—to making a go of it.

KATE: How?

YOUNG MAN: You've got to play it their way, haven't you?

KATE: *Whose* way?

YOUNG MAN: Keep out of trouble with the bogies. Work. Save a bit of money. [*pause*] I mean, you've got to keep out of trouble, and I've always been in it. [*pause*] They picks me up on a job one night, the others got away—and I was standing there crying. *Me.* Crying me bleeding eyes out. What for? It was nothing. [*pause*] A few years like that . . . things like that. Well. I went straight. Then I starts going off me nut—ends up in here. [*pause*] I've had some of that electric shock, it's O.K., you don't feel nothing. Don't know nothing about it. [*pause*] A bit dazed, after—you know. The old memory goes off a bit. [*pause*] But here, they know what they're doing. *Nobody* outside knows. [*pause*] You got to get rid of all the nonsense, haven't you? Well that's it—I'm better and I'm off out soon. [*pause*] See what I mean, here, it's a bit like the army. I was in the army. You know where you are. It's all regulated, that's what people need—or they goes off the rails. You've got your meals, and that . . . at set times. You got your bed, your own bed. Some of the others in my ward, mind—the old ones! They're a bit far gone. But what can you do for them? It's too late, isn't it? You can't get through to them, they won't take the discipline they're past it. [*pause*] The staff and that, in here, they're kind, see? You soon catch on. [*pause*] Gawd! I thought, when I first come in. I was a bit confused you know. I thought: it's like being a kid again, like being back home with the old bastards. But that's missing the point, isn't it? You're not a kid and they know it here, I mean it, you can put it across like you're adult, which you *are*, aren't you? If you can do that, they're on your side. Start roughing it up, and naturally it's away with a few of the old privileges. I seen it in the army—you let men get bolshy, and bolshy they *are*. And where's it end? In the glass house! [*pause*] None of that rubbish here, what I mean they give you a chance and it's up to you.

KATE: I know it's up to me—

YOUNG MAN: There you are, then.

Pause.

KATE: Have you finished your painting?

YOUNG MAN: Nearly.

KATE: Shall we go for a bit of a walk?

YOUNG MAN: A walk?

Pause.

KATE: Yes. Anything wrong with that?

Pause.

YOUNG MAN: Some of them doesn't like it.

KATE: Who?

YOUNG MAN: Staff. All I'm saying, it makes some of them a bit nervous—see what I mean?

KATE: What on earth for?
Pause.
YOUNG MAN: It's dodgy, that's all.
KATE: Why?
YOUNG MAN: After all, we're their responsibility, look at it like
that.
KATE: Well? We're not doing anything.
YOUNG MAN: How do they know that? Some of the inmates here
—gawd! Enough to drive the bleeding staff out of their minds.
Pause.
KATE: What if we did do something?
Pause.
YOUNG MAN: Is that what you're after?
KATE: No. But I'm asking. Is it any of their business?
YOUNG MAN: Course it's their business! We're in here aren't we?
In their charge, aren't we? [*pause*] You got a lot to learn!
KATE: I just want to know . . . supposing you and me or anybody
else . . . supposing we were attracted . . . and we . . . it'd
be *us*, wouldn't it? Sort of just to do with us.
YOUNG MAN: Nothing of course to do with why we're in here.
KATE: Well—no. No I don't see that it is.
YOUNG MAN: You're an ill person, aren't you? Am I right? Or
you wouldn't be here.
Pause.
KATE: I suppose so.
YOUNG MAN: Well then. Look at it their way—are you fit to be
going on like when you're outside? It's not the same, is it?
Till they're discharged, nobody's really fit to know for them-
selves, are they?
Pause.
KATE: I don't "go on" when I'm outside.
YOUNG MAN: Go on! I can see. Looking at you I can see—
KATE: What?
Pause.
YOUNG MAN: You're fond of it, aren't you? You like it, darling—
Pause.
KATE: I'm not promiscuous. You've no right—
The YOUNG MAN *looks at her for a long moment.*

YOUNG MAN: Right. You're right. [*pause*] You be along here tomorrow the same time—we'll have a little walk.

SCENE 24

Int. ward.

KATE *is lying on her bed. On the other beds, one or two patients—quiet and hunched—lying with the covers pulled round them.*

We see the ceiling, and a pan of the ward from KATE'S *point of view. A* NURSE *approaches, but stops at one of the other patients. The ceiling, from* KATE'S *angle.*

VOICE: Like one of them space places. Cape Kennedy, is it? [*pause*] A room all dials and flickering lights. And wires reaching underground . . . under the sea . . . reaching inside people. Into my head. [*pause*] Somebody presses a button, it'll move my arm. Go on, then. Press it. [*we see* KATE'S *arm rise into shot*] Another button . . . thousands of miles away—

Her other arm rises into picture. The NURSE *approaches.*

NURSE: Kate?

She gently presses KATE'S *arms down.*

KATE: I'm in the charge of a machine—

NURSE: Are you?

KATE: But I know what I'm doing,

NURSE: I'm sure you do.

Pause.

KATE: What do you want?

NURSE: I want to talk to you. Will you come into my office? There's a cup of tea.

KATE: No. I don't want to.

NURSE: Now Kate, we aren't going to—

KATE: We? Who's we?

NURSE: You know who I mean.

KATE: Me and her?

NURSE: You know very well what I mean. Now Kate—

KATE: All right.

The NURSE *goes down the ward, outside and into her room.* KATE *gets up and follows. We go with her down the ward, into the* NURSE'S *office.*

SCENE 25

Int. office.

NURSE: I've got a nice cup of tea for you—

KATE: What do you want?

NURSE: Don't we want our tea, then?

KATE: What do you want?

Pause.

NURSE: Sit down, Kate—[*they sit down facing each other*] It's about Paul Morris—

KATE: Yes?

Pause.

NURSE: He's going out soon.

KATE: Yes.

NURSE: Well. You've struck up quite a little friendship, haven't you?

KATE: I don't really like him—

NURSE: Anyway, it's—not quite the right thing to be doing, you know.

KATE: Isn't it?

NURSE: You know it isn't.

KATE: You sound like my mother.

NURSE: I think that's something I needn't be ashamed of. [*pause*] And they're coming to see you, tomorrow is it?

KATE: Yes.

Pause.

NURSE: And—I don't want you taken advantage of.

KATE: I know what I'm doing.

NURSE: I didn't say you didn't.

KATE: I can look after myself.

NURSE: Of course you can. But for the time being, you see—

KATE: Am I misbehaving?

NURSE: Shall we say, a little self-willed? A bit thoughtless, no more than that.

KATE: Is that what it is, then?

Pause.

NURSE: We can't have . . . it's not easy to explain . . . I don't

think, well you and Paul, I don't think it's suitable. [*pause*] I've heard that . . . it doesn't mean anything serious, I've heard your little walks upset Paul. Do you follow what I mean, Kate?
Pause.

KATE: No.
Pause.

NURSE: I think he's not been so well, since you—you know, since you got pally.

KATE: You mean *I've* made him unwell again?

NURSE: Don't be silly! What an idea to get in your head. [*pause*] Only he might be anxious about you, and how to put it? Embarrassed? Would that be it?

KATE: What have I done then?

NURSE: You haven't done anything. I'm not saying it's you, it's your walks and talks together—when he's thinking of going out of here, you see.
Pause.

KATE: Have *I* been worse?

NURSE: You haven't been too well lately, dear. [*pause*] You've been very good, and taking your pills. Only I think if you were to try and see Paul's side of it. [*pause*] You have to be extra careful don't you? When you're not feeling too good.

KATE: I don't feel so bad.

NURSE: Do you think you know better than the doctors, and the rest of us?
Pause.

KATE: No.

NURSE: There. I knew you'd understand how it is. You're a bright girl—
KATE *gets up and leaves. She goes into the ward, to her bed. Stands staring at a wooden chair beside the bed. After a moment, she picks up the chair and begins to tap it up and down on the floor, firmly and quietly—very intense. The* NURSE *has followed her into the ward. As she comes towards* KATE, KATE *lifts up the chair and stands holding it as if bewildered and uncertain what to do next.*
The NURSE *and two other nurses have seen this—in a moment they are on to* KATE, *grabbing for the chair. There is a scuffle. The chair is wrenched away and* KATE *is held by two of the nurses.*

SCENE 26

Int. ward.

KATE *is being tucked into bed very firmly—the bedclothes pulled tightly across her and pushed under the mattress. Finally, she is completely immobilised from chin to feet, one arm outside the bedclothes. The* NURSE *bends over her smiling, as another nurse brings an injection tray.*

NURSE: There, that's better isn't it?

KATE: I don't want to be in bed.

NURSE: We can't have you up if you're going to create such a fuss, now can we?

KATE: I wasn't.

NURSE: What was that, then? With the chair? Now we'll give you something to let you have a nice sleep.

KATE *snatches her arm away. The* NURSE *takes it in a firm grip.*

NURSE: You'll feel lots better when you've had a rest, Katie—

The tray is brought to the bedside, and we see KATE *given an injection.*

SCENE 27

Int. visiting room.

MRS. WINTER: I don't know what to make of it Kate. I really don't.

WINTER: The nurse is real put out, and she has a right to be. But there you are, Katie—now have we been right all these years or have you?

Pause.

KATE: I don't know.

WINTER: You don't know! She doesn't know! Attacking the staff with a chair. You *said* you knew what you were doing, it isn't as if you were . . . as if you were ill at that minute, is it?

KATE: I *said* . . . I wasn't attacking anybody.

MRS. WINTER: And then there's this boy. What's going on *there*?

KATE: Nothing.

MRS. WINTER: Is it nothing, that ends up with you going wild?

KATE: I didn't go wild.

MRS. WINTER: What else was it? We've heard their story and we've heard yours. You admitted picking up the chair . . . nobody's lying. I think you get things the wrong way round in your mind afterwards, not that you can help *that*. But giving trouble to all these people.

WINTER: Can you not see how it is that you, you see *you* Katie go your own way . . . you do as you like, and then your mother and I, it's *we* have to take the consequences. I didn't know how to look that nurse in the face.

KATE: That kind of thing, it does sometimes happen in here—

MRS. WINTER: Well I suppose it does. We're not *getting* at you Katie don't you see?

WINTER: If you don't co-operate with these people—after all they're doing their best . . . well you could be in here for ever. *Pause.* KATE *suddenly looks her mother straight in the face.*

KATE: I sometimes think—if I *do* co-operate, *that's* how I'll be in here for ever.

MRS. WINTER: Now that's plain bad-mindedness Kate. What's the use of you coming in here for your illness and just making things worse for everyone looking after you. [*pause*] To say nothing of the other patients.

KATE: I went for a few walks with Paul. I didn't do any harm. [*pause*] That nurse is trying to dominate me, always trying to put me down.

MRS. WINTER: Is that dominating? To give you a bit of advice and guidance?

KATE: That nurse doesn't like me, and she persecutes me.

WINTER: Why should she do that? She's put here . . . I mean it's their vocation, and they're trained. Trained, you see Kate? Some of these doctors, they've spent years . . . how you've got to look at it, the way you are, it's no different than well . . . than some ordinary physical disease. In the body, if you see. Any other way of seeing it, it's old fashioned. People don't have those old attitudes no more. There's books, and telly programmes—it hasn't got the sort of . . . stigma, that it had at one time. In my day, for example. [*laughs*] No different, in a manner of speaking, than a broken arm, really. That's how I've heard it said. [*pause*] Nothing to be ashamed.

KATE: I'm *not* ashamed.

WINTER: I didn't say you were ashamed, but it would be understandable. The amount of ignorance there is about these days, and then people they don't want to know either. Don't want to look at anything square. Can never happen to them—that type of mentality. [*pause*] Well, now, a nurse in this hospital —she's got the *training*, if you see what I mean. [*pause*] She's looking at the outside, isn't she? What you'd call professional. And she can see you the way you can't see yourself. [*pause*] So you see Katie, to talk of persecution . . . I hope you don't say that to her, you'll only put her against you. Won't you? *Pause.*

MRS. WINTER: The little girl *I* brought up wouldn't have . . . well, you know, with the chair. Can't you see what a strain you put on people? If you didn't know you were doing these things . . . if you said *that* . . . well I'm sure we'd all understand.

KATE: What would that prove?

MRS. WINTER: It . . . doesn't it show lovey that you're not *my* Katie when you go round doing things like that? D'you see? *Pause.*

KATE: Whose bloody Katie am I then?
Pause.

MRS. WINTER: That's another thing. [*pause*] The swearing. The bad language. [*pause*] I've . . . I believe you use some awful language . . . to the staff . . . and they know it isn't you of course. But they're entitled to your respect, same as me and your father.

KATE: You and Dad use swear words.

MRS. WINTER: *Everybody* uses an oath now and then. It's not quite the same thing. I know you . . . such expressions couldn't pass your lips when you're well, only—

KATE: You're a bloody liar!

The WINTERS *exchange sympathetic looks, contriving to seem outraged at the same time.*

WINTER: Kate—

KATE: I'm sorry. [*pause*] Sorry Mum—

MRS. WINTER: It's all right darling. I know you didn't mean it.

KATE: No.

MRS. WINTER: Because I've never lied to you, have I?

Pause.

KATE: No.

MRS. WINTER: Nobody's lied to you. [*pause*] I think, if you've turned things round in your mind . . . got the wrong side of things . . . your father and I understand. We want you to know that—

WINTER: That's right. We've got faith in you, Katie love.

Pause.

KATE: Will you ask that nurse if she tried to stop me seeing Paul?

MRS. WINTER: She's told us *all* about it. Nobody's got anything to hide, you see—

KATE: Well then. Did she stop me? Say I shouldn't?

MRS. WINTER: What else should she say? Where would they be if they had that on their hands at every verse end?

WINTER: Do you not see her point of view?

Pause.

KATE: Have *I* got a point of view?

WINTER: Has anybody denied that? Tried to take it away from you?

KATE: My head aches. I can't hardly see anything . . . or hear anything. [*pause*] Your voices, they're coming from a long way away . . . I—I—

She breaks down and begins to cry. MRS. WINTER *nods at her husband, gets up and goes out.* WINTER *reaches across to touch* KATE'S *arm.*

WINTER: Now don't upset yourself Katie—

KATE: They're jerking at me . . . pulling at me—

WINTER: Who is love?

KATE: With the wires. They've got these wires attached . . . they run inside my head, into my brain . . .

WINTER: Katie!

KATE: There's this great big machine . . . at the centre of the earth, and it controls everybody. Me, you, *her* . . . all of us. [*pause*] I can hear it throbbing. I can hear it. The walls are shaking with it. Look at my hand—

She puts her hand out—it is shaking.

WINTER: There's no machine, Katie—

KATE: If I don't do what it wants, it'll kill me.

WINTER: Nothing's going to kill you. You're all right. [*pause*]

You're *going* to be all right, if you give yourself *time*.

MRS. WINTER *returns, with the* NURSE. *They are all tremendously relieved—the* NURSE *to get* KATE *back into the ward, the* WINTERS *to be away from the strain of the encounter.*

NURSE: Come along then, Kate . . . come along—

MRS. WINTER: I think we'll be getting away, then—

NURSE: Say goodbye to Mum and Dad, then—

KATE *stands up, and she and her mother face each other.* KATE *is half vacant, but also watchful.*

Her mother comes to her with her arms outstretched. KATE *reaches towards her—at the last minute* MRS. WINTER *seems to become rigid herself, and her gesture becomes perfunctory. She is frightened. She pecks* KATE *on the cheek.*

MRS. WINTER: We'll come again soon darling—

KATE *looks from her mother to her father. Turns and walks away. After a few steps, she turns and looks back.*

The NURSE *is talking in a low voice to her parents. We hear a growing whisper. The whisper gets louder and louder until it is intolerable. Still shooting from* KATE'S *point of view we see what she sees as she runs out of the room, down a corridor and into the ward. She flings herself onto her bed, and as her face touches the pillow, fade out.*

SCENE 28

Int. ward. Morning.

KATE *is sitting on her bed. The* NURSE *comes. The ward scene is as usual—calm, neat, one or two patients lying hunched on their beds, the sun is shining.* NURSE *comes into close-up.*

NURSE: Not going out this morning, Kate? [*pause*] You had a good night, didn't you? [*pause*] Kate? [*pause*] Such nice people your mother and father. I think we were a little bit naughty, weren't we? Naughty with them—after they'd come all this way to see you. And then to go making your mother . . . you remember, don't you . . . making her all upset? When they love you, and just want you to be their Kate . . . and you think we're all in a tizz about that window, when we're not, are we? What's a little pane of glass? It's nothing, and it's of no consequence . . . your poor father, offering to pay for it, and of course there's no such necessity, it's a question of not losing our temper, isn't it?

During the last few words, the NURSE'S *voice is faded. There is a moment of silence, the* NURSE'S *mouth working in speech—then* KATE'S *voices begin to crowd in. Superimpose the sound of the voices over close-up of the* NURSE.

MRS. WINTER'S VOICE: It isn't the way I'd go on, you see. I have to call it badness . . . I have to say, there's the matter of sex . . . you have to be careful, and obtain a man's respect. You give them what they want, and there's no respect, and no future. You're no better than a prostitute, and one thing leads to another. You've learned nothing but what's right and good from me and your father, and that's what you have to go by. I hardly recognise you sometimes . . . I have to say it, you're a disappointment, and this with men it's dirty, and until you learn some self-control—

WINTER'S VOICE: I love you, I have since you were little, and I've tried . . . I think I can say I've been a good father . . . and what have you done? Pushed it back in my face, because you're self-willed, I don't know what it is . . . stubborn . . . you don't seem to know right from wrong, good from bad, what's moral like, and what's immoral. I wash my hands. Your mother, and I—she's a good woman and I can't stand to see the effect . . . what you're doing . . . what you do to *her*, you'll see, I know you *can* see if you'll forget yourself a minute, that it's undermining her. Undermining her health . . . I'm ashamed of you, can't hardly put my mind or *think* of what you are, the way you behave . . . if she has a breakdown or anything, it'll be on your conscience my girl! We're not in this world to do as we like, and I don't care how free . . . Well to be free, you'll find that comes out of . . . d'you see Katie, not self-indulgence, but doing what's right and what you owe people. It's like debts, and when you owe nobody nothing, that's when

you're free, only you can't live as if you're the only one breathing
—now can you girl?

Fade in NURSE'S *voice.*

NURSE: And so what we're trying to do in the hospital . . . it's
to help you help yourself. You can't say you're regimented and
pushed about . . . there's no one here to give orders, to expect
things of you dear. Everything has its purpose, and we know
what that purpose is, I think. In the end, it's for you to walk
out of those gates and never come back, isn't it?

Camera pans, takes in the ward—moves in and out, picks out details,
finally recedes until the NURSE *is in long shot. We cut to* KATIE'S
hands clutching her knees, and there is the sound of loud sobbing.
Darkness.

SCENE 29

Int. lecture theatre.

A small lecture theatre, with a bench and demonstration space. A
CONSULTANT *is addressing a number of students.* KATE *stands nearby,*
with a NURSE. *She is docile, mostly expressionless but occasionally*
smiles to herself, or mumbles under her breath.

CONSULTANT: Good morning, Kate. How are you this morning?

KATE: No.

CONSULTANT: Not very well?

KATE: I haven't, no . . . I haven't . . . I really haven't . . . I
really . . . no. I'll let you. I *will* let you. *Anything.* Good
morning. I *can* good morning—listen.

The CONSULTANT *turns to his students.*

CONSULTANT: In many ways a fairly typical case-history. Happy
sociable, until her late teens—then in and out of various jobs
for a while. A reputation for inefficiency, bad temper, rudeness
. . . often alienated from the people she worked with, through
the notion that they were somehow plotting against her, or
disliked her, or were trying to make a fool of her. Out of work
for a time, and the parents noticed some improvement then—

from all accounts she became childish and tractable, and the mother seems to think this was one of Kate's "well periods". [*pause*] Eventually, she worked again, then it seems a series of unfortunate affaires, culminating in a pregnancy which was terminated at eleven weeks. [*pause*] She was referred after an attack on her mother with a knife, this apparently the climax of a long period of increasingly abnormal behaviour which her parents contained until they found her to be unmanageable. This included: rigidity, withdrawal, vagueness, thought disorder (as you saw just now), and so on. Finally, as I say, the incident with her mother, and a period of hospitalization. [*pause*] The case notes here include thought-blocking, over-inclusion, emotional apathy, automatic obedience—she was in seclusion part of the time, and gained a reputation for smashing in states of catatonic excitement. There were delusions of persecution —for example, that her mother was killing her, had killed her aborted child . . . that she was under the control of some sort of all-powerful, cosmic machine. Family history negative, and apparently no detectable relationship between her various symptoms and her environment. [*he goes to* KATE, *addressing the students still*] Notice the posture, the occasional grimaces, the tendency to mumble things to herself. I think the clinical picture is a fairly clear one, and the present condition of the patient what one might call a logical expectation given the case history. [*pause*] Now . . . a diagnosis?

STUDENT: Schizophrenia.

CONSULTANT: Treatment.

STUDENT: Tranquillizing drugs, for example Largactil. Possibly convulsive treatment. At a later stage occupational therapy with a view to rehabilitation—

CONSULTANT: Yes. Thank you. [*turning to* NURSE] Thank you Nurse—

Close-up KATE. *The* NURSE *gently turns her and they leave the lecture theatre.*

SCENE 30

Int. ECT room in hospital.
KATE is anaesthetized and awaiting electric convulsion therapy. As the machine is brought up and the electrodes placed in position, we hear a DOCTOR'S VOICE fragmentarily.

VOICE: Patient completely anaesthetized, you see . . . feels nothing . . . notice how the electrodes are placed . . . something between the teeth . . . afterwards some temporary loss of memory . . . you know how this treatment originated? . . . yes . . . it was pigs . . . more or less an accident, really . . . Naples I think . . . of course we don't know how it works . . . all we know is that it *does* work . . . quite remarkably . . . main object is to get the patient functioning again . . . back to normal life . . . my god, if we waited until we found out *why* these things work!

Titles over this sequence.

Fade out.

THE PARACHUTE

CHARACTERS

WERNER VON REGER

KLAUS

BARON GEORG VON REGER

HELEN VON REGER

ANNA

HELMUT

KOEPFER

MAN

SCHACHT

FRAU SCHACHT

CORPORAL

SERGEANT

OFFICER

HOLZ

SOLDIERS

GUESTS

GERMANY, 1913-1945

SCENE 1

Newsreel: A parachute dropping exercise. The sky is filled with parachutes—billowing, drifting, some just opening. Several shots of men swinging in harness high above the earth. The parachutes are blossoming everywhere like huge flowers.

MILITARY VOICE: . . . The new parachute, therefore, must allow of maximum speed of descent with minimum risk to the troops. It cannot be emphasised too strongly that this matter is *urgent. Extremely urgent.*

CLOSE UP: WERNER, swaying in harness.

TITLE: THE PARACHUTE.

We see one of the soldiers reach the earth. He rolls over and over, the cords pulling at him. The parachute is blown over him.

SCENE 2

The dormitory in a Luftwaffe barracks. Night. Time—1940. It is dark, but a faint light filters through the windows. There are ten beds with men sleeping. Open on WERNER'S *bed. He is entirely covered by the sheet. As we cut to this scene, he sits up, pulling the sheet down, and reaches for a cigarette. Lighting the cigarette, he turns on his side and lies smoking, staring in front.* WERNER *is in his late twenties—lean, intelligent, a rather bitter face.*
In the next bed, KLAUS *is also lying awake. He whispers.*

KLAUS: I'm scared.

WERNER: Why?

KLAUS: The new rag we're testing tomorrow. Everybody knows it's too small. Are we committing suicide or are they murdering us?

WERNER: *smiling*] Both. [*pause*] It's relatively safe from the tower.

KLAUS: Relatively!

WERNER: Go to sleep—

235

KLAUS: Why did *you* volunteer?

WERNER: Why did you?

Pause.

KLAUS: It's better than fighting. That's what I thought. [*pause*] But maybe it isn't.

WERNER: Go to sleep—

KLAUS *turns the other way.* WERNER *rolls onto his back, still smoking. Cut to:*

SCENE 3

A balcony. A woman, expensively dressed in the period of 1918, *lifts up a small boy of about four. She is* WERNER'S MOTHER.

MOTHER: Look, Werner—

Cut to: Newsreel of street. A column of German soldiers is marching past. A band plays vigorous German military music. Cut back to: Balcony. WERNER'S MOTHER *lifts his arm.*

MOTHER: Wave, darling! Wave—

BOY: I want to see the Kaiser!

She sets him down, crouches in front of him. He looks at her steadily.

MOTHER: Your father's coming home.

BOY: I want to see the Kaiser!

She kisses him. He moves away—goes to the balustrade and peers between two of the stone supports. Cut to:

Street newsreel. The soldiers march past. The music blares out stirringly. Cut back to:

SCENE 4

Barracks. WERNER *closes his eyes. We now see* KLAUS'S *face from the side away from* WERNER.

KLAUS: Werner?

WERNER: What?

KLAUS: I wish I was at home. In the milking shed. [*pause*] I like cows—

WERNER: Be quiet!

KLAUS: Why? [*plaintively, almost*] *We* know each other!

WERNER: No one knows anyone.

KLAUS *turns to him, grinning in the faint light.*

KLAUS: *Poet!*

WERNER *turns to him seriously.*

WERNER: I told you. I wrote poems. I didn't say I was a poet.

KLAUS: You made a living out of it—

WERNER: I made a living from translations.

KLAUS: *turning away*] What an intellectual!

Pause.

WERNER: No. I was rather stupid. [*pause*] *Am* rather stupid.

KLAUS: It shows less, when you're educated—

WERNER: It shows more.

KLAUS: That's beyond me.

WERNER *laughs quietly to himself.*

KLAUS: What's up *now?*

WERNER: I was thinking . . . how intelligent of *you*, to prefer
the cows.

KLAUS: Who'll they pick for the first jump? And do you think
when he's dead, they'll call the whole thing off?

Pause.

WERNER: Nobody's going to die.

KLAUS: How do *you* know?

Pause.

WERNER: That tower's high enough to make a crippled Hero of
the Reich. But not high enough to guarantee death. [*smiles
gently*] It's quite poetic, really.

He stubs out his cigarette. Lies back with his eyes closed. Cut to:

SCENE 5

*A drawing room—Berlin, early twenties. A string quartet is playing.
Ten or fifteen guests are sitting and standing, intent on the music.
Somewhat to the back,* WERNER'S MOTHER *sits in a chair listening. On*

the floor beside her, WERNER, *now about ten, is writing in a copy book.*
He writes:

> Her beak was like a sword,
> Her wings were like a fan—

He hesitates, chewing his pencil. His mother looks down at him, smiling.
He smiles back at her. Writes:

> The sky was blue around her
> As underneath I ran—

WERNER *makes a heavy full stop at the end of the last line. Cut to:*
The doorway. A tall, stern, *rather emaciated man—*WERNER'S FATHER—
has just entered unobtrusively. He stands a moment listening, then
quietly walks over to his wife. We now see the page and the poem
spread out in front of WERNER. *A foot comes down firmly on the page.*
We pan up to his FATHER'S *face.*
The FATHER *stares down at* WERNER *quite neutrally. The boy stands up.*
The music has finished and everyone is clapping. WERNER'S FATHER
stands clapping, smiling and nodding round the room. WERNER *is moving*
backwards slowly to the door. The guests begin to move about, chatting.
WERNER'S MOTHER *gets up and faces her husband.* WERNER *stops—*
stands watching them. They say nothing. The FATHER *has a half smile*
on his face. The MOTHER *is stony. After a moment, she picks up the*
book and takes it to WERNER. *With a look over her shoulder at her*
husband, she takes WERNER *out, her arm round his shoulders.*

SCENE 6

Barracks. Morning. WERNER *is sleeping but the others are up and*
moving about with a lot of noise—dressing, pulling on boots, etc. KLAUS,
in singlet and trousers, is shaking WERNER. WERNER *sits up yawning.*

WERNER: What's the weather like?
KLAUS: *looking out*] It's pissing down.
WERNER: *Good.*
KLAUS: The rain'll go when it gets lighter—
WERNER: *Bad.*
KLAUS: We've got six minutes.

WERNER: Before what?

Laughing, KLAUS *does a caricature of running on the spot.* WERNER
laughs—jumps out of bed. We follow KLAUS *to the washroom. At
a row of basins, several men are washing and shaving. As* KLAUS
fills his basin, WERNER *comes to the one beside him. They both begin
to shave.*

KLAUS: I dreamt about you.

WERNER: I'm touched.

KLAUS *turns to look at* WERNER, *who stares fixedly into the mirror.*

KLAUS: You're not liked, you know—

WERNER: I know.

KLAUS: I don't know why.

WERNER: Yes. [*drawing the razor up his cheek*] You like me Klaus,
don't you!

This was said sardonically. KLAUS *is hurt. He hesitates a moment,
then:*

KLAUS: In the dream—

Pause.

WERNER: Either tell me or don't.

KLAUS: There were huge flowers. [*pause*] Instead of blossoms they
had billowing parachutes. [*pause*] It was . . . pretty. [*pause*]
Do you understand anything about dreams?

WERNER *steps back holding his razor away from his face. He regards*
KLAUS *with a wry face—speaks lightly, but with a faint edge.*

WERNER: The interpretation of dreams is decadent Jewish filth.

This subdues KLAUS. *He goes on shaving. But* WERNER *persists.*

WERNER: And how was I involved?

KLAUS: *grinning now*] You were mowing the flowers down. With
a scythe. [*pause*] And the parachutes blew away.

WERENER: How very sophisticated!

KLAUS *turns to him slowly, struggling to say something. It is as if his
mind has great difficulty in finding the words to catch the essence of
a feeling, or intuition.*

KLAUS: I embarrass you, don't I?

WERNER: *smiling*] I don't know why the Luftwaffe bothered to
pull you out of the cowshit!

KLAUS *looks round. The washroom has emptied. He grabs* WERNER'S
wrist.

KLAUS: You ought to be frightened—

WERNER *gently disengages his wrist.*

WERNER: Ought I?

He bends over the basin and rinses his face. KLAUS *stares at his back, thoughtfully rubbing his face with a towel.*

KLAUS: I don't mean the 'chute trials.

WERNER *reaches for his towel.*

WERNER: *What* do you mean, then?

KLAUS *hesitates—collects his shaving tackle together.*

KLAUS: Your father could have kept you out of—out of all this. Couldn't he? A rich industrialist, you said. The first time we spoke to each other in the mess. I don't know how it came up. My father's a powerful man, you said.

WERNER: One of my bad habits. I tell people too much . . . too soon. However, about my father I was telling the truth—but I was being ironic. Do you see?

KLAUS: No. And we'd better get a move on.

KLAUS *exits.* WERNER *dabs at his face with a towel. Goes to the window of the washroom. We see a bleak barracks—rows of long, low buildings and a parade ground.* WERNER *turns his back to the window. He walks slowly to the door and goes out, pulling it gently to behind him. Cut to:*

SCENE 7

Another door opening. Through it comes a man padded and masked for fencing. He closes the door behind him and stands holding a foil. We see the room from his angle—a largish private gymnasium. In the centre of the room stands WERNER, *this time fifteen or sixteen. He too is dressed for fencing and stands quite still, the button of his foil resting on the toe of one shoe.* WERNER'S FATHER *goes towards him.*

FATHER: Ready, Werner?

WERNER: Yes, father.

They address each other formally, and begin to fence—which they obviously do well together. The performance is light, elegant, and restrained. Suddenly, the FATHER, *whom we now hear laughing,*

goes in under WERNER'S *guard and rips the padding on his chest.*
They stand back, removing their masks.

FATHER: All the same, you're getting quite good.

WERNER: Thank you.

FATHER: I hear you are very popular at school. [*pause*] Good
   academically—good at sports. [*pause*] A rather sardonic twist of
   mind, so they say.

WERNER: Who says?

FATHER: Your teachers.

WERNER: I find things easy—and that amuses me . . .

FATHER: It *is* amusing.

WERNER: I'm glad we agree, father.

FATHER: I've always found perfection of accomplishment in human
   beings slightly hilarious. One should achieve everything—then
   have the good sense to despise what one has achieved.

The FATHER *stares solemnly at* WERNER, *then bursts our laughing.*
WERNER *laughs.*

FATHER: You seek my approval—I seek your . . . complicity.
   There's the basis of an excellent father-son relationship!

WERNER: Complicity? You want my—

FATHER: *cutting in*] Where is your mother this afternoon?

WERNER: In the Tiergarten.

FATHER: How *is* your mother?

WERNER: Why don't you ask her?

FATHER: *turning away*] You must have realised by now that I leave
   that kind of thing to you. What's the point of having a son if
   he doesn't assume some of his father's more . . . irksome
   responsibilities.

He goes to a table at the side of the gymnasium, takes out a box of
small thin cheroots and lights one. WERNER *is perfectly relaxed—*
stands watching his FATHER.

WERNER: *drily*] I do my best.

FATHER: We both have a delicate enough sense of humour. Why
   else would I have taken the trouble to guarantee you a perfect
   parody of a German upbringing and education?

WERNER: Is that what I've had?

FATHER: Hadn't you realised it?

WERNER *bursts out laughing—his* FATHER *puffs at his cheroot.*

WERNER: Of course I realised—

FATHER: My maternal grandfather was a Polish aristocrat—have we been through all this before? [*as* WERNER *shakes his head*] No? Good. And what you must understand is that the Poles temper their ferocity with irony. A nation which has suffered one humiliation after another acquires a great sense of history. This is what grandfather conveyed to my mother in order to punish my father for being German. My mother, in whose death before your own birth you are extremely fortunate, was a somnolent Polish countess who preferred German industry to Polish fantasy. If I seem to you a frivolous man in some respects, you must take all this into account. Your conception was an absurdity to which I have never quite reconciled myself. For me, copulation was a pleasure. For her it was a duty. I wouldn't even say she *conceived* you, my boy—she sprang you on me. Perhaps that's why you like her so much, you feel that at least she got her own back. I'm pleased you don't *fidget*. So many boys of your age *fidget*. There we are. Everyone is satisfied. Your mother sees you as a living rebuke to me; I see you as a vehicle for my detestation of her; and you see yourself in a good position to exploit the pair of us. [*he flourishes his foil*] Shall we go on?

WERNER: I expect mother feels your frivolousness was a criticism of her—

His FATHER *goes to him and pats his cheek.*

FATHER: Aren't you *precocious*!

WERNER *walks to a rack by the wall and puts away his foil.*

WERNER: You've rather put me off. Why not try the sabres with Helmut?

His FATHER *goes to the door and bawls out.*

FATHER: Helmut! [*coming back into the room*] Do you know what he spends his time doing these days? Concocting illiterate pamphlets demanding the deportation of Jews and Bolsheviks. Poor Helmut! [*racks his foil—goes to another rack for a sabre*] That's the *real* trouble with the Weimar Republic, its frustrating incompetence turns otherwise amiably stupid little Germans into visionaries.

He hesitates. Takes a step towards WERNER. *Speaks facetiously.*

FATHER: Would you say that's better, or worse, than turning

stupid little visionaries into Germans?

WERNER *turns away. Their mood is somehow broken.*

WERNER: I don't know what you're talking about.

FATHER: I'm told you versify competently. Aren't poets sometimes visionaries? Though I must say at your age I preferred brothels to rhymes. Do you find that squalid?

WERNER: *rounding on him*] Mother said recently: your father is a rather sensitive man who finds uneasy refuge in seeming brutal.

FATHER: That was charitable of her—

He breaks off, throws his head back and bawls out:

FATHER: Helmut!

HELMUT *enters. A heavy, yet still athletic man of middle age. He has a rough, brooding face—deferential, but with a grievance.*

HELMUT: Sir!

FATHER: My son would like to see what we can do with the sabres—

HELMUT *goes to a wall rack, takes two sabres down.*

FATHER: But first of all—

Pause.

HELMUT: Sir?

FATHER: Tell him what you think of the Jews.

HELMUT *looks at him for a moment, then turns to* WERNER, *who is watching and listening neutrally.*

HELMUT: He knows.

FATHER: I wonder—

WERNER: *to* HELMUT] What about them?

HELMUT: *defensively*] Everybody knows.

WERNER'S FATHER *goes to him, takes one of the sabres.* HELMUT *holds the other uncertainly. The* FATHER *raps his sabre against* HELMUT'S *chidingly.*

FATHER: Come along, come along! [*he pokes his sabre gently into* HELMUT'S *stomach, smiling*] You soft-gutted Bavarian weasel—[*shouting*] let's have it!

HELMUT *now speaks in a mounting crescendo of feeling, as if something within him has burst.*

HELMUT: Jackals, vermin, lice, ponces, criminals, pederasts, we ought to shoot the bloody lot!

WERNER'S FATHER *turns to him ironically.*

FATHER: There you are, you see. The authentic voice of Germany! Why is that, Werner? Why do you think Helmut is so frightened?

HELMUT: *almost naively*] I won the Iron Cross under your very own command, sir!

FATHER: Indeed you did! Haven't I always been proud of you?

HELMUT: *uncertainly*] Why . . . yes, sir.

FATHER: And gave you work—

HELMUT: *even more bewildered*] Yes, sir.

FATHER: And laughed at your boozing and whoring?

HELMUT: I expect so—

FATHER: I'd say I've been very civil with you.

WERNER: Father—

FATHER: I think *you* ought to take him on.

He throws his sabre to WERNER, *who catches it by the shaft. He goes out.* WERNER *and* HELMUT *face each other clutching the sabres.* HELMUT *tentatively raises his*—WERNER *suddenly starts laughing, leans on his sabre laughing and shaking his head from side to side.*

SCENE 8

Parade ground outside the barracks. It is raining and dismal, the ground very muddy. An N.C.O. *conducts* WERNER'S *platoon at P.T. As we open on them they are doing legs astride and arms raised.*

N.C.O.: One two, one two, one two, one two, *stop!*

They stop at attention. We pan down their faces to WERNER *and* KLAUS. *Hold* WERNER'S *face. Apart from the sound of the rain it is very still. Almost dreamlike—the platoon and the* N.C.O. *quite motionless.*

A loudspeaker on one of the huts begins to whine and howl. There is a burst of electric crackling. Then, softly at first but getting louder and louder the speaker begins to relay brass band music.

The N.C.O. *smiles. He suddenly yells:*

N.C.O.: *Down!*

The platoon flop down on their stomachs in the mud.

N.C.O.: *Up—*

They stand up.

N.C.O.: Down—

They flop down again. As we see WERNER *go down into the mud:*

SCENE 9

Cut to: The swinging blade of a scythe in a hayfield. As we pull back, the man with the scythe stops work, takes a stone and begins to sharpen the blade. Camera pans across the field. In a hollow, at the edge of the high grass, we see WERNER—*still seventeen or so—kneeling over a girl of the same age in a white summer dress. She is beautiful, serene, gentle.*

WERNER: Why not?

ANNA: I can't.

WERNER: You don't want to!

ANNA: I do.

WERNER: But you can't!

Pause.

ANNA: No.

WERNER: *lying down*] You're frightened?

ANNA: No.

Pause.

WERNER *turns on her, sneering.*

WERNER: My *darling* cousin—

ANNA *stretches her arms, laughing.*

ANNA: I do dream about you—

WERNER: *Ach!*

He picks up a book from his side and pretends to read. Cut to: The man scything. We follow several long, rhythmic, even sweeps. Cut back to:

WERNER: Dream what?

ANNA: When I do, it's moonlight. And we lie in the deep grass by the lake and . . . make love. [*pause*] I have such intense feelings in the dream. Then I wake up crying. [*pause*] It's funny, isn't it, that your family should have Polish connections—

WERNER: Funny why? Anyway, you're not Poles. You're Germans.

ANNA: We've got Polish blood.

WERNER: I suppose the thought of actual copulation disgusts you?

ANNA: Nothing disgusts me.

WERNER: Nothing at all?

ANNA: Perhaps, being dead.

He reaches out his hand. She takes it. He pulls her towards him. As they are about to kiss, WERNER hears something. He pulls away startled and looks up. The man with the scythe stands looking down at them.

SCENE 10

Parade ground. WERNER is lying face down in the mud. Over him stands the N.C.O. The N.C.O. takes two paces back then calls out to the platoon.

N.C.O.: Up!

They get up.

N.C.O.: Down.

They go down.

N.C.O.: Up—

They get up again.

N.C.O.: To the showers, then. Quick march, one two one two one two—

As the platoon marches off through the rain, mix to:

SCENE 11

A row of showers, WERNER and KLAUS are soaping and rinsing themselves.

KLAUS: That's the third time this week he's made us do that.

WERNER: Do you mind?

KLAUS: Of *course* I bloody mind!

WERNER: Why?

KLAUS: S'all right for raw recruits, but—

WERNER: Oh? *Is* it?

KLAUS: You know what I mean. Well. What I mean—there's a question of human dignity involved.

WERNER *turns off his shower, stands staring in front of him.*

WERNER: I don't mind going down in the mud at all. It's clean. It smells of rain, and earth. No. I don't mind that. [*pause*] My dignity's in there [*taps his head*]—where no one can get at it.

KLAUS: I'm not talking about the mud.

*One of the other men—*KOEPFER—*has been listening. He approaches* KLAUS.

KOEPFER: Why don't you hit him?

KLAUS: Eh?

KOEPFER: Why don't you thump your poncy friend?

KLAUS: What's the matter with you?

KOEPFER: You know what I've heard?

KLAUS: What?

KOEPFER: You're the first jump today.

KLAUS: So?

KOEPFER: You know so! We all think Reger should go first.

KLAUS: *They* decide who goes first.

KOEPFER: *to* WERNER] Why aren't you an officer, anyway?

KLAUS: Lay off him—

KOEPFER: Couple of fairies, are you?

KLAUS hits him. Several of the others gather round. WERNER *watches the whole thing impassively.* KOEPFER *laughs. Two of them grab* KLAUS *by the arms.*

KOEPFER: Not him. [*turning to* WERNER] This one. It's this one we don't like. Isn't it?

Some showers are still on. The place is steamy. We hear the drip of water and men breathing heavily. WERNER *says nothing.*

KOEPFER: Who says Reger jumps first?

They all raise their arms.

KOEPFER: Answer me, Reger.

Silence.

KLAUS: Bloody well say something.

WERNER: I don't care who jumps first.

KOEPFER: I knew you were a hero. Underneath. A long way underneath.

WERNER: You dislike being ignored, don't you Koepfer?

KOEPFER: By you?

WERNER: Yes.

KOEPFER: I love you Reger.

KOEPFER *laughs. The others join in.*

WERNER: See you after the war.

KOEPFER: I'm here now. You can see me now. You stinking old German families. Your stinking money. Your influence here and there and everywhere. Why aren't you an officer?

WERNER: Would you prefer that?

KOEPFER: I can smell something pretty bad about you, Reger. I wonder what it is? I wonder why daddy hasn't got you a crack regiment? Why you aren't already dead for the Fuhrer?

WERNER: The only thing you can smell is your own stench. [*he sniffs*] Yes. I think that's what it is. Cabbage water with dead rats. Vintage Koepfer—

KOEPFER: *smiling*] *That's* what I wanted to hear.

He turns to the others. The two holding KLAUS *pull him away, the rest move in on* WERNER, *who makes no attempt to stop them.*

There is a crush of men's bodies—a writhing mass which surrounds WERNER. *The beating is brief, and they leave him under a shower bleeding at the mouth. Grinning,* KOEPFER *turns the water on. It comes splashing down on* WERNER, *plastering his hair down, making watery rivulets of the blood on his face. Close-up* WERNER'S *face.*

SCENE 12

Cut to: An exploding revolver.

In a long, bare shooting gallery, WERNER'S FATHER *is shooting at clay pipes.* WERNER *and* ANNA *watch. He hits three of the pipes and puts the gun down smiling.*

FATHER: There *will* be a war of course. That depraved little man who calls himself the Fuhrer . . . [*picks up another gun*] that squalid paranoiac of ours . . . is determined to have one. And he'll have one. He'll stuff our good Germans with Nordic gods, Wagner, German destiny, warrior heroes . . . we shall go to war, be triumphant for several years and then suffer a total humiliating defeat.

WERNER: Is that what you predict, father?

His FATHER *shoots down three more pipes, and turns to* WERNER.

FATHER: German history is the history of German fantasy. But never mind. If we aren't overrun by the Bolsheviks, the Americans will punish us for our sins and then subsidise the creation of an even stronger Germany—*[grinning]* a restless, *democratic* Germany! Shall I get you out? Shall I send you to Switzerland? *[pause]* Anna?

He holds out his gun to ANNA. *She takes it and shoots the remaining pipes.*

FATHER: Shall I send you and WERNER to Switzerland, ANNA? Geneva? Think of that beautiful lake. The swans. The mountains. Charming. *[pause]* The only problem is the Swiss. Are you his mistress?

ANNA: Not yet.

FATHER: After all these years of lolling in fields, and rowing boats, riding my horses, moonlight assignations in my woods? The servants *expect* you to be his mistress by now. You confuse me.

ANNA *turns to* WERNER *and looks at him for a moment.*

ANNA: I don't know what he is.

FATHER: *I* think he's a Swiss. You know? I think he'll become a fat professor in Zurich. Probably develop asthma as well.

ANNA: And I?

FATHER: My charming Anna, *you* should have been English. You have the soul of a suffragette. There's nothing I like better in a woman than beauty combined with inflexibility. *[pause]* You must give up your silly communist games, chérie. If not, those very *unfunny* men in black will come early one morning and take you away.

ANNA: What do *you* know about it?

Pause.

FATHER: I know *everything* about it.

Pause.

ANNA: Am I under suspicion?

FATHER: You people are very *boring* with your Marx and Engels . . . your historical necessity . . . your romantic oversimplifi- cations. That's the trouble with my family. Every now and then we throw up some disastrous idiot who cares about "the people". Usually a woman. Werner's mother, who as you know is my second cousin, has a touch of it. Werner inherited the trait, but I think I've done rather a good job on him. Don't you? I think I can confidently assert that Werner believes in *nothing*. [*pause*] Stalin betrayed the German Communist Party, in effect. Why shouldn't you?

ANNA: *turning to* WERNER] *Has* he done a good job on you?

WERNER *goes to his father.*

WERNER: You are destructive—

FATHER: Have I ever pretended otherwise?

WERNER: No.

FATHER: Are you going to whine?

WERNER: No.

FATHER: The German resistance movement, in so far as there *is* one . . . is a puerile farce.

ANNA: It is *not*!

FATHER: Werner has visionary dreams during the night you know. It's got to a point where Helmut has to sleep on the couch in Werner's dressing-room. [*pause*] When my son wakes up sweating and shouting, our brutal old retainer pacifies him like a mother. Helmut—of all people! [*pause*] When it happens, I won't allow my wife in there. [*pause*] I believe it is her dearest wish that you two should marry.

ANNA *goes to* WERNER.

ANNA: Dreams? [*pause*] Visions?

FATHER: If only you'd condescend to sleep with him—you'd find out. Wouldn't you?

WERNER: *shouting*] Leave her alone!

FATHER: Do you think I can protect her?

WERNER: You already have—

ANNA: It's not true—

FATHER: My darling child, you've dangled by a thread from my fingers like a puppet. There! Now you *are* upset. I know it's not amusing to think one's life depends on anybody—let alone a man one despises for ideological reasons. [*pause: Brusquely*] The point I am labouring to make is that my efforts on your behalf are exhausted. I'm very fond of you. But I have reached the limits of the indulgence of . . . certain people.

Pause.

ANNA: *quietly*] I don't despise you.

FATHER: Do you love me?

ANNA: Yes.

FATHER: *turning away*] How schizophrenic people are.

Pause.

ANNA: And I love Werner—

FATHER: *turning back, shouting*] And you cling to your preposterous faith in the Soviet Union? Do you know that your friends there turned over German communists to the S.S.? Do you know that their means are indistinguishable from ours? And their ends forgotten? Do you know *anything*?

He strides out of the room. WERNER *goes to the row of pistols— selects one and stands shooting at the second row of clay pipes. As he stops shooting:*

ANNA: Werner—

WERNER: What?

ANNA: When you all go to Laugstein tomorrow—I'm not coming.

WERNER: I think mother's expecting you to.

ANNA: She is.

WERNER: So?

ANNA: I can't.

WERNER: What do you want me to say.

ANNA: I want you to stay in Berlin. [*pause*] With me.

Pause.

WERNER: We always go to Laugstein on May the fifteenth. On May fifteenth the von Regers take up residence at their country seat. Mother would have left father years ago if she'd been denied her summers at Laugstein. [*pause*] She recuperates from winter with father. [*pause*] It is an understood thing that father also recuperates—from mother, in Berlin, with Fraulein Bechner, who is Berlin's favourite ballerina. [*pause*] Do you know, my mother supervises the bottling of fruit and berries at Laugstein? She's always been dedicated to those activities which my father finds contemptible.

ANNA: I'm very fond of your mother.

WERNER: It seems—you love us all.

ANNA: Collectively, I hate our family. [*pause*] Individually—

WERNER: What *is* the Party line on individuality?

ANNA: *Please*, Werner—

WERNER: You've seen what I'm like. My father paralyses me. Utterly. [*pause*] I respect his intellect. I admire his virility. I envy his detachment. I'm devoted to his sense of humour. [*pause*] He seems already to *be* everything I might have aspired to. It's an uncanny feeling.

ANNA: *shouting*] I am *not* a communist!

WERNER: What are you?

Pause.

ANNA: They're building a camp near Laugstein.

WERNER: Are they?

ANNA: Yes.

WERNER: Well. They *do* build camps you know. For the army, the Hitler Youth—

ANNA: *Stop* it!

WERNER: Sober local citizens cut planks, boil glue, hammer nails —we're an industrious nation.

Pause.

ANNA: Why do you try to humiliate me?

WERNER: Laugstein isn't Germany. It's a self-perpetuating dream. They can erect camps near Laugstein . . . demolish camps near Laugstein. In twenty years' time, my father will still be taking his mistresses there in winter—when, as you know, it's mother's custom to do her duty by father in Berlin. [*pause*] I should think Fraulein Bechner will be dead by then. She drinks too much. [*pause*] I hope *I'm* dead by then. Long before then.

WERNER *exits.* ANNA *goes to the pistols, takes one and starts shooting at the pipes.*

SCENE 13

A counter at the parachute depot. We see men filing past—girls hand them their parachute packs. KLAUS *and* WERNER *collect their parachutes with the others—the shed is dark, oppressive, no one speaks.*

SCENE 14

A canvas-covered army transport lorry. Benches down both sides. The men sit huddled as the lorry jolts along, with their packs on their knees. KLAUS *offers* WERNER *a cigarette and they light up. We see stretches of flat desolate country on either side.*

KLAUS: Laugstein—

WERNER: You know it?

KLAUS: I only left our farm once. To Munich. [*laughs*] I was there three days. I was drunk all the time and went home with the clap. [*pause*] Do you understand what happened this morning? In the showers—

WERNER: You've been talking about me. Haven't you?

Pause.

KLAUS: Yes. [*pause*] You talked to *me.* [*pause*] Well. I was drunk. [*pause*] I was *boasting.*

WERNER: You're pathetic.

KLAUS: You picked me out for a friend. [*pause*] I'm nothing. [*pause*] It . . . it worries me sometimes. I don't know what you want.

WERNER: I don't want anything.

KLAUS: Sometimes you . . . touch me, you know. On the arm. The hand. I don't mind. I don't think you're . . . what they said. [*pause*] But I feel ashamed. [*pause*] When I was drunk, I think I . . . *infected* them.

WERNER: With this shame?

KLAUS: I don't know what I mean. Koepfer said—listen we were *pissed*—he said: I saw Reger touch you, lilly-boy. [*pause*] Werner —I *blushed.* [*pause*] I hated you. I made them laugh. Koepfer grabbed me by the ears and kissed me on the cheek. They hauled me onto the table, I seemed to be paddling in beer. I cried. Then suddenly I was making fun of you to them.

Pause.

WERNER: Have you a girl at home?

KLAUS: No. [*pause*] Have you?

WERNER: She's not at home. I don't know where she is. I don't know if she's alive, even.

Pause.

KLAUS: Look. There's the tower. [*pause*] My guts are crawling.

WERNER: I shall go first.

KLAUS: *You?*

WERNER: I think it's been arranged.

KLAUS: We're guinea-pigs. That's all.

WERNER: It doesn't matter who goes first. There's no real danger.

 KLAUS *puts his hand on* WERNER'S *arm.* WERNER *looks down at* KLAUS'S *hand, then at* KLAUS—*who withdraws it.*

KLAUS: Does your family still have Laugstein?

WERNER: Yes. My mother's there. [*pause*] She's insane.

KLAUS: I'm sorry.

WERNER: She's deluded that it's before the war. [*pause*] Before Hitler. [*pause*] There are hardly any servants left, of course. [*pause*] In the summer she bottles fruit. [*he smiles*] Compulsively. [*pause*] And sometimes when she sees me, she plays a sly game. She seems to think that she's . . . Anna.

KLAUS: Your girl?

 The lorry lurches to a stop beside a field. A CORPORAL *jumps down from the cab and runs round to the back. Dropping the tail-flap, he shouts:*

CORPORAL: Out out out. Come on then. Let's have you—

 The men begin to jump down from the lorry into squelching mud. KLAUS *takes* WERNER'S *arm, pointing.*

KLAUS: The tower—

 Close-up WERNER'S *face.*

SCENE 15

The dining room in the Von Reger's house. At a long table, WERNER, *his* FATHER *and* MOTHER *sit at one end. The* FATHER *pours wine for himself and* WERNER—*all three are eating fruit.*

MOTHER: I still can't think *why* Anna didn't tell me she would be out for dinner.

FATHER: Kronfeld is bankrupt. I've bought four of his horses. Beautiful animals. [*pause*] Doubtless we shall be eating them before very long. [*pause*] I *could* have bought Kronfeld. [*coldly, to* WERNER] *Should* I have bought Kronfeld?

MOTHER: She *will* marry you, Werner. She loves you. I know.

WERNER: I haven't asked her, mother.

FATHER: Kronfeld is a very boring man. Very devoted to the
Fuhrer. Teutonic mythology oozes out of his ears. He has that
charming German habit of presenting his arse to the mirror so
as not to have to look at his own face. [*pause*] If you see what
I mean. [*pause*] Fraulein Bechner once inserted the tip of her
parasol in his nose. The old frog's duelling scars turned livid.
"Fraulein Bechner," he pleaded—

WERNER: With her parasol in his nose?

FATHER: With her parasol in his left nostril, to be precise. "Fraulein
Bechner"—I admit his tone was somewhat nasal—"What does
this mean, Fraulein?"

WERNER: And what did Bechner say?

FATHER: She said: I thought it was a baked potato. [*turns to the*
MOTHER] Fraulein *Bechner*, you know—

WERNER *is laughing.* MOTHER *peels an apple carefully.*

MOTHER: Yes. I know.

FATHER: Helenka—you're an artful woman.

MOTHER: I think we've been tolerably happy together. You have
your whores. *I* have Laugstein.

FATHER: Bechner is *not* a whore!

MOTHER: I don't know what else she is. Gifted people are so
unstable, aren't they?

FATHER: Bechner is *delectable*!

MOTHER: I'm surprised at you. With that pride of yours. [*pause*]
After all, you took her over from Kronfeld. I can't think why
else he should permit the business with the parasol. Unless you
were joking, that is.

FATHER: Kronfeld, my darling, is impotent.

MOTHER: And that's what you're afraid *you* are—isn't it Georgie?

FATHER: He did *not* permit the parasol—he *endured* it.

Pause.

MOTHER: Comes to the same thing.

FATHER: *to* WERNER] How about a game of billiards?

MOTHER: And tomorrow we shall go to Laugstein.

FATHER: *to* MOTHER, *rising*] One of us will undoubtedly go insane.
I fear it will be me.

He exits.

MOTHER: I wish your father and I had *some* secrets from you Werner. [*pause*] But he has never allowed that. He's quite logical. He insists that human beings are nothing more than complicated machines . . . that they exist only to afford each other cruel amusement. [*pause*] I have never fought him on the point, since I believe his self-respect depends upon it.

Pause.

WERNER: And *your* self-respect?

MOTHER: You think I'm weak, don't you?

WERNER: Each evening when you're in Berlin, there's this . . . degrading charade. It revolts me, bores me, baffles me—and I've never known you speak to each other in any other way.

MOTHER: We have no other way.

Pause.

WERNER: Are you—fond of him?

MOTHER: My feelings have atrophied into something like . . . like what? I don't know. Yes I do. [*pause*] Watchful fascination.

WERNER: Watchful?

Pause.

MOTHER: I'm entitled to protect myself.

WERNER: What from?

Pause.

MOTHER: He relies on me to . . . to impose rigid limits on my collusion with him in these encounters.

WERNER: Relies on *you*—?

MOTHER: *rising*] Your father has always feared he will go mad one day, Werner.

She exits. WERNER *drinks the rest of his wine.*

SCENE 16

A staircase. HELMUT *mounts it with* WERNER *over his shoulder.* WERNER *is swinging an empty bottle and laughing. They reach the landing— go through the door to* WERNER'S *bedroom.*
The bedroom. HELMUT *tips* WERNER *onto the bed and takes the bottle off him.*

WERNER: Music—

HELMUT: Ah, come on sir!

WERNER: *Music.*

HELMUT: What we goin' to do with you?

WERNER: Try doing what you're told.

HELMUT: Which record?

WERNER: Any bloody record.

HELMUT *roots about in a pile of records. He selects one and puts it on.*

WERNER: The wolves, Helmut—

HELMUT: You've heard that yarn a hundred bleedin' times.

He puts out all the lights except one near the bed, sits down resignedly.

HELMUT: It was in winter.

WERNER: In Poland.

HELMUT: I come to the station to fetch you and your mother, on the sledge.

WERNER: I was wrapped in furs.

HELMUT: You was wrapped in furs. You looked like a bloody badger.

WERNER: And we went to my great-uncle's castle through the forest.

HELMUT: It was a bitter night.

WERNER: But moonlight.

HELMUT: A fine full moon.

WERNER: And the sledge runners sang on the snow.

HELMUT: I never said that.

WERNER: *I* say it.

Pause.

HELMUT: Fanciful!

WERNER: There were charcoal burners under our feet.

HELMUT: I give you some chocolate.

WERNER: My mother took it away when you were packing our luggage onto the sledge.

HELMUT: She looked like a saint. That pale face of hers under her little fur hat.

WERNER: The wolves were running in packs that year. A hungry winter. Through the Polish forests. [*pause*] I was frightened, but you made me giggle. [*pause*] You bloody well made me giggle!

HELMUT: When I put your hands in your muff—I tickled your palms, sir.

WERNER: And our breath froze in the moonlight—

HELMUT: The pack followed us . . . in and out the trees . . . far as Krejczyn . . . far as—

WERNER: The runners *did* sing on the snow.

HELMUT: Sleep now, sir—

WERNER: And the wolves—

HELMUT: Did no harm. Stayed in the pines. [*pause*] You slept. [*pause*] A fat little bundle you was. Like a badger. [*pause*] And that night your mother . . . at the ball in your great-uncle's house—

WERNER: Danced the mazurka—

Pause.

HELMUT: That she did sir.

WERNER: With a distinguished Polish civil servant.

HELMUT: A gentleman. In white gloves. Red sash. [*pause*] Your father having remained in Berlin.

WERNER: Something to do with the Deutschmark.

WERNER *is falling asleep.* HELMUT *watches his eyes close, then covers him with the counterpane.*

SCENE 17

A sledge. Night. Moonlit forest. The adult WERNER, *wrapped in furs, sits beside his* MOTHER. *Her fur hat is inclined, her collar turned up— we see nothing of her in fact but her furs.*
The sound of the horses' hooves thudding in the snow. The hiss of the sledge runners. The jingle of sleighbells. In front is HELMUT. *We hear* HELMUT *shouting at the horses and cracking his whip.*

WERNER: Mother—

She neither replies nor moves.

WERNER: Mother—

No response. He turns to her, touches her arm. The fur coat collapses and the hat falls away—there is no one there. WERNER *screams.* HELMUT *turns, cracking his whip at* WERNER. WERNER *puts his arms up to defend himself and tumbles off the sledge.*
*A white expanse—*WERNER *lies, a dark shape against the whiteness.*

At the rim of the white, the moon rises—it is huge, and rises quickly like an enormous disc bouncing.

Close-up WERNER'S *face. There is only the moaning of the wind now. The overlarge moon hovers. There is the distant baying of wolves. We hear a horse breathing heavily.*

WERNER'S FATHER—*dressed as an Uhlan, mounted and carrying a lance, enters picture. He is wearing a cloak which reaches to his stirrups. Slowly he goes up to* WERNER, *and circles round him.*

Completing one circle, he reins the horse motionless. WERNER *looks up. With the tip of his lance, the* FATHER *gently prods him in the chest.*

FATHER: Werner—

Pause.

WERNER: Father—

Pause.

FATHER: Look—

Groping behind him, he drags something from behind the saddle and heaves it into the snow. It is a dead wolf.

FATHER: It's a long way to the castle. And I am due there to dance the mazurka with your mother. [*pause*] I shall wear white gloves. A red sash. [*pause*] My decorations. [*pause*] Though I warn you—the Polish branch of the family is very boring. [*pause*] Do you know what they've done to your cousin Anna? They've put her in a long white dress . . . and tied up her hair . . . and put her feet into little black patent leather shoes . . . and told her she shall dance the mazurka with you. [*pause*] Are you pleased? [*pause*] One day we shall bring Anna with us to Berlin. Naturally, the girl must be educated in Berlin. [*pause*] Warsaw, for all their ridiculous claims . . . is a village.

He circles WERNER *once again, and comes to a halt raising his lance.*

FATHER: Get up, my boy.

WERNER *stands.*

FATHER: Come here—

WERNER *approaches.*

FATHER: Have you been good?

WERNER: Yes father.

FATHER: Did you eat Helmut's chocolate?

WERNER: No father.

Pause.

FATHER: You must never eat Helmut's chocolate. [*pause*] He is poor, and the chocolate should go to Pomerania. To his children. You understand?

WERNER: Yes father.

FATHER: Are you a good German?

WERNER: Yes sir.

Pause.

FATHER: A fanatical German?

WERNER: Yes sir.

FATHER: And how do we regard this?

WERNER: You and I sir?

FATHER: You and I.

Pause.

WERNER: As a joke, father.

FATHER: We laugh, don't we?

WERNER: Yes father.

FATHER: Because?

WERNER *draws himself stiffly up to his full height and chants:*

WERNER: Because the aristocrat owes allegiance to nothing and no one. The true aristocrat has a duty to . . . to insulate himself from all forms of vulgarity. He transcends nationality, race and religion. His purpose is to accomplish only—himself. His role in society is one of detachment . . . of vigilant irony. [*pause*] The aristocrat —

FATHER: Enough!

WERNER: Sir.

FATHER: Excellent. [*pause*] Here—

*He throws his lance—*WERNER *catches it.*

FATHER: Fraulein Bechner—

Pause.

WERNER: Sir?

FATHER: Is nimble with both lance and parasol!

He starts laughing. WERNER *laughs. Slowly, the* FATHER *rides away.* WERNER *stirs the dead wolf with his foot.*

Still holding the lance, he turns to see the moon. It is growing larger and larger. There is a sudden loud yipping and baying. WERNER *turns to the wolf—it is gone.*

He hurls the lance away from him and kneels. The moon grows until it fills the screen.

SCENE 18

WERNER'S *bedroom. He lies quite still, his face running with sweat. The telephone rings in the dressing room.* WERNER'S *eyes open— otherwise he doesn't move.* HELMUT *enters.*

HELMUT: *quietly]* Sir?
WERNER: I'm awake.
HELMUT: On the telephone—Miss Anna. I said I'd fetch you. But she gave me an address and rang off.
   WERNER *sits up.* HELMUT *looks sullen.*
WERNER: Is she in trouble?
HELMUT: Could be—
   Pause.
WERNER: Do you know anything about it?
HELMUT: What would I know?
   Pause.
WERNER: You'd denounce her, wouldn't you!
HELMUT: I'm three monkeys in one, sir. Hear no evil, speak no evil, see no evil.
WERNER: Get my coat, and write the address. *Quickly—*
   WERNER *gets up and prepares to leave.*

SCENE 19

A briefing shed near the parachute tower. KLAUS, WERNER *and the others sit at desks. Facing them, a blackboard. A Wehrmacht* OFFICER *addresses them.*

OFFICER: Everything possible has been done to assure the safety of this parachute. It has been tried and tested to the point where only one further proof remains—that it should bear a fully equipped soldier to the ground. [*pause*] For this work you have all volunteered. [*pause*] I would remind you of the words of the Fuhrer: the heroism of the German people is invincible. Poland fell to us like a rotten apple. Our men and machines are the best in the world. We are a united nation. We require from our people in Germany sacrifices no less than those of our soldiers at the front—

Close up WERNER, *who is sitting at a desk next to* KLAUS. *The* OFFICER'S *voice becomes distant and muted.*

SCENE 20

A Berlin street. WERNER *approaches the back door in an office building. There is a deep portico. As he enters, two men come forward out of the darkness.*

MAN: Your name?

WERNER *hesitates.*

MAN: I said: Your *name?*

WERNER: von Reger. [*pause*] Are you—with Anna?

MAN: Come on—

He enters the building. WERNER *follows.*

A small office overlooking the main street. ANNA *sits by the window. The door opens—the* MAN *motions* WERNER *inside, then closes the door remaining in the corridor.* WERNER *stands looking at* ANNA— *the room is illuminated only by light from the street.*

ANNA: *smiling*] Well. You've made *one* decision!

WERNER: Is that what you wanted?

ANNA: I don't really expect to be alive tomorrow.

WERNER: Do your friends agree?

ANNA: They don't pretend not to be frightened.

WERNER *crosses to the window. A hunting rifle with telescopic sights is leaning against the sill. He picks it up.*

WERNER: Who?

ANNA: Schacht.

WERNER: Where?

ANNA: In that restaurant across the street. [*she smiles*] He's devoted to his mother. Every Tuesday evening they dine together over there. They go in at ten, and leave at twelve. [*pause*] Last week

I dined at the next table. She asks him about his laundry, his drinking . . . his women. He's rather evasive about the women.

WERNER: Does it help, knowing that Schacht is a homosexual?
Pause.

ANNA: Why should it?

WERNER: What you're doing—it's not only puerile, it's farcical. And ringing me! What an amateur you are! I'm surprised your friends haven't deserted you.
Pause.

ANNA: Schacht will be commandant of the camp at Laugstein. [*pause*] Would have been.

WERNER: If you miss—*will* be. In any case, they'll appoint another man at once.

ANNA: I didn't think you'd come. I was a bit hysterical when I rang you. If I'd waited a few minutes longer . . . it passed off.

WERNER: I came to stop you.

ANNA: That's not possible.

WERNER: It's ridiculous.
Pause.

ANNA: I admit that what I want to know more than anything . . . is whether I can do it. [*pause*] And if I can . . . what you'll make of it.

WERNER: I know now. It's—irrational. [*looks out of the window*] I wonder what Schacht is eating. Drinking. I wonder what he and his mother are talking about. [*pause*] I pity them.

ANNA: There'll be war this autumn.

WERNER: I know.

ANNA: Do you pity those they'll take to Laugstein?
Pause.

WERNER: Yes.
Pause.

ANNA: A moment before you came I realised, it does make a difference that Schacht is a homosexual.

WERNER: You're killing the homosexual?

ANNA: I'm killing Schacht.

WERNER: But you *are* uneasy—

ANNA: No. [*pause*] I'd still be doing it if he wasn't. [*pause*] I knew

you'd pick on that. Why do you? [*pause*] They'll be out soon.
She takes the rifle and tries the bolt.

WERNER: What *kind* of difference does it make that Schacht's queer?

Pause.

ANNA: You know.

WERNER: Do I?

ANNA: Yes.

WERNER: What? [*he goes to her and shakes her*] What?
He steps back. ANNA *can hardly speak.*

WERNER: It excites you! Yes? However little. And what follows is that you've how shall I put it? Lost your arbitrariness. Haven't you?

Pause.

ANNA: Yes.

Pause.

WERNER: No one's execution is arbitrary. [*pause*] The *choice* of Schacht is arbitrary, at the most.

ANNA: Leave me now.

He wrenches the gun from her.

WERNER: Shall I do it?

ANNA: *Could* you?

Pause. He hands back the gun.

WERNER: I think not.

ANNA: So—leave me.

Pause.

WERNER: You hoped I might.

ANNA: Your father will be amused. After all, he taught me to shoot. [*pause*] Well. We both know what it is to adore someone who understands everything and feels nothing. [*pause*] You and your father seem to be invulnerable. It can't be so. You both seem to think my revulsion and anger are some kind of unfortunate aberration. If he saw me here now with this rifle he'd screw his eyes up and laugh. So gently . . . so tenderly . . . like a man bending over a child in a cradle. Pauvre Anna chérie! [*pause*] Are you going to plonk a bullet between the eyes of the redoubtable Schacht? You might at least allow him to digest his supper first—

WERNER: *smiling*] I think that's *exactly* what he would say.

ANNA: He notices what people do—but not what they are. If he has an insight about someone, he regards it as some curious invention of his own.

WERNER: Better than putting his trust in cheap psychology.

Pause.

ANNA: Do you believe I shall kill Schacht?

WERNER: The people in your organisation must be out of their minds.

ANNA: They aren't involved.

WERNER: And those two outside?

ANNA *laughs. She goes to the window.*

ANNA: They are boys. They believe in *me*. I'm sure that will irritate you.

WERNER: I see. But they don't believe in *you* to the point of doing your assassinating for you—

ANNA: Why should they believe in me as much as that?

WERNER: Schacht's death . . . the death of any one of them . . . is completely irrelevant now.

ANNA: It's unlike you to state the obvious.

Pause.

WERNER: I dreamt this evening that I was going to Wyslowo. To your grandfather's. Do you remember the night of that ball? When wolves followed our sledge from the station? [*pause*] You and I were turned out like little dolls. We danced the mazurka. Everyone laughed and clapped.

ANNA: We took a plate of hot piroshki away, and ate them in one of the bedrooms.

WERNER: And we tried . . . as you put it then . . . to "do what grown-ups do", under the bed.

ANNA: I'd had two glasses of champagne.

WERNER: Helmut gave me vodka—in the kitchen.

ANNA: And I solemnly assured you the next day that I was pregnant!

Pause.

WERNER: And now—we're here!

Pause.

ANNA: But I was always happiest at Laugstein—

WERNER: I shall go down into the street. I shall wait for you *not* to do it. Then we'll go home. And tomorrow we'll go to Laugstein.

ANNA says nothing. Turns away from him. WERNER goes out.

The street. The entrance to the restaurant. Opposite, WERNER stands lighting a cigarette.

SCHACHT and his mother emerge. He stands a moment, puffing at his cigar. His mother is pulling her gloves on. He sees WERNER— he is pleased.

SCHACHT: My dear young von Reger! All alone?

WERNER: Well, I—

SCHACHT: Come and meet my mother—mother, it's George's boy.

After the briefest hesitation, WERNER crosses the street. SCHACHT shakes his hand. The three of them are now close together.

SCHACHT: Mother—Werner von Reger.

She smiles and shakes hands.

MRS. SCHACHT: I used to know your father quite well. But I hardly ever go out now. [*turning to SCHACHT*] Only when Heini takes me to dinner—

SCHACHT: How *is* your father? Oh, he's a terror! I was with Goering only the other day and he mentioned George, you know. That von Reger! Such men—backbone of the nation. But he's so difficult. A naughty man! It isn't true that Goering lacks a sense of humour. Are you waiting for a girl?

WERNER: I am, as a matter of fact.

SCHACHT: Don't let us keep you, my boy. Mother, show him what I bought you.

MRS. SCHACHT: Oh Heini—

SCHACHT: Come along, come along—

She fumbles in her coat and pulls out a pendant. SCHACHT takes her other hand and kisses it.

SCHACHT: Now what do you think of that? Here, take a proper look—

SCHACHT takes the pendant, holding it up. WERNER has no option but to bend towards it in the poor light. A shot rings out—WERNER is hit. As he falls, SCHACHT catches him in his arms. MRS. SCHACHT screams. SCHACHT nods towards the restaurant entrance, as he takes WERNER in both arms.

SCHACHT: In there. *Quickly.*

MRS. SCHACHT *hurries into the restaurant.* SCHACHT *reaches the portico, and looks round. Another shot rings out and ricochets off the wall by* SCHACHT'S *head.* SCHACHT *kneels in the shadows and puts* WERNER *down. A head waiter emerges from the ante-room of the restaurant.*

SCHACHT: The police. Telephone. And be quick about it. Ambulance as well.

The waiter goes back. SCHACHT *kneels by* WERNER—*touches his neck gently where the wound is. His hand comes away covered in blood.*

SCHACHT: Werner . . . Werner—

He takes one of WERNER'S *hands, holds it between his own. Then he presses it to his cheek.* WERNER'S *eyes open slightly. He half smiles.*

WERNER: What are you doing, Heini?

Immediately, SCHACHT *releases* WERNER'S *hand.*

SCHACHT: Is it something you're mixed up in, you silly bastard?

WERNER: It's funny. I'd have expected you to panic. You look like a smug pig when you're exerting self-control Heini! Shall I live?

SCHACHT: Of course you will—

WERNER: What a pity!

WERNER'S *eyes close.*

SCENE 21

The briefing room at the tower. The men rise from their desks and move out, orderly fashion.

Outside, they line up. They are marched across the field to the tower. The field is deep in mud. Near the tower, they are lined up again, and stood at ease by the CORPORAL.

CORPORAL: Now then, here's the jumping order. As yer name's called, break out smartly and get up that bloody tower. Right? Reger, Koval, Breuer, Savitsky, Redl—you five first. You know what to do and how to do it. Any man breaks a limb, he'll find me standing on his neck—breaks his neck, [*with a grin*] he wants his head examining.

The other men whose names have been called break ranks. WERNER *seems not to have heard.* KLAUS, *who stands beside him, shakes his arm.*

CORPORAL: Reger—what you waiting for? A printed invitation? Chop chop—

WERNER *breaks ranks and heads for the tower. At the base of the tower, a* SERGEANT *checks their equipment.*

SERGEANT: Right. [*to* WERNER] You first son. Come down in one piece and it's free booze tonight and a medal when they've had a word in the Fuhrer's shell-like.

WERNER *goes to the tower and begins to climb. Part of the way up he looks down. We see the rest of the men in long shot.* KLAUS *waves.*

SCENE 22

WERNER'S *bedroom. His* FATHER *stands smoking by the window.* WERNER, *with his neck in bandages, sits in a chair with a rug over his knees.* HOLZ—*a plain clothes man—is talking.*

HOLZ: I'm asking you, Baron, to make the young man speak. [*pause*] In both your interests.

We see the street from WERNER'S FATHER'S *point of view. A black saloon car, and a man lounging against it.*

FATHER: What does Schacht have to say?

Pause.

HOLZ: Schacht killed himself two days ago. [*pause*] His mother was away. He went into her bedroom. Got into her bed. And killed himself. With brandy and sleeping pills. [*pause*] You'll appreciate, I shouldn't be talking to you like this. [*pause*] Schacht was a degenerate.

HOLZ *goes close to* WERNER—*bends down and looks into his eyes.*

HOLZ: The bullet was intended for poor Schacht, of course—

WERNER: I don't know.

Pause.

HOLZ: I told you. We have the girl here. In the street. In a car. [*pause*] Shall I bring her up?

WERNER: Do what you like.

HOLZ: Baron . . . I can do nothing. I am, as it were, under orders to do nothing. I believe I have you to thank for that.

FATHER: Does it irritate you?

Pause.

HOLZ: I have a servile temperament. And like all servile people I have a masochistic admiration for those who humiliate me. [*pause*] I am intelligent, ambitious, ruthless . . . I was a lawyer once, you know. And here I am talking to you like this. [*pause*] Why is that? Because you are beyond the reach of my power . . . there aren't many of you who are. [*pause*] And one wonders how you . . . maintain . . . how you . . . achieve this splendid immunity. [*pause*] If . . . well let me put it like this, Baron. I am allowed to offend you—between these four walls. But I musn't threaten . . . or damage . . . or I shall get my knuckles rapped. [*pause*] How do I feel then? I feel like a precocious child—but still a child. [*pause*] My world is a cellar, really. I'm a cultured man. And in my cellar, as you well know, I have to do the most uncivilised things. [*pause*] I will say Baron . . . you give one a sense of freedom. You permit one to feel that one may talk. And instantly—I feel ashamed. You give me the authentic moral "frisson" Baron! Why is that? Not for what I am; but for what I am in relation to what you are. And what is that? [*pause*] That, regrettably, is something I don't understand.

FATHER: Werner—

WERNER: Yes?

FATHER: Are you listening?

WERNER: Yes.

HOLZ: The boy . . . and Schacht. Do you understand? That's what I mean. Something there. Something one has to know. Because Schacht left a note. More of a scrawl. Barely decipherable. Two or three words. [*pause*] Darling Werner . . . I want to tell you . . . and at that point he gave up.

He crosses again to WERNER.

HOLZ: *What* did he want to tell you? Darling Werner—

WERNER: I—

HOLZ: Did it concern—Laugstein?

WERNER: How should I know?

His FATHER *crosses to him as* HOLZ *moves away with a smile.* FATHER *takes* WERNER'S *face between his hands tenderly.*

FATHER: I can have this man shot. [*pause*] I really can arrange that. [*pause*] He knows. [*pause*] You need say nothing about Schacht . . . Or Anna. You need say nothing at all.

He turns away. HOLZ *looks pleased.* WERNER *lifts his head.*

HOLZ: That is absolutely true. I'm here . . . how shall I put it? On sufferance. On your father's sufferance. [*pause*] He permits me in his house . . . because the girl is out there in the car. Because he doesn't want to test his authority too far. He daren't seek its limits!

FATHER: The one thing you people respect me for is my contempt!

HOLZ: Oh, we *respect* you Baron!

FATHER: If there's anything at all in the idea of racial characteristics . . . that is the German discovery: that people who despise them with confidence make them want to obey!

HOLZ: What a ribald cynic your father is!

WERNER: I spent one evening with Schacht. [*to his* FATHER] Fraulein Bechner took me to a private room in a restaurant where he was dining. [*pause*] I'd spent the afternoon in bed with her.

FATHER: Now that *is* extraordinary!

WERNER: No. Not at all. [*pause*] I got drunk . . . I went to her flat. I said: are you as nihilistic as my father?

FATHER: Callow boy!

WERNER: She was sitting there . . . sipping cointreau.

FATHER: Which you loathe—

WERNER: She said: I know what *you've* come for!

FATHER: People with limited imaginations have a nasty faculty of knowing what one *is* after—

WERNER: So—

FATHER: So you had a charming incestuous afternoon.

WERNER: I—

FATHER: Bechner is skilful without being patronising—that's what a young man needs, isn't it?

Pause.

HOLZ: Can we . . . get back to Schacht?

FATHER: Holz—if you don't let him get round to it in his own way I shall have you thrown out.

HOLZ: I *beg* your pardon!

FATHER: After all, it's *I* who am the aggrieved party—

WERNER: Are you, father?

FATHER: You might have told me. I'd have given you Bechner *any* time. Her collar bones are beginning to irritate me.

WERNER: I went with her to theatre. Met her afterwards. She said: I'm dining with Schacht. [*pause*] She said: some women *need* a queer in their lives.

FATHER: They do! It's the most harmless form of aggression they ever go in for.

WERNER: We got into this private room. She introduced me. She said: this is von Reger's boy . . . doesn't he look sullen? He looks sullen because he humped me this afternoon. Humped me till I'm sore. I danced badly. I feel very fractious . . . and *he* feels sordid for going with his father's mistress.

Pause.

HOLZ: Well?

Pause.

FATHER: *Well?*

Pause.

WERNER: We all drank ourselves stupid.

FATHER: And then?

WERNER: Bechner left us. [*pause*] I believe she was seeing you that night.

FATHER: I'm beginning to ask myself whether some small part of me *might* be capable of resentment! [*pause*] That's very tedious—

HOLZ: And you and Schacht—?

WERNER: Went back to his flat.

Pause.

FATHER: For high jinks?

Pause.

WERNER: He wanted—

Pause.

FATHER: But you—?

Pause.

WERNER: I was full of maudlin pity.

FATHER: Schacht *was* capable of inspiring one to that. [*pause*] So you—

WERNER: I hit him.

FATHER: Hard?

WERNER: No. But he collapsed on the floor and cried. Then he got up and started screaming at me. [*pause*] So I left.

SCENE 23

Close-up WERNER *on the tower ladder. He is clinging tightly—not climbing. Cut to:*

The ground below. KLAUS *and the others are standing around.* KLAUS *lights a cigarette with difficulty—the wind sighs and moans across the field. Some distance away—*KOEPFER *and the others who attacked* WERNER *in the showers. Camera pans across their faces.* KOEPFER *is looking up at the tower—he smiles to himself.*

A long high shot of the men in the field from WERNER'S *point of view. Close-up* WERNER. *He resumes climbing. The wind is very loud.*

SCENE 24

WERNER'S *bedroom. He lies in bed—a doctor is withdrawing a hypodermic needle from his arm.* WERNER'S FATHER *stands watching.* WERNER *smiles at him.*

WERNER: What happened?

FATHER: You started screaming at Holz. Then you collapsed.

WERNER: And—Holz?

FATHER: Has left. Temporarily, no doubt.

  Pause.

WERNER: Anna?

  Pause.

FATHER: Here.

WERNER: I must see her.

FATHER: You are going to sleep now.

WERNER: I *must*.

FATHER: When you wake.

WERNER: Holz . . . has released her?

Pause.

FATHER: They have no real evidence. But then, they never need any. [*pause*] She's here with a guard. [*smiling*] He thinks he's being subtle. He needs something. [*pause*] Otherwise he'd have a bullet put through her neck in what he calls his "cellar". [*pause*] She looks well. Even quite truculent! It's me Holz wants. And knows he can't manage it. Very frustrating for him.

WERNER: Father—

FATHER: Now go to sleep.

WERNER: Do you remember that night at Wyslowo?

Pause.

FATHER: The ball?

WERNER: Yes.

FATHER: I wasn't there.

WERNER: You were. It was the night you killed a wolf.

FATHER: You're already dreaming, Werner.

Pause.

WERNER: Yes. I'm confused. [*pause*] I often confuse what happened and what I dreamed. And sometimes, I dream that I only dream what I believe really happens.

FATHER: *laughing*] You *are* confused!

WERNER: I loved Wyslowo—

Pause.

FATHER: They'll take Poland in a matter of weeks.

WERNER: And then?

FATHER: *shrugs*] France. Belgium. Holland. The English will fight. The Americans will decide it all, one way or the other.

WERNER: *Have* you ever killed a wolf?

FATHER: I did shoot one near Wyslowo. When you were a baby.

WERNER: I'm feeling drowsy, now—

FATHER: I'll leave you, my boy.

WERNER: Wait until I'm asleep.

He closes his eyes, putting his hand out over the covers. His FATHER *takes his hand, sitting on the bed. After a moment, he bends down, presses* WERNER'S *hand to his cheek. Then he leaves.*

WERNER'S *hand comes up and touches his bandaged neck—rests there. Softly, far away, we hear a piano playing a Chopin mazurka. Close-up* WERNER.

SCENE 25

A row of high concrete posts, curved at the top and connected by barbed wire—part of the perimeter of a camp.

On one side is a wooden inspection platform. On the far side of the wire, a row of chairs. On one of the chairs sits ANNA, *dressed as described by* WERNER'S FATHER *in the first dream—white dress etc. The mazurka continues, underlaid by the sound of a rising wind.*

WERNER *and* HELMUT *come into shot.* WERNER *is in the full dress uniform of a high-ranking Wehrmacht officer.* HELMUT *leads a black Alsatian dog. They ascend the steps onto the platform.* WERNER *stands with both hands on the rail, looking through the wire.* HELMUT *remains just behind him. The music gets louder.* WERNER *raises his arm in the Nazi salute.* ANNA *looks up. She stands, curtsies, and begins to dance the mazurka.*

She dances a few moments, then we hear the heavy sound of marching feet. Crowds cheering. The dog barks. WERNER *turns to look at* HELMUT, *who smiles and points.* WERNER *turns back.*

A montage of rally sequences from the thirties—troops, banners, tanks and guns. Cheering and singing. Cross cuts from WERNER *with his arm raised to the montage sequences.*

Suddenly everything stops and we close up ANNA, *who is finishing her dance with a curtsy.* WERNER *now stands in front of her. The dog is raging up and down the wire behind him, barking.*

Silence, except for the wind.

WERNER *clicks his fingers. Arc lamps all round switch on. He and* ANNA *stand in a pool of glaring light.*

WERNER: Fraulein Bechner?

ANNA: Baron von Reger?

WERNER: What can I do? How can I protect you?
  Pause.

ANNA: If you love me—
  WERNER *looks round. Begins to shout.*

WERNER: This is *not* Laugstein!
  Pause.

ANNA: But it is. Look—
  She points at the chairs. On one of them slumps SCHACHT—*dead. She leads* WERNER *to him.*

WERNER: Schacht—
ANNA: You see. It *is* Laugstein.
  WERNER *kneels beside the chair.*
WERNER: *Schacht—*
  He turns away—to see HOLZ *emerge from the shadows, smiling.*
HOLZ: *softly*] Darling Werner—
WERNER: Listen—
  HOLZ *points at* ANNA.
HOLZ: No *you* listen! [*pause*] She's yours.
WERNER: *rising*] And—am I *yours?*
  HOLZ *laughs and walks away into the shadows. He stops and turns*
  before disappearing.
HOLZ: I ordered the sledge. Why don't you take her to Wyslowo?
  [*exits*]
  The lights go out except for two spots on WERNER *and* ANNA'S *faces.*
WERNER: Shall I?
ANNA: Yes. I'm tired.
  We hear the thud of horses hooves . . . sleigh bells. ANNA *takes*
  WERNER'S *hand—they walk into the darkness.*

SCENE 26

A sunny garden. Through a door in a wall, WERNER *leads* ANNA *by the*
hand. They are both dressed in light summer clothes of the twenties.
There is a children's garden swing. On it, standing, is WERNER'S FATHER
in morning clothes and top hat.

WERNER: The snow's gone!
FATHER: You know I never come to Wyslowo in the winter.
WERNER: Where's mother?
  FATHER *points. Some distance away,* WERNER'S MOTHER *stands quite*
  still, shading herself with a parasol.
WERNER: You sent for us—
FATHER: *swinging*] Bechner . . . you look delicious.
ANNA: You look rather silly yourself.
  He steps down from the swing, comes to ANNA.
FATHER: You have betrayed me with my own son.
ANNA: Don't be tiresome, Georgie.

FATHER: I wouldn't say I trusted you. On the other hand, mistrust should go unconfirmed if it is to remain enjoyable.

WERNER *goes to his* MOTHER. *She smiles.*

WERNER: Listen to those two bickering!

MOTHER: She *is* delightful though—

WERNER: On the way here . . . there was snow. Why is there no snow here mother?

Pause.

MOTHER: Darling, it's spring in Wyslowo.

WERNER: Do you really like her?

MOTHER: I think she is adorable.

WERNER: And father—?

MOTHER: Your father told me he's beginning to find her a shade scrawny.

WERNER: He's jealous!

MOTHER: He wants you to be happy.

WERNER *points up the garden. A huge four poster stands on a lawn, with fine filmy curtains lifting slightly in a breeze.*

WERNER: Is that where we shall be married?

MOTHER: Yes darling.

WERNER: Immediately?

MOTHER: At once. Then your father and I will return to Berlin.

WERNER: Listen—

They listen. We hear the sound of bells—softly, then gradually swelling in volume. He turns. His FATHER is coming towards him with ANNA on his arm—she is smiling radiantly.

WERNER *takes his* MOTHER'S *arm. The four of them—*WERNER *and* ANNA *in the middle—walk to the bed.*

At the bed, the four stand immobile for a moment. Then the parents kiss WERNER *and* ANNA. FATHER *pulls the bedclothes back at one side—*ANNA *gets in.* MOTHER *does the same for* WERNER.

WERNER *and* ANNA *sit with the sheets up to their chins.* FATHER *snaps his fingers. Two footmen enter picture—one to each side of the bed. They carry silver salvers containing Russian meat patties.*

ANNA: Piroshki!

WERNER: Piroshki!

The salvers are placed on the bed and the footmen withdraw. The parents smile indulgently.

FATHER *looks at his watch.*

FATHER: Helmut will be waiting with the sledge—

MOTHER: We must go, children—

FATHER: Brace up, boy—

MOTHER: Fraulein Bechner . . . he is . . . inexperienced, you know—

FATHER *raises his hat.*

FATHER: Versailles was a farce. The mark is deteriorating. Some upstart in Bavaria is making trouble. [*pause*] One returns to one's responsibilities.

MOTHER: I'm not sure that he *knows* what grownups do!

FATHER: What's more, you'll inherit those responsibilities. So make the most of things now—

He replaces his hat, moves away.

MOTHER: Goodbye children—

ANNA: Goodbye mother—

WERNER: Goodbye mother—

MOTHER *and* FATHER *exit. Silence. The mazurka begins again, softly.*

WERNER: He's one of the most powerful men in Germany.

ANNA: Isn't.

WERNER: *Is* then.

ANNA: *Isn't* then.

WERNER: *Hindenburg* came to our house in Berlin.

ANNA: *That* old josser!

WERNER: He ruffled my hair.

ANNA: *That* old winkle!

Pause.

WERNER: *What* do grownups do?

ANNA: I told you.

Pause.

WERNER: They don't.

ANNA: They do then. I've seen them.

WERNER: Who?

ANNA: Them.

WERNER: Liar.

Pause.

ANNA: It's like fighting.

Pause.

WERNER: I feel peculiar in the stomach.

Pause.

ANNA: So do I.

WERNER *kneels.*

WERNER: Father says . . . he says . . . that Germany is rotten, but one will learn to ignore the smell.

ANNA *giggles.* WERNER *smiles at her.*

WERNER: Can I touch you?

ANNA: If you like.

WERNER: It's all right. We're married.

ANNA: I don't care.

WERNER: Well then—

ANNA: Well then—

WERNER *laughs and pulls the sheets over them. There is a lot of giggling and movement under the sheets. The mazurka plays louder.*

SCENE 27

WERNER'S *bedroom. He wakes with a start. The door is opening.* ANNA *comes into the room and slowly walks towards the bed.*

*The tower—*WERNER.

*The ground—*KLAUS.

Close-up WERNER*—the mazurka.*

WERNER'S *bedroom.* ANNA *stands by the bed.*

WERNER: Holz?

ANNA: Coming soon.

WERNER: To take you away?

ANNA *shrugs.*

WERNER: I dreamt we were at Wyslowo.

ANNA: I dozed on a sofa. Me at one end. The guard at the other.

Pause.

WERNER: And—father?

ANNA: Pacifying your mother. She's hysterical.

Pause.

WERNER: There was nothing between me and Schacht.

ANNA: I know nothing about you and Schacht.

Pause.

WERNER: No. [*pause*] It was me you shot, after all.

Pause.

ANNA: I went to a flat . . . friends . . . in Leibnitzstrasse. That's where they found me. I don't know how. [*pause*] There was nothing to associate me with the shooting. [*pause*] They took me to their headquarters . . . and into what Holz calls his "cellar". [*pause*] They gave me coffee and cigarettes. [*pause*] When Holz arrived, he said: Strip her. So they did. [*pause*] One of them even apologised. [*pause*] Since I was a child, no one has seen me naked. I wanted to cover myself. But I kept my hands by my sides. [*pause*] I thought of you lying in the street . . . dead . . . or wounded . . . I didn't know. I thought of what you said about being arbitrary. I thought: is Holz arbitrary in all this?

WERNER: Schacht killed himself. [*pause*] He was in my dream. Dead. At Laugstein camp.

ANNA: Are you in pain?

WERNER: No.

ANNA: Do you want me to stay?

WERNER: Yes.

ANNA: Something's happened to me. I feel so detached . . . since the cellar. Almost cold. [*pause*] Towards you. [*pause*] I don't care what happens to me. [*pause*] I was trying to kill Schacht for you. To show you what could be done. [*pause*] Is that how women always function? Is it? [*pause*] I tried to act passionately for you. Perhaps—to make you ashamed. But then, you were ashamed to begin with. None of us lacks shame. What we lack is the will to turn it into something else. [*pause*] Women suffer from being able to see so clearly what men *ought* to do! It's a bitter, poisonous insight. It ignores men, really. [*pause*] Well. You see how it ended up. Shall I tell you more? What a rough concrete floor feels like under your bare feet? What it's like in a room full of uniformed men to look down and see your own bare breasts . . . and your nipples stiff with the cold air? [*pause*] I noticed . . . after a moment or two . . . a gutter in the floor. I thought: one day all this will become a kind of mythology . . . that the world will slowly turn more and more deaf to. [*pause*] It will become *embarrassing*. And suddenly—I started laughing. I thought: Werner could be dead. And I am here. And Holz is looking me up and down. I thought: if any of us survive—shall we understand it? [*pause*] I laughed. [*pause*] My breasts shook. [*pause*] They found that . . . exciting. [*pause*] And then I was sick. They watched that. Holz was smoking. [*pause*] Does all this mean anything to you?

Pause.

WERNER: My father will have it stopped.

Pause.

ANNA: I thought they would hurt me. Rape me. [*pause*] At that moment all I could think was: I wish Werner and I had slept together. [*pause*] But all they did was stare. I think they know instinctively what damages people most. I suddenly realised that torture is infinitely complicated . . . and can be subtle.

WERNER: You knew that before—

ANNA: Not in the same way.

WERNER: You went to a room with a gun. With a purpose. Didn't you? You knew all about it. We're not among those who'll ever be able to plead ignorance. [*pause*] You know the politics of it. The history of it. The psychology of it. [*pause*] So do I.

ANNA: They left the cellar, all except one. He was ordered to make me stand there and he did. [*pause*] What with fear . . . and exhaustion . . . I was amazed to find myself drowsy. I was swaying on my feet, half asleep and half awake.

WERNER: So, there wasn't really an interrogation?

ANNA: If you mean questions—no.

WERNER: But they knew who you were.

ANNA: Yes.

Pause.

WERNER: Holz came here to ask his questions.

ANNA *can't help smiling at this.*

ANNA: I *am* sorry!

Pause.

WERNER: My father's the only one who knows exactly what is happening.

ANNA: Yes. All we have to do is wait for him to pull a few strings—

Pause.

WERNER: I see what it is I don't like.

ANNA: *What?*

Pause.

WERNER: It's your sense of rectitude. Your superiority. [*pause*] Your high moral tone.

Pause.

ANNA: You always seem to be quoting your father.

WERNER: And you turn suffering into a form of blackmail!

ANNA: That's true. [*pause*] I can't help it. I find it as nauseating as you do.

WERNER: No. I don't. It just makes me feel—helpless.

ANNA: You know . . . I *could* have given you a highly comic version of what happened in the cellar. I could have made you laugh, I think. If I hadn't been pleading for your concern.

WERNER: For a concern which you think I simply . . . lack.

ANNA: It doesn't matter any longer.

WERNER: You want to say: Werner would have been different, if it weren't for his father.

ANNA: Maybe one day *you* will want to say that.

WERNER: Then you understand neither him nor me.

Pause.

ANNA: Don't you *see?* Your mother understood him. She shut herself off from him. [*pause*] She *survived*.

WERNER: My mother had the advantage of being relatively adult when she met him! I believe my first encounter with him was when I was twenty-five minutes old. She did well to shut herself off from him! It was probably then when he began to take a diabolical interest in me. [*pause*] I'm not a bit like him. I don't emulate him. [*pause*] I *approve* of him. I approve of his style, his money, his irony. I think in his way, he's a profound man. No one could ever use him, or manipulate him. [*pause*] He's been outmoded, that's all. [*pause*] Outmoded, *without* being usurped! [*pause*] I digress, don't I? [*pause*] What you want me to concentrate on is you naked in Holz's cellar and your feelings about it.

Pause.

ANNA: Yes. That's what I want you to concentrate on.

WERNER: I sometimes think you're obsessed with my redemption!

ANNA: Redemption from?

Pause.

WERNER: Perhaps—detachment.

ANNA: Standing in the cellar, I had a kind of dream about Wyslowo. [*pause*] We were in the house. You took my hand. We ran upstairs, into one of the bedrooms. [*pause*] Your father was sitting in one of the chairs—dead. [*pause*] I awoke. The guard was looking at me. I said: Won't you let me sit down? [*pause*] He said: Lie down. [*pause*] So I did. [*pause*] He came and knelt in front of me. He brought his gun towards me. I curled up. He said: If you move, I shall shoot. [*pause*] I just lay there. [*pause*] Werner, listen. He put the barrel of his gun into me. Not far. It wasn't painful. [*pause*] He said: Are you a virgin? I said: Yes. He laughed. He said: How'd you like to be deflowered with a bullet?

WERNER *turns over, buries his face in the pillow.*

ANNA: Werner *listen! Werner!*

WERNER: Get out.

ANNA: Werner—

WERNER: *Get out!*

Pause.

ANNA: That was all, Werner.

WERNER: *Please—*

Pause.

ANNA: If you know what they are capable of—why can't you listen?

WERNER: *Out!*

ANNA: What won't you *admit?*

WERNER *begins to sob.* ANNA *looks at him for a moment, then turns and slowly walks out of the room.*

SCENE 28

The tower. Close-up WERNER. *He is running his fingers over his parachute harness.*
The ground: KLAUS.

The tower. The wind is high. WERNER *looks round him once—and jumps.*
The ground—big close-up of KLAUS'S *face. He registers* WERNER'S *jump. After a second his face clenches with horror.*

KLAUS: *Werner—*

Track KLAUS *running across the field.* WERNER *lies sprawled and twisted in a very muddy part of the field. His parachute is crumpled beside him.*
We see the SERGEANT *blow a whistle. An army ambulance at one end of the field begins to rev and plough through the mud.*
KLAUS *reaches* WERNER *first. He kneels beside him.*

KLAUS: Werner . . . Werner—

The SERGEANT *comes running up. He kneels down, pushing* KLAUS *aside.*

SERGEANT: The silly sod. The stupid bastard.
KLAUS: What do you mean? The chute opened.
SERGEANT: Didn't it then! *Didn't* it!

He bends over WERNER, *pulling at his tunic. The ambulance approaches.*

KLAUS: He's dead—
The SERGEANT *has his head down on* WERNER'S *chest.*
SERGEANT: He's not bloody dead. He ought to be. [*looking up at* KLAUS] You saw. He ballsed it up. He bloody ballsed it—
Pause.
KLAUS: Or else the chute—
SERGEANT: Don't talk to me about the bloody chute, sonny boy. He went off that tower like a bleeding sleepwalker. What's the matter with you? What've I spent weeks training you twats for? Now get back there, will you?
The ambulance pulls up shrieking in the mud beside WERNER. KLAUS *goes back to the others and joins them in line. From their point of view we see the stretcher bearers get* WERNER *onto a stretcher and into the ambulance. The* SERGEANT *stands close by, watching them.*
Camera pans along the faces of the men.
The SERGEANT *turns and comes to the line. He goes to* KLAUS, *jerks*

his thumb in the direction of the ambulance.

SERGEANT: Go on, then! Go with him.

KLAUS *goes to the ambulance, stops and looks up at the tower—
gets in.*

SCENE 29

Inside the ambulance. KLAUS *crouches by the stretcher.* WERNER *opens
his eyes.*

WERNER: Klaus?

KLAUS: I'm here.

Pause.

WERNER: So. [*pause*] I'm alive.

KLAUS: Are you in bad pain?

WERNER: I'm—numb. I can't feel anything. [*pause*] Do you know
what happened?

KLAUS: No.

WERNER: The chute did open—

KLAUS: Yes. [*pause*] Not soon enough.

Pause.

WERNER: My back's broken.

KLAUS: Now listen—

WERNER: Do you think I deliberately—?

Pause.

KLAUS: I don't know.

Pause.

WERNER: Why should I?

KLAUS: It's a miracle. That you're alive. [*pause*] The mud—

WERNER: Do you think I—

KLAUS: *Did* you?

Pause.

WERNER: I don't know.

KLAUS: You *must* know!

Pause.

WERNER: Well. I'm out of the war.

KLAUS: Yes.
Pause.
WERNER: I suppose that could seem like a motive.
KLAUS: Except that it was nearly certain death.
Pause.
WERNER: I'm crippled.
KLAUS: *Stop* it Werner!
Pause.
WERNER: When I come out of hospital . . . I want to go to Laugstein.

SCENE 30

A terrace overlooking the grounds at Laugstein. WERNER'S MOTHER *sits vacantly in a chair. Windows open into a large room. A horizontal invalid carriage appears, with* HELMUT *pushing, between the folded back windows.* WERNER *lies in it, an open book face down on his chest.* HELMUT *wheels the carriage to a spot on the terrace facing* HELEN VON REGER'S *chair.*

HELMUT: There, sir. Now I'll go and get you unpacked.
WERNER'S MOTHER *stirs. She looks at him.*
MOTHER: Georgie?
WERNER: No, mother.
MOTHER: You look like George.
Pause.
WERNER: It's Werner, mother.
MOTHER: You *are* George!
WERNER: Helmut told you. Father was killed in an air raid on Berlin a month ago.
Pause.
MOTHER: I'm so young. [*pause*] So young. [*pause*] When you first took me to Wyslowo I said: you want me? George van Reger wants me? [*pause*] Every young woman in Vienna and Berlin wants you! [*pause*] Rich . . . titled . . . arrogant. [*pause*] You teased me for saying it George. I remember how my face burned.

You put your fingertips on my cheeks. [*pause*] They were cool. [*pause*] Your fingers smelled of lilac, George.

WERNER: Mother—

MOTHER: I know, I know. Your back was broken in an air raid. [*pause*] You'll never ride again. Never shoot. [*pause*] There'll be no more Fraulein Bechners for *you*, Georgie.

She laughs. WERNER *looks away from her.*

WERNER: There are papers for you to sign mother—

MOTHER: Oh, yes! Papers! [*pause*] You'll have to make way for Werner *now*, won't you? [*pause*] How you hurt me!

Pause.

WERNER: Fraulein Bechner was sent to a concentration camp—

MOTHER: You could have prevented that, George. I think you were tired of her. She was a nuisance. Pretty. Yes. Pretty. [*pause*] *Not* a very good dancer. [*pause*] And she drank too much. Oh yes. You wouldn't mind them taking her away. [*pause*] You let *me* go away. Didn't you?

Pause.

WERNER: Do you seriously expect me to carry on with everything? The country is shattered. We're being squashed flat between the Russians and the Americans. [*pause*] The cities are ruined. [*pause*] There won't be much left—

Pause.

MOTHER: You must have faith in Werner. [*pause*] When they took Anna away, he was . . . he was—

WERNER: What was he?

MOTHER: My little Werner—

WERNER: *What* was he?

Pause.

MOTHER: He cried in my arms. He didn't want *you*, George. He wanted me. *Me.*

WERNER: I thought he wanted—Anna?

Pause.

MOTHER: I know I'm ill, George. Ill in my mind. [*slyly*] You're humouring me!

Pause.

WERNER: They say . . . I might walk again. [*pause*] *Might.*

MOTHER: *indifferently*] Yes, dear.

WERNER: *very quietly*] You are ill. I am Werner. Father is dead. Anna—probably dead. [*pause*] We have lost the war. As I hoped we would. As father predicted we would. [*pause*] I've spent nearly four years in various hospitals. [*pause*] I somehow think . . . you could cease to be ill now . . . if you wanted, mother.

MOTHER: One doesn't *choose* one's mental state dear—

WERNER: No?

MOTHER: I loathe *them*. But I love Germany. [*rises*] Werner won't fail us. He'll be everything you were . . . and more. [*pause*] Thank God he lacks your indifference . . . your . . . your terrible aloofness, Georgie. [*pause*] Whatever has been destroyed, he will rebuild. [*she giggles*] You once said . . . oh you were often so *vulgar* . . . you said: the von Regers are strong enough to *piss* on history! [*she turns away to the balcony of the terrace*] Isn't it a beautiful day?

WERNER: Listen—

Far away, they hear a steady rumbling.

MOTHER: Thunder!

WERNER: No. Artillery.

There is a sudden burst of much louder fire.

MOTHER: In ten years, everything will be just as it was. Werner will see to that—

WERNER: *Shut up!*

MOTHER: I understand how you feel. You were so active. My poor man! You're *jealous* of our son—

WERNER, *with a terrible, painful effort, raises his head and looks at her.*

WERNER: Helenka—

She turns to him calmly.

WERNER: I *hate* your son—

Pause. MOTHER *turns away.*

MOTHER: I thought . . . in your own way . . . you loved him. WERNER *lowers his head, exhausted. She goes to him, stands behind the carriage and puts her hands over his eyes.*

MOTHER: I want you to remember something Georgie—

WERNER: Go on.

She looks out from the terrace.

The artillery fire rumbles and roars much louder.

MOTHER: We came here on our wedding day. You had insisted

on driving down in one of the new motor cars. We arrived in
the late afternoon. Do you remember?
Track in on her eyes. Cut to her fingers on WERNER'S *eyes. Cut back
to her eyes. Cut to the drive through the grounds to the terrace.*

SCENE 31

A 1913 motor car drives up, with HELMUT *at the wheel—*WERNER'S
parents behind. All are in motoring clothes of the period, MOTHER *in a
veil and the two men wearing goggles.*
The car stops at the steps leading to the terrace. Laughing, VON REGER
*and his wife get down. He takes her hand—leads her laughing up the
steps, across the terrace, into the room beyond.*
A bedroom. VON REGER *and his wife are taking off their motoring clothes.
There is a knock on the door.*

FATHER: Come in—
  A grinning HELMUT *comes in with an ice bucket containing a bottle
  of champagne. He sets it down on a table and leaves.* VON REGER
  begins to pour two glasses.
FATHER: Well. We escaped them all—
MOTHER: *smiling*] I wanted to.
  He hands her a glass.
FATHER: Let's drink to the first thing we shall do. What's that?
MOTHER: We'll drink to it—and I'll tell you after.
  They drink. He kisses her.
MOTHER: I promised myself—
  She hesitates.
FATHER: Yes?
MOTHER: Will you be pleased?
FATHER: How do I know?
  Pause.
MOTHER: I promised myself . . . if we came here this afternoon
  . . . after the wedding . . . I would give you a child. [*pause*]
  I *know* I shall give you a child the first time.
FATHER: How do you know?

MOTHER: *laughing*] I just do.
He smiles. Looks at her. Goes to her and holds her face in his hands.
FATHER: If it's a girl—I shall divorce you!
They both laugh.
MOTHER: You shall have a son, George.
Pause.
FATHER: Yes?
Pause.
MOTHER: Yes.
He picks her up—puts her on the bed. Fills his champagne glass, comes to lie beside her with the glass to his lips.
FATHER: Here's to a son, then?
He drinks—she drinks from the same glass. He looks at her seriously.
FATHER: There's going to be a war, Helen.
MOTHER: Is there?
Pause.
FATHER: I want a son very much.
He bends over her, begins to kiss her. Camera pans to open window —light curtains billowing . . . bright sunshine.

SCENE 32

The terrace. WERNER'S MOTHER *stands with her hands over his eyes. We hear the guns. Close-up* MOTHER.

MOTHER: Do you remember? [*pause*] The following day you had an urgent call to Berlin, on business. [*pause*] The following night—you were in a brothel. [*pause*] You never lied to me about your activities—
She removes her hands, and turning quickly sweeps into the house. WERNER *opens his eyes, blinking. We see the sky from his point of view. It is filled with parachute troops.*
WERNER: *calling*] Helmut. [*pause*] Helmut!
We see the sky alive with tumbling men and opening parachutes. HELMUT *comes onto the terrace.*

WERNER: Look—[*pointing*]

HELMUT: *looking*] Yes, sir.

Pause.

WERNER: Russians.

Pause.

HELMUT: Yes sir.

More shots of parachutists.

HELMUT: Shall we try to move out, sir?

Pause.

WERNER: No. [*pause*] We shall stay here.

*The sky—the parachutists—*WERNER'S *face superimposed. We see some of the troops land, rolling over, their parachutes collapsing.*

End.

THE POLYTECHNIC OF WALES
LIBRARY
TREFOREST